The Japanese Pharmaceutical Industry

The Japanese Pharmaceutical Industry

The New Drug Lag and the Failure of Industrial Policy

L.G. Thomas, III

Goizueta Business School
Emory University, USA

Edward Elgar
Cheltenham, UK • Northampton, MA, USA

Published by
Edward Elgar Publishing Limited
Glensanda House
Montpellier Parade
Cheltenham
Glos GL50 1UA
UK

Edward Elgar Publishing, Inc.
136 West Street
Suite 202
Northampton
Massachusetts 01060
USA

A catalogue record for this book
is available from the British Library

Library of Congress Cataloguing in Publication Data

Thomas, L.G., 1953–
    The Japanese pharmaceutical industry: the new drug lag and the failure of industrial policy / L. G. Thomas III.
        p. cm.
    Includes bibliographical references and index.
    1. Pharmaceutical industry – Japan. 2. Pharmaceutical policy – Japan. 3. Drugs – Japan.
    I. Title.

    HD9672.J29 T46 2001
    338.4'76151'0952 – dc21

                                                    00–066244
ISBN 1 84064 580 6

Printed and bound in Great Britain by MPG Books Ltd, Bodmin, Cornwall

Contents

Figures

Tables

Introduction

In the early 1970s, several studies famously documented the 'drug lag' suffered by the United States (Wardell, 1973a, 1973b, 1974; Wardell and Lasagna, 1975). Many innovations in the global pharmaceutical industry at that time were launched in the USA several years after becoming available in Western Europe. And some international medicines never even made it into the US market. American patients were thus denied therapeutic benefits of numerous new medicines. Several of the delayed or excluded pharmaceutical innovations were quite important, notably new cardiovascular products such as beta-blockers. And, indeed, the drug lag was perversely as large for more significant innovations as for more incremental ones (Grabowski, 1980).

A firestorm of criticism was leveled at the US Food and Drug Administration (FDA) after documentation of the US drug lag (US Congress, 1979; US GAO, 1980). The bureaucratic and adversarial regulations of the FDA were identified by all as causing the lag. In due course, the FDA approval process in the USA speeded up (Kessler, et al., 1996), Western European approval mimicked parts of FDA standards (see the studies in Wardell, 1978), international approval lags converged to roughly common levels (Parker, 1988) and, by the end of the 1970s, the US drug lag largely disappeared.

Today, a new drug lag has emerged, not in the USA but in Japan. A staggering 87 percent of significant pharmaceutical innovations in the most recent years are unavailable in Japan, while only very few of these products have failed to make it into the various markets of Western Europe or the USA. As before, patients are denied therapeutic benefits of important new medicines. But unlike the earlier case, government safety regulations for new drugs are only partly the culprit. In the United States, new FDA regulations were layered onto a system that was fundamentally healthy, with sensible doctor demand, excellent university research in biomedical sciences, and a highly innovative domestic industry. In Japan, recent problems with the registration process for new drugs have been interjected into a system that has long-standing problems. Thus, the new drug lag in Japan has its own distinct characteristics rather than being a simple repetition of a great USA bureaucratic mistake. First, greater exclusion of significant new drugs from Japan began quietly and slowly some seven years before the Ministry of Health and Welfare (MHW) announced reforms to its registration process in 1992. The vastly greater magnitude of the new drug lag after 1992 has made it more visible, but is not the whole story. Second, and consequently, reforms in Japan to end the new drug lag must start with the registration process, but they will have to go well beyond that to solve the problem. Significant additional reforms are needed for the MHW price regulation process, the biomedical research process in Japanese universities, and the nature of doctor (hence patient) demand for pharmaceuticals. Third, and again consequently, the Japanese system for pharmaceuticals exhibits significant pathologies beyond limited availability of new medicines. It is now quite clear that the various parts of the Japanese drug system, operating together, have created excess costs threatening the financial stability of the Japanese health care system. And the domestic Japanese drug system has undermined the global competitive capabilities of domestic Japanese pharmaceutical firms. Even at its worst, FDA regulation never generated such consequences in the United States.

This book presents an analysis of the nature, causes, and consequences of the new drug lag in Japan. The outline of the argument is as follows. Chapter 1 sketches the magnitude and nature of the new drug lag, contrasting it with the 1970s drug lag in the USA. The powerful role of Japanese domestic politics is outlined in shaping the pharmaceutical industry in that nation. The second chapter examines how industries are socially constructed from their surrounding *domestic ecosystems*, or the total collection of actors that affect pharmaceutical innovation, production, and consumption. This framework is important since the new drug lag in Japan results from the interaction of numerous distinct policies, not just the pre-market registration process for new drugs. The third and fourth chapters outline the domestic ecosystem surrounding the Japanese pharmaceutical industry. These chapters identify key features of the ecosystem, indicate how these features interact, and demonstrate the pathologies of the system as a whole. Chapters 5 through 8 document the mechanisms of delay and exclusion for new drugs from Japan. The ninth chapter indicates why the existing domestic ecosystem in Japan is not sustainable, and the prospects for change. The final chapter discusses remedies for the new drug lag from the perspective of a US government seeking to sustain and promote global pharmaceutical innovation.

This study emerged and draws from a decade of research I have conducted on the global pharmaceutical industry (see Thomas, 1990, 1994, 1998). The focus of that research has been not on trade, but rather on the role that government industrial policy plays in creating or destroying competitive advantage. In the course of this research, however, it became clear not only that Japan was significantly disconnected from the international pharmaceutical industry, but that this disconnection was sharply increasing in the 1990s, verging on isolation. Half of this disconnection is due to the profound competitive weakness of Japanese ethical drug firms, and their inability to penetrate foreign markets. The other half, however, is caused by mounting exclusion of foreign innovations and firms from the Japanese home market. Investigations into the nature and causes of this exclusion resulted in this book.

Thanks are in order to Chris Clancey, who managed the calculations for this study of comparable pharmaceutical prices in Britain, Japan, and the USA, and to Gail Mooney, who composed the many figures and tables for this book. Their careful effort and patience are very much appreciated.

Nature of the new drug lag

Every year, hundreds of new drug products are introduced throughout the world into the pharmaceutical industry. Most of these products are of quite minor significance, both commercially and medically. Some are repackagings, reformulations, and combinations of drugs already on the market. Some are generic products: chemically identical imitations of existing drugs. Other drugs are minor molecular manipulations of existing products, chemically distinct and thus patentable, but just as clearly imitative. Finally, there are truly innovative new products, a handful at most of which will become blockbuster products. These blockbuster drugs provide the revenue that sustains the entire innovative process (Grabowski and Vernon, 1990; US Congress, OTA, 1993).

There is generally some competitive or medical purpose for each component of this broad array of new product launches in the global pharmaceutical industry. But it is unsurprising that most of these new products do not widely diffuse in the global marketplace, precisely because they are imitative of products that already exist in various nations. Indeed, even if we exclude generics, combinations, and reformulations, over half of the distinct new molecules launched throughout the world are never sold in more that one or two nations (Thomas, 1996). In contrast to these 'local products', only 25 percent of the distinct new molecules introduced diffuse to six or more nations. These widely diffused innovations, which will be called 'global products', are the focus of this study.

Figure 1.1 traces the diffusion into the five most important pharmaceutical markets of all global products launched since 1963. Each product is dated by its year of first launch into any nation, and the innovations of all nations are included, not just those of the five target markets listed. Examining Figure 1.1, we see that, until 1981, the USA was the most exclusionary of the major markets for global products. Only 75 to 80 percent on average of these significant innovations made it past the burdensome and non-transparent pre-market approval regulations of the FDA, regulations that created the original US drug lag. The most inclusionary nation of the five is Germany, with over 95 percent of global

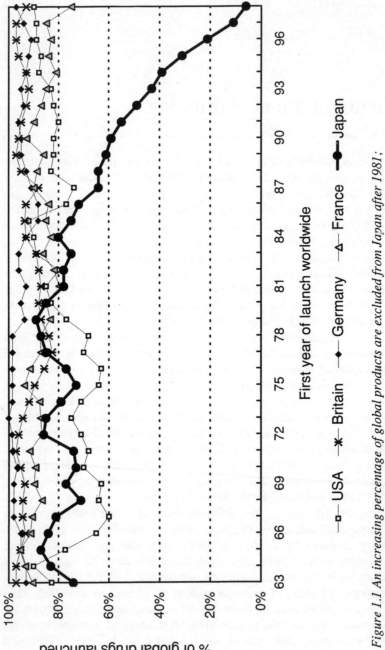

Figure 1.1 An increasing percentage of global products are excluded from Japan after 1981; percentages are three-year moving averages.

products gaining access. Clearly, Japan has become steadily more exclusionary since 1981, with a stunning and even more severe level of exclusion since 1991. Of the 230 global products launched since 1985, only 100, or 43 percent are now available in Japan. Of the new global products since 1990, only 33 percent are available in Japan, and only 13 percent of global products since 1995 have been launched into this large and wealthy nation, despite the fact that it offers the second largest pharmaceutical market in the world. Note that during the time that Japan became steadily more exclusionary, there is only minimal fluctuation in access rates for the Western nations.

THE ORIGINAL DRUG LAG: THE USA

The drug lag in Japan, of course, is not the first in an important pharmaceutical market. The original drug lag occurred in the United States, roughly from 1966 to 1976. Two factors caused this first drug lag. First, there was a scandal. Thalidomide is a minor tranquilizer that is safe and effective for almost all patients, except pregnant women. Unfortunately, the manufacturers of thalidomide choose to sell this drug to precisely this small patient group, as a treatment for morning sickness during pregnancy. Many expectant mothers who took thalidomide gave birth to children with severe deformities. The ghastly nature of these side-effects, combined with the fact that many safe tranquilizers were already on the market, created an enormous public uproar.

Thalidomide never actually received FDA approval for launch in the USA, but it was distributed to some women for clinical trials. The national outcry over even these few actual side-effects and the public praise for regulators who delayed the launch of thalidomide made a profound impression on the FDA. Ideally, national regulation of pharmaceutical safety should weigh the costs and benefits of approval for any new drug. Put differently, safety regulation involves an inherent trade-off between deaths and suffering due to side-effects from approved drugs, and deaths and suffering that arise because important drugs are delayed or withheld from the market. Responsible regulators should minimize the sum of these deaths: a grisly but inescapable calculus. The thalidomide scandal, however, severely tilted the incentives for the FDA in its consideration of new drugs. Any significant new side-effects from approved medications would clearly generate tremendous public attention. The FDA quickly discovered, however, that virtually no public attention was paid if approval for new drugs was delayed, even for years. This asymmetry of public attention resembles that paid to transport deaths. Airline crashes are always front-page or lead-story news, while the far more numerous deaths from motor vehicle accidents are virtually ignored by the press.

The second source of the original drug lag in the USA was, oddly enough, an important regulatory reform. Partly in reaction to the thalidomide scandal, the Congress in 1962 amended the Food, Drug, and Cosmetic Act to require premarket proof of effectiveness as well as safety. Proof of safety had been required in the USA since 1934. In contrast, proof of effectiveness was a very new concept, and not only the FDA but the entire range of actors in premarket testing for drugs lacked the capability to sensibly design and effect such tests. The situation resembled the current banking industry in Thailand, where the need to move to evidence-based banking is clear. Loans in the Thai banking industry have historically been made on the basis of personal connections and impressionistic judgments as to the financial soundness of investments. Yet the generation, evaluation, and response to financial evidence require a systemic upgrading of capabilities in Thailand: in accounting firms, in regulatory agencies, in banks, in securities firms, and in capital markets. The social construction of standards, processes, culture, and capabilities, however, takes time, particularly in the absence of strong leadership determined to advance rapidly this collective process. In the US pharmaceutical industry, the FDA grossly failed to provide adequate leadership for the complex task of launching evidence-based medicine after 1962. Indeed, it was not until 1972 that the FDA finally issued Good Clinical Practice (GCP) guidelines, ten years after Congress required proof of effectiveness for new drugs.

The impact of scandal and regulatory reform in the USA after 1962 may be seen in Figure 1.2. The top of Figure 1.2 gives the average years of delay for launching new global drugs into the USA. Note that, after 1962, the mean period of delay rose sharply from two years to six years, and remained at that level until the mid-1970s (circled). By that time, the 'drug lag' had become so prolonged and pronounced that it finally caught public attention. After criticism of the FDA from the press and Congress over the drug lag, the agency accelerated its reviews of new drug applications, and the drug lag abated.

It is important to recognize that delay for drugs that were eventually launched in the USA was only one component of the original drug lag. An additional component was a drop in the access rate for significant new drugs. The lower portion of Figure 1.2 reproduces the access rate data of Figure 1.1, but only for the USA in isolation, so that trends there are more visible. Note that, during the period of the drug lag, 1966–76, the access rate for global drugs fell to an average of 75 percent (circled), the worst performance among major markets. With the fading of the drug lag, the US access rate rose above 80 percent, but it did not register sustainable

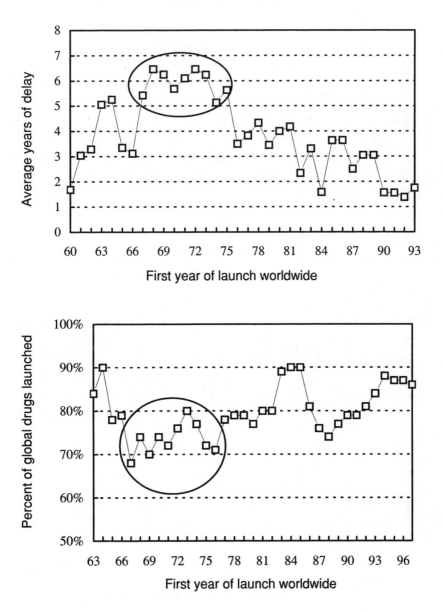

Figure 1.2 Delay and exclusion in the US drug lag, 1966–76. Chart data are three-year moving averages and include all global drugs launched into the USA. Ovals denote delay (at top) and exclusion (at bottom).

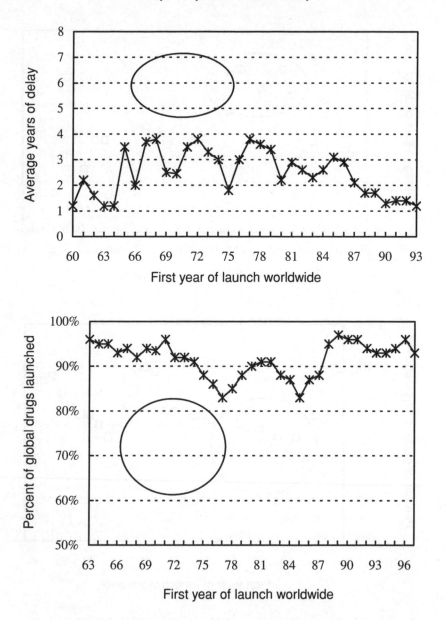

Figure 1.3 No drug lag in Britain, neither delay nor exclusion. Chart data are three year moving averages and include all global drugs launched into Britain. Ovals are replicated from Figure 1.2 for reference to US drug lag.

improvement until the Republican-dominated Congress adopted reforms in 1992 to speed drug approvals. These reforms are discussed in detail in the final chapter of this book.

A drug lag, then, is a mix of delay and exclusion for significant new drugs, caused by regulatory overreaction to scandal and regulatory mismanagement of reform. It is important to recognize that only two major markets have suffered a drug lag: the USA for ten years after 1965, and Japan for the last ten years or so. There is nothing inevitable about a drug lag. For example, thalidomide was actually approved and sold in Britain, and Britain joined the USA after 1966 in forcing stringent regulation of drug effectiveness in addition to drug safety. Yet there was no drug lag in Britain, as can be seen in Figure 1.3. The circles for the US drug lag from Figure 1.2 are reproduced in the exact same location in Figure 1.3 for easy reference. Note that Britain experienced deteriorations in neither delay nor access for new drugs.

THE NEW DRUG LAG: JAPAN

How the new drug lag in Japan will play out remains to be seen. As mentioned above, of the 230 global drugs since 1985, 100 are now available in Japan and 130 are unavailable. Of these 130 currently unavailable drugs, 90 are currently undergoing clinical trials or regulatory review in Japan. Most of these 90 global drugs will eventually be launched there, though exactly when depends on the course of regulatory policy in that country. Because of the public nature of the regulated premarket review process for drugs, we may use published dates for clinical trials to forecast what will happen to these 90 drugs. The assumptions used for this forecast are discussed in detail in Chapter 6. For the moment, suffice it to say that the assumptions behind this forecast are reasonable, but optimistic in that they presume that full regulatory reform for the Japanese pharmaceutical industry will be implemented immediately.

Figure 1.4 traces the forecast pattern of the new drug lag in Japan if reform is promptly adopted. Comparison of Figures 1.2 and 1.4 indicate that the forecast drug lag in Japan may well look very much like that of the USA 20 years earlier. In Japan, the average delay may well be seven years (against six years in the USA) for those drugs actually launched, while the access rate for global products will fall to around 70 to 75 percent (with almost the same rate historically in the USA). This finding may be put quite simply: if Japan reforms promptly, the American and Japanese drug lags will be quite similar. If, however, Japan delays reform, the Japanese drug lag will become correspondingly worse than that of the USA.

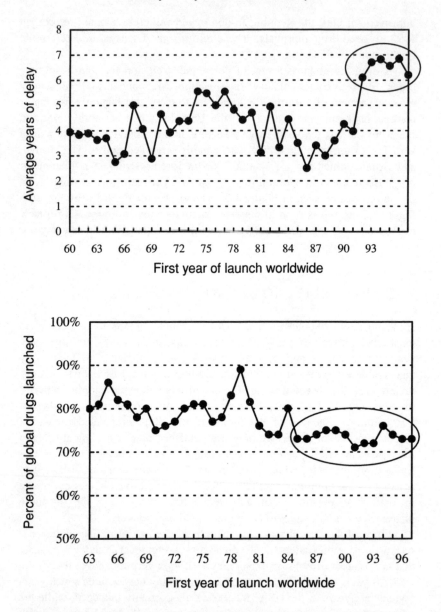

Figure 1.4 Forecast drug lag in Japan, delay (at top) and exclusion (at bottom). Chart data are three year moving averages and include all global drugs forecast to be launched into Japan. See text for forecast method.

Many of the drugs not now available in Japan are significant innovations, with important therapeutic effects. A listing of significant global products currently unavailable in Japan is given in Table 1.1. Aricept (donepezil) by Eisai is especially interesting as it was discovered by a Japanese firm, Eisai, but has not yet been marketed in Japan. Note that even Japanese innovations suffer from the new drug lag.

The fundamental origins of the new drug lag in Japan are almost identical to those of the original drug lag in the USA: scandal and regulatory reform. First, and as described in detail in Chapter 3, Japan and MHW have suffered not one but rather a series of quite prominent scandals with its drug approval process. In 1994, however, a scandal with Sorivudine finally eliminated public patience with MHW. The subsequent brutal drubbing MHW received in the Japanese press caused a severe overreaction by the ministry that has since virtually shut down the registration process for new drugs in Japan. Second, and as also described in Chapter 3, MHW has sought to reform the clinical trial and registration process in Japan to bring it into conformity with Western standards. In 1992, MHW proposed and in 1994 required Good Clinical Practice (GCP) guidelines that fundamentally changed the clinical trial process in Japan. While this regulatory reform is actually good news in theory, in practice MHW has provided very little direction or support for the Japanese pharmaceutical industry as this reform has been implemented. An important reason for this lackluster implementation of regulatory reform is that the politics surrounding MHW in Japan are far greater than those for the FDA in the USA, and perhaps greater than those confronting any other important pharmaceutical regulatory agency. To fully understand the nature of the new drug lag in Japan, we must examine these political constraints.

DOMESTIC POLITICS IN JAPAN AND THE DUAL STATE

The inefficiency and non-competitiveness of the Japanese pharmaceutical industry may represent a significant surprise for many readers. The images of Japanese industrial policy and corporate strategy that persist in the American press are those of the automobile, camera, consumer electronics, semiconductor, and steel industries. In each of these industries, export promotion by the Ministry of International Trade and Industry (MITI) and aggressive expansion by firms such as Toyota, Canon, Sony, Hitachi, and Nippon Steel resulted in great economic success. What is far less well known by Americans is that these successes are in the export sector of the Japanese economy that makes up less than 20 percent of total national

Table 1.1 Significant drugs not available in Japan as of December, 1988

Significant drugs delayed

atorvastatin	Lipitor	Warner Lambert	both
azithromycin	Zithromax	Pfizer	top 200
cladribine	Leustatin	Johnson & Johnson	FDA Priority
donepezil	Aricept	Eisai	FDA Priority
dorzolamide	Trusopt	Merck	top 200
fexofenadine	Allegra	Hoechst	top 200
fluvastatin	Lescol	Novartis	top 200
gabapentin	Neurontin	Warner Lambert	both
ketorolac	Toradol	Roche	FDA Priority
lamotrigine	Lamictal	Glaxo Wellcome	FDA Priority
latanoprost	Xalaton	Pharmacia & Upjohn	both
levocabastine	Livostan	Johnson & Johnson	top 200
loratadine	Claritin	Schering Plough	top 200
losartan	Cozaar	Dupont Merck	top 200
mivacurium	Mivacron	Glaxo Wellcome	FDA Priority
mupirocin	Bactroban	SmithKline Beecham	top 200
nefazodone	Serzone	Bristol-Myers Squibb	top 200
norgestimate	Cilest	Johnson & Johnson	top 200
paroxetine	Paxil	Novo	top 200
salmeterol	Serevent	Glaxo Wellcome	top 200
sertraline	Zoloft	Pfizer	top 200
sumatriptan	Imitrex	Glaxo Wellcome	both
zolpidem	Ambien	Synthelabo	top 200

Significant drugs excluded

atovaquone	Malarone	Glaxo Wellcome	FDA Priority
buspirone	BuSpar	Bristol-Myers Squibb	top 200
colfosceril palmitate	Exosurf	Glaxo Wellcome	FDA Priority
flouoxetine	Prozac	Lilly	top 200
fosinopril	Monopril	Bristol-Myers Squibb	top 200
ramipril	Altace	Hoechst	top 200
rifabutin	Mycobutin	Pharmacia & Upjohn	FDA Priority
tacrine	Cognex	Warner Lambert	FDA Priority
venlafaxine	Effexor	American Home	top 200

Note: Of the 130 global drugs launched since 1983 but not available in Japan as of December, 1988, 90 molecules are delayed and are undergoing clinical trials in Japan, while another 40 molecules are excluded and are not undergoing clinical trials in Japan. All drugs listed in this table are ranked as Priority Drugs by the FDA during its review of them, or are among the top 200 most prescribed drugs in the USA in 1996, or both.

output. In much of the remainder of the domestic-oriented economy, productivity is quite poor. Overall standards of living in Japan are an average of the dynamic high-productivity export sector and the stagnant low-productivity domestic sector. There are thus 'two Japans' or a dual state.

Academic analyses of Japan focused until recently on the export sector of Japan, and its relations with MITI (Johnson, 1982; Wade, 1990; Odagiri and Goto, 1996; World Bank, 1993). These analyses have stressed MITI's political autonomy from domestic political pressures that turn most industrial policy efforts into destructive 'pork barrel' politics. The undisputed political importance of national economic growth in Japan, and the prestige and long tenure of MITI bureaucrats, sheltered them from most humdrum political pressures. MITI officials were free to promote national economic growth, by rewarding export-oriented firms with cartels, occasional subsidies, and protection from imports. Precisely because of this autonomy, MITI was able to demand and receive a *quid pro quo* from Japanese firms. Only those firms that succeeded with the simple metric of exports would continue to receive the support of MITI. Those firms that were able to improve quality, lower costs, and advance technology sufficiently to be able to sell their products in global markets would receive MITI support, and hence financial funding from the banking sector. These firms were continually forced to peddle their wares in the most sophisticated markets of the world, especially the USA. They succeeded through continuous accumulation of corporate capabilities, nurtured by implicit financial support from MITI and their protected home market, but also challenged by the need to export to the USA. MITI thus conducted an implicit tournament among firms, encouraging a vigorous rivalry among them that eschewed price competition at home but was vigorously competitive in terms of capability enhancement. Firms that used the benefits of cartels and import protection to enjoy monopoly profits without improvement of corporate capabilities would find themselves without new capital, licenses for technology import, and other administrative requirements for expansion. This characterization of the export sector is summarized in the top of Figure 1.5. Note that the political autonomy of MITI is critical to its ability to refuse support to inefficient firms.

The political benefits of the export sector for the ruling Liberal Democratic Party (LDP) in Japan are large and important. These benefits include political legitimacy and prestige for the LDP, both within Japan and internationally. The export sector also provides growth and wealth for the economy as a whole, generating taxes that fund government expenditure and campaign contributions that fund LDP activities. The success and prestige of the export sector have long provided political cover for a very

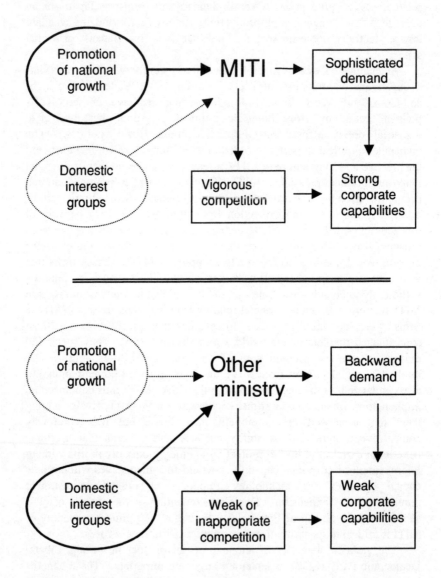

Figure 1.5 Political pressures and industrial policies in the two economic sectors of Japan, export sector (above) and domestic sector (below)

different dynamic in the domestic sector. The domestic industries that make up almost 80 percent of the Japanese economy export little of their output and contribute little to improvements in the national standard of living for Japan. There is no *quid pro quo* extracted from firms in these industries by the government: no requirement of productivity enhancement in exchange for government support. Administrative techniques such as import protectionism and cartels thus work in these industries as they do in the rest of the world, encouraging economic stagnation and low productivity. Most important, LDP politicians manipulate regulation of the domestic sector to secure their individual re-election and retention of power for the party. The political economy of the domestic sector of the Japanese economy is represented in the bottom of Figure 1.5.

The decades-long political preeminence of the LDP masks the important fact that the individual members of the Diet (LDP and otherwise) suffer among the greatest electoral vulnerability and shortest legislative tenures in the developed world (Calder, 1988). The source of this vulnerability lies in a peculiar feature of Diet elections, where historically virtually all candidates for the Lower House and many for the Upper House are elected from multi-member districts. Each voter has only one non-transferable vote, yet districts will elect from two to six members of the Lower House. The LDP thus must field multiple candidates in most districts, and somehow carefully balance and split the vote of its supporters in order to elect as many of these candidates as possible. Since votes are non-transferable, this is no easy task. The time-honored solution to this conundrum is for individual LDP candidates to cleverly differentiate themselves from other candidates of the same party. They achieve differentiation by creating a personal support network (or *koenkai*), comprising specific special-interest groups. Individual Diet members thus personally tie to themselves the votes of support group members.

Assembly and maintenance of a personal support network is a complex and all-consuming task for Dietmen. Over 40 percent of LDP Dietmen are second generation in that they inherited a preexisting personal support network from family or a mentor (Ramseyer and Rosenbluth, 1993). A staggering one-third of LDP voters historically have belonged directly to special-interest groups or grassroots political organizations tied to specific LDP Dietmen (Calder, 1988). The average Diet member expends $1 million (¥120 million) a year on services and even personal favors for members of his district, such as gifts of money at weddings and funerals or subsidies to support group activities (Ramseyer and Rosenbluth, 1993). Flanagan and Lee (2000) calculate that these expenditures render the cost of parliamentary office in Japan to be four times as expensive as any other country. Most important, Diet members use government expenditures and regulations to ensure support of their personal networks. In his excellent study of the Japanese political system, Calder has vividly and understandably labeled these personal support groups 'circles of compensation'.

One of the strongest special-interest groups in Japan is the Japan Medical Association (JMA). There are roughly 210,000 doctors in Japan, one for every 600 Japanese (Howells and Neary, 1995). Each doctor is said to 'carry 100 votes in his medical bag' owing to influence over patients and co-workers in clinics and hospitals (Steslicke, 1973), though this is surely an exaggeration today. More important, the JMA is one of the largest financial contributors to political parties (widely regarded as one of the top three contributors, along with the construction industry and rice farmers, other beneficiaries of LDP government largesse). Indeed, one estimate is that contributions from doctors and dentists account for 15 percent of LDP income (Howells and Neary, 1995). Finally, the JMA has been well organized and aggressive over the decades, and has established itself as a significant political force. With its political influence, it has pushed for generous financial treatment of ambulatory care and pharmaceuticals, the principal sources of doctor incomes (Calder, 1988). JMA pressure has thus moved the pharmaceutical industry firmly into the domestic sector of the Japanese economy.

It is important to recognize that the export sector and the domestic sector of the Japanese economy, the two components of the dual state, do not simply sit side by side. Rather, they make each other possible. The LDP is able to refrain from excessive political interference with MITI and the export sector precisely because it has such extensive pork-barrel activities in the rest of the economy. And the large firms of the export sector acquiesce in the inefficiency of the domestic sector precisely because this buys them protection from political interference with their growth. Many of these large firms were historically highly leveraged to enable maximum growth, and in this vulnerable financial position they could not afford to pick quarrels with the LDP. The wealth generated by the large firms in the export sector buys them, and MITI, significant autonomy from LDP political interference.

It is also important to recognize that the dual state is not absolute. For example, some MITI activities are really part of the domestic sector in Japan. Under pressure from the LDP, MITI has used protectionism and subsidies to delay essential economic restructuring in several declining industries, rather than to promote efficiency (Uriu, 1996). The political economic outcomes for one such industry in Japan, textiles, look very much like standard pork-barrel politics in the USA, and nothing like the 'autonomous' workings of an 'elite' bureaucracy. Conversely, even in the most politicized segments of the domestic sector, much of political administration promotes interests of the nation as a whole. Thus, while industries and government agencies may in general be readily identified as in one sector or the other of the dual state, some aspects of each sector will be found in the other.

The obvious inefficiency and legalized 'corruption' of the domestic sector of the Japanese economy have on occasions led members of the LDP to seek political reform. The chance to reduce the burdens of intra-party competition on the LDP surely enhances the appeal of such reform. In 1956, 1960, 1972, the LDP tried but failed to move Japan to single-member electoral districts (Calder, 1988). In 1992, facing public outrage over a seemingly never-ending series of scandals and public fear over economic recession, the LDP splintered, with defectors forming three new parties. For the first time since its formation in 1955, the LDP no longer ruled Japan. The non-LDP coalition government elected in July, 1993 quickly proposed extensive electoral reform, and in January, 1994 the Diet adopted a new national election law. In October, 1996, Japan held the first Diet elections under the new system (Christensen, 1998; Cox, Rosenbluth, and Thies, 1999; Masaru, 1997; Seligmann, 1997). The pre-1994 lower house of the Diet comprised 511 seats sorted into 129 districts. The new lower house is made up of 300 seats from single-member districts, with an additional 200 seats filled by proportional representation in 11 regional blocks. In these regional blocks, each party receives a proportion of seats approximate to its share of the regional vote. Each Japanese voter has two votes: one for a particular candidate in a single-member district and one for a particular party in a regional block. Oddly, candidates may choose to run simultaneously in single-seat and proportional representation lists, so that a loss in the single-seat district may be 'saved' in the region if the candidate is listed high enough in his party's electoral roster.

While the 1994 electoral reform raised hopes for a transformation of Japanese electoral politics, several factors have prevented realization of these hopes. In each case, blocking factors preserve the extreme high cost of Japanese national elections and thus retain the need for *koenkai* and special-interest monies. The first factor is that the 1994 reform is only partial. Only 8 percent of candidates in the 1996 election ran exclusively in their single-member district, while over 70 percent ran as 'double' candidates in both district and regional lists (Cox, Rosenbluth, and Thies, 1999). Second, the number of individual districts increased from 129 to 300. This proliferation of districts combined with the fluidity of party affiliation in 1996 acted to simply sort candidates among districts with their *koenkai* largely intact (Seligmann, 1997). Indeed, the sorting process strongly exhibited bandwagon effects, where those candidates with the strongest *koenkai* soon became the consensus party nominee in single-member districts (Christensen, 1998). Candidates with weaker *koenkai* were pushed into regional party lists or withdrawal from the election. Third, Japanese electoral regulations severely restrict electioneering.

> Strict campaign regulations make it nearly impossible for candidates to effectively reach voters in numerous ways. Candidates and campaign workers are not allowed to canvass voters door to door. Campaigns may create only officially approved campaign posters and these posters may be placed only in publicly provided and designated locations. Campaigns may produce only two types of brochures and the total number that may be distributed is limited by regulation. Direct mailings to voters are limited to an officially approved postcard that is sent at government expense to a limited number of voters. Media advertisements by candidates, when allowed, are strictly limited to a few government-approved settings in which all candidates follow identical regulations concerning content and format. The number of campaign offices and cars and the amount of expenditures on campaign workers are also closely restricted or regulated by government. (Christensen, 1998)

Under these regulations, *koenkai* remain essential for candidate access to voters.

As a consequence of these blocking factors, the nature and costliness of Japanese Diet elections have not changed despite the new electoral law (Mulgan, 2000). With failure of these reforms, individual Diet members must fall back on the gross materialism of traditional Japanese politics to manage re-election.

THE 50-YEARS WAR: JMA VERSUS MHW

The 'domestic' nature of the Japanese pharmaceutical industry is clearly not some technological given. Rather, it is the outcome of political interactions over the years among the LDP, the JMA, and the MHW. To learn the determinants of the domestic focus of the drug industry, then, we must examine political history.

The origins of the JMA would seem to suggest a strongly pro-innovation focus for that group. With the 1880s Meiji restoration, the government of Japan sought to promote Western medical science and to repress Chinese *kanpo* traditions. The Greater Japan Medical Association (GJMA) was founded in 1893 to support these government efforts and raise scientific standards for government practice. But the political efforts of the GJMA and subsequent rival organizations soon turned to more mundane issues. Key among these was the separation of dispensing and prescription of drugs (*bungyo*) and regulation of the medical profession by its own association (Steslicke, 1973). The GJMA opposed *bungyo* and supported self-regulation. From the Chinese tradition, Japanese doctors both prescribed and dispensed drugs, and drug sales to patients constituted a significant portion of doctor incomes. Thus, from the very outset, Japanese medical associations demonstrated a focus on autonomy from government ministries and protection of pharmaceutical-based income. These issues would recur in several notable post-1945 battles between the JMA (the ultimate result of mergers among initially competing medical associations) and the MHW.

Battle of 1954
During the American military occupation after World War II, US military leaders proposed importing American medical practice by imposing *bungyo* on Japan. After the occupation, MHW officials themselves pushed forward this initiative by introducing pro-*bungyo* bills in the Diet. The Federation of Health Insurance Associations added its support for the MHW plan, expecting that *bungyo* would reduce medical costs and improve patient care. The JMA opposed this threat to its members' incomes, quietly during the American occupation and steadily more forcefully afterwards. In 1954, JMA opposition reached its peak. JMA deployed sound trucks in Tokyo to blare its opposition to MHW and the *bungyo* proposals, and staged a 'sitting to the death' in protest at the Diet building. As a reward for its boisterous actions, the JMA attained initial postponement and ultimate defeat of the MHW *bungyo* proposals (Steslicke, 1973). Hostilities between JMA and MHW were thus joined, reversing close pre-war ties. The JMA began to refer to MHW as totalitarian in its regulation of doctors and medical practice.

Battle of 1961
By 1960, relations between the JMA and the MHW had deteriorated to the point where JMA had withdrawn from the Central Social Insurance Medical Council (or *Chuikyo*), the forum that advised MHW on national medical care. In August of that year, the JMA presented the MHW with 'The Four Demands' to increase doctor fees and decrease regulation of doctors by health insurers. The JMA was careful to craft its proposals insultingly as 'demands' rather than requests. The MHW responded to these demands with the sort of vague promises that so often emanate from Japanese bureaucrats. MHW also strongly urged the JMA to rejoin the Central Council and resolve disagreements through negotiations there. The JMA refused, then went over MHW to negotiate directly with senior LDP officials, in the absence of any MHW representation. To advance its

political case, the JMA declared a 'medical holiday' or one-day strike by its members, on February 19, 1961. Roughly 85 percent of Japan's doctors refused to work that day, with many of them joining in political rallies and marches. By threatening further 'holidays' and even mass resignations from insurance schemes, the JMA forced the LDP to negotiate directly a compromise settlement. After 1961, the JMA established direct ties with the LDP and autonomy from the MHW. Any hope for MHW to exert MITI-like control over the medical sector vanished. From this point on, medical care in general and pharmaceuticals in particular were firmly established as part of the domestic sector of the Japanese economy.

Battle of 1971
The compromises attained in 1961 soon proved inadequate. After ten years of continued protests and occasional repeats of the February 1961 'medical holiday', the JMA finally deployed its ultimate political weapon. During July and August of 1971, 50,000 doctors boycotted health insurance schemes, requiring patients to pay for services directly. The boycott was ended only after direct negotiations with the most senior LDP officials including the Prime Minister, who promised basic revisions to the health insurance systems sought by the JMA.

Battle of 1981
By the 1970s, the political power of the JMA had significantly distorted welfare policy in Japan. Medical expenditures as a share of total welfare costs were over 40 percent in Japan, compared with a range of 22 to 27 percent in other developed nations. Within medical costs, pharmaceutical expenditures accounted for almost 40 percent, compared to a range of 10 to 20 percent abroad (Calder, 1988). Both these percentages demonstrate the commitment of the JMA to protection and expansion of its members' incomes. By the mid-1970s, the Ministry of Finance (MOF) had become alarmed by these huge socialized costs, and began pressuring the MHW to rein them in. In 1981, the MHW sharply reduced regulated pharmaceutical prices (an action discussed in detail below). This action made little policy sense. High pharmaceutical costs in Japan were caused by excess prescriptions by doctors, not high prices from pharmaceutical firms. Given the stinging defeats suffered by MHW in its earlier confrontations with the JMA, however, it is perhaps understandable that MHW would hope that this indirect approach might have some pay-off. Certainly, it was safer to attack the politically weak pharmaceutical industry than the politically strong JMA, and it bought relief for a time from MOF pressure. More aggressively, also in 1981, MHW proposed a series of reforms designed to reduce health-care expenditures for the elderly. The Health Care for the

Aged Law was adopted by the Diet within one year, a limited triumph for MHW.

How was MHW able to achieve limited success in the 1980s? First, it now stood not alone against the JMA but with the politically more powerful MOF. Second, it adopted what in the US would be described as a 'stealth strategy'. The most contentious aspects of MHW proposals were capitation of physician fees for certain illnesses (replacing fee for service) and creation of retirement homes. Both features were strongly opposed by the JMA. Capitation would eliminate income from overprescription of drugs for the elderly, and retirement homes would compete directly with doctor-managed hospitals that housed 75 percent of the institutionalized elderly. These two policies were supposedly dropped from the new law as adopted in 1982, but both were subsequently implemented by MHW through its administration of that law and subsequent laws passed by the Diet. Third, the political influence of the JMA has declined somewhat over time (Howells and Neary, 1995; Mikitaka and Campbell, 1996). Younger doctors are less likely to join the JMA or to work in the small private practices that the JMA most benefits. Also, a series of scandals and tax evasions by doctors have damaged the image of the medical profession.

The domestic nature of the Japanese pharmaceutical industry is thus the outcome of 50 years or more of political struggle. The domestic focus is a political equilibrium, or routine, for the key players in the industry: regulators (MHW), doctors (JMA), and pharmaceutical firms. The source of the routines underpinning the domestic focus of the industry is clear: they are a truce to specific political battles. Nelson and Winter (1982) have well described the powerful hold of truce-derived routines (though their argument reproduced below focuses on battles and truces within a single firm):

> Like a truce among nations, the truce among organization members tends to give rise to a peculiar symbolic culture shared by the parties. A renewal of overt hostilities would be costly and would also involve a sharp rise in uncertainty about the future position of the parties. Accordingly, the state of truce is ordinarily considered valuable, and a breach of its terms is not to be undertaken lightly. But the terms of a truce can never be fully explicit, and in the case of the intra-organizational truce are often not explicit at all. The terms become increasingly defined by a shared tradition arising out of the specific contingencies confronted and the responses of the parties to those contingencies. ...
> The apparent fragility of the prevailing truce and the implied need for caution in undertaking anything that looks like a new initiative is thus reinforced by the defensive alertness (or alert defensiveness) of organization members seeking to assure that their interests continue to be recognized and preserved. The result may be that the routines of the

organization as a whole are confined to extremely narrow channels by the dikes of vested interest. Adaptations that appear 'obvious' or 'easy' to an external observer may be foreclosed because they involve a perceived threat to internal political equilibrium.

The next chapter examines general issues of industrial policy, and how industrial policy affects the performance of industries.

Industrial policy and domestic ecosystems

Industrial policy is a controversial concept, at the heart of an extensive debate over the proper interface between government and industry. On the one hand, conservative critics of industrial policy argue that government has no role to play in direction of industry activity and ought to be 'neutral' in its economic impact (for discussions of this view see CEA, 1984; Lawrence, 1984; Quick, 1984; Schultze, 1983; Weidenbaum, 1988). By 'neutrality', opponents believe that government should not favor one firm over another, one industry over another, or one technology over another, all relative to some (quite conceptual) market in the absence of government. These critics define industrial policy as explicit government intervention into the 'normal' market-place. This definition reduces industrial policy to 'artificial' interventions, such as import protectionism, public subsidies for private firms, or government-sanctioned cartels. These tactics are seen to distort and worsen the superior workings of unregulated competitive markets. From the perspective of static efficiency, industrial policies are seen as raising prices to consumers, thus immediately lowering national standards of living. From the perspective of dynamic efficiency, industrial policies are seen as having even worse consequences in the long run, since they shield incompetent firms from the rigors of global rivalry. Domestic labor and capital, that could be put to work in new and more competitive ways, stay locked in protected incompetent firms. Critics of industrial policy readily point to a string of actual failures, in multiple industries, all over the world.

Advocates of industrial policy largely argue that traditional economists are only attacking a straw man (Johnson, *et al.*, 1989; Johnson, 1993; Kuttner, 1984; Reich, 1983, 1985; Zysman and Tyson, 1983). Of course, protectionism usually fails, for reasons of both static and dynamic efficiency, but appropriate industrial policies are misdefined as artificial interventions in the market. Rather, appropriate industrial policies actually create and define the market. There are innumerable ways for a government to organize and administer taxation, government procurement, labor markets, capital markets, technology development, international

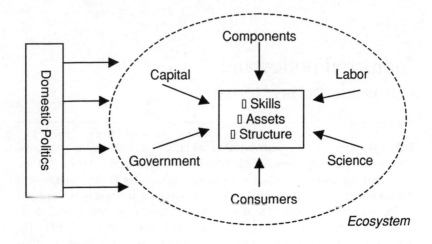

Figure 2.1 The ecosystem model: Firm capabilities in a social network

trade, anti-monopoly restrictions, corporate governance, and on and on. These national patterns of commerce will be called the *domestic ecosystem*, illustrated in Figure 2.1. As has been stressed in the previous chapter, politics drive construction of the domestic ecosystem. In the very act of defining this institutional environment, a government inescapably favors certain firms, industries, and technologies, and this favoritism is large and durable. Put plainly, there are many forms of capitalism, and the very act of choosing a particular form creates predictable favoritism. Thus the only real choice for government is not 'yes' or 'no' as to pursuit of industrial policy, but either to explicitly recognize and optimize government impact on industry or to blindly ignore government impact so that it occurs in a fragmented and conflicting manner. In other words, the only choice for government is explicit versus implicit industrial policy.

An alternative expression of this new view is the *environment–conduct–performance model*, illustrated in Figure 2.2. The environment or ecosystem that surrounds a firm significantly determines the general conduct of the firm, such as the strategic assets it accumulates, the strategies it follows, its organizational design, its financial structure, and so on. This conduct directly determines how the firm performs in the world. Thus, if we analyze the domestic ecosystem surrounding a firm, we can predict the capabilities and resources this firm possesses, and also the

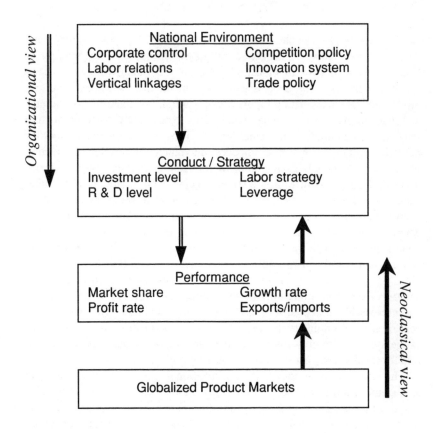

Figure 2.2 Environment–conduct–performance model

resources it lacks. A useful metaphor here is that industrial policy is very much like child rearing. If you have a good home, a child develops good habits and good skills, and the child performs well. If you have a bad home environment, you raise a juvenile delinquent that behaves badly, and does not do well in the outside world. Also like child raising, good industrial policy is a balance between nurture and challenge. An overly harsh environment will destroy firms, while an environment that is too lenient will never force development of sufficient internal skills and resources to compete globally.

DOMESTIC ECOSYSTEMS: FIRMS AND INDUSTRIES

At the root of the debate over industrial policy is a more fundamental debate over the nature of firms and industries. At one extreme, underlying conservative criticisms of industrial policy, is traditional (or neoclassical) economics theory. The neoclassical model of the firm is a black box, or a production function relating inputs (labor, capital, raw materials) to outputs and stripped of any institutional detail. This exogenously given production function is essentially the same for all firms in the industry, and for potential entrants. Nothing impedes movement along this production function. The neoclassical model of industry is equally simple: clearly defined, legally distinct, arm's-length agents who relate to each other exclusively through market prices. There are no spillovers (or externalities) from the economic decisions of one actor onto other economic actors. Of course, most economists and even most conservative economists do not regard spillovers as never occurring. Rather, significant spillovers are seen as rare, and readily identifiable. Government intervention in the market-place is appropriate only in these rare instances, to restrict negative spillovers (such as pollution) or to promote positive spillovers (such as basic research). It is precisely this view of firms and industries that enables conservative economists to regard markets as neutral aggregations of exogenously given consumer valuations and supplier costs, and to find no role for the domestic ecosystem or industrial policy.

In contrast, new views in organizational economics and strategic management have coalesced around new models of firms and industries. The most prominent new theory of the firm is the *resource-based* view. A resource is an asset that is firm-specific (hence costly to transfer across firms without permission of firm owners), scarce (hence costly to imitate), and valuable (hence costly to substitute). Some resources are external market positions, such as patents, brands, or distribution networks. But arguably the most important resources are the internal capabilities of the firm. (For studies that view the firm as a collection of resources and skills, see Barney, 1986, 1991; Penrose, 1959; Rumelt, 1984; Wernerfelt, 1984; and Teece, *et al.*, 1997.)

The most prominent new theory of industry is social networks, drawn from economic sociology (Piore and Sabel, 1984; Granovetter, 1985; Powell and Smith-Doerr, 1994). A network is a pattern of informal relations, among a group of loosely tied actors, sharing similar social practices, and buttressed by common politics. A social network can thus be considered to have three basic attributes: *sources* or the political factors that sustain shared practices, *mechanisms* or the practices, culture, and cognition that network members maintain in common, and *outcomes* or the implications of shared practices.

From a social network perspective, the immediate local interactor ties of the domestic ecosystem dominate ties with foreign actors The most basic and least controversial reason is that these ties provide resources for the firm, which enable and constrain its activities (Pfeffer and Salancik, 1978). Sales and purchases create an obvious flow of financial funds into and out of the firm, and a less obvious flow of information, about customer preferences, supplier capabilities, competitor strategies, regulatory requirements, possibilities for innovation, and the future direction of technology. The first reason, then, that local ties dominate is that they are more frequent and have greater magnitude, and hence offer more resources to firms.

Yet acknowledgment of the importance of resources is in the end no answer at all, as it begs the question of why the firm has surrounded itself with one particular configuration of resources and not some other. From the perspective of neoclassical economics, the observed resource configuration for a firm is presumed optimal, because firms costlessly and instantly reconfigure external resources to achieve this optimality. Outside the theories of such economists, resource change is neither costless nor instantaneous, precisely because firms are *embedded* in their current networks of ties (Granovetter, 1985; Zukin and DiMaggio, 1990; Barber, 1995; Baum and Dutton, 1996). By 'embedded', we mean that these ties are *constructive* for the firm, creating and sustaining its very nature and existence. Thus the culture, cognition, structure, and politics of the firm's current network of resources strongly determine the culture, cognition, structure, and politics of the firm itself (Dobbin, 1994; Hamilton and Biggart, 1988; Whitley, 1994).

The other side of this second reason for domestic ties dominating offers a third: the firm is *disembedded* (Giddens, 1991) from networks that are *dissonant* or culturally distant. The capabilities of firms derive from domestic culture, cognition, social patterns, and politics, and are optimized through adaptation over time to work best in the domestic institutional environment. As these capabilities are deployed in foreign markets, they will have diminished value in foreign institutional environments that reject and conflict with norms 'back home'. As the cultural distance between such norms increases, local firms become steadily less adept and less capable in foreign networks.

Actually, modern firms maintain ties simultaneously in several, conflicting networks. Global firms operate in multiple nations, each with potentially distinct networks of consumers, regulators, and suppliers of labor and capital. The technology-induced crumbling of industrial boundaries places many firms in a fast-changing array of industry networks. Most firms thus maintain at once different levels of embeddedness and disembeddedness in various networks. Some scholars argue that trends in culture, technology, and economics are steadily disembedding firms from their original national networks, creating a new class of stateless or 'transnational firms' (Bartlett and Ghoshal, 1989). The disembedding mechanisms include changes in communication, transport, and information technology that reduce the costs of ties to external networks and hence pull firms out of their local environment. Other disembedding mechanisms center on greater competition due to reduced barriers to entry, higher fixed costs (especially R&D and marketing), and shorter product lives that force firms to seek global scale and push them into foreign environments. Other scholars argue that the same trends force firms to effect ever greater strategic focus (Quinn, 1992) and competitive excellence, which forces increased ties to specific national networks (Porter, 1990; Tyson, 1991). The extent to which modern firms are embedded or disembedded in local and foreign markets is ultimately an empirical issue.

This book seeks to integrate and thus add to the resource-based view of firms and the social network view of industries. The integration is achieved by emphasizing that internal capabilities are accumulated though interactions over time with actors in a particular social network. The dependence of corporate resource on capabilities of the local ecosystem was recognized as early as Marshall (1919, 1920), who cited 'good choice of workers' (local factor supply), 'subsidiary trades' (localized upstream and downstream industries), and shared 'mysteries of the trade' (corporate technology capabilities) as key features of the local ecosystem. And he regarded this local ecosystem as the driver for productivity, competitiveness, and regional clustering of successful firms in an industry, such as textile manufacturing in 19th-century Manchester. An eclectic but important collection of academic research builds on Marshall's initial insights, ranging from evolutionary economics (Nelson and Winter, 1982), economic history (Chandler, 1990; Freeman, 1987), strategic management (Porter, 1990, Kogut, 1993), the economics of innovation (Nelson, 1993; Foray and Freeman, 1993), to economic sociology (Piore and Sabel, 1984; Granovetter, 1985; Powell and Smith-Doerr, 1994).

The capabilities firms accumulate are those rewarded and enabled by the local ecosystem, while other possible capabilities are discouraged by the environment and wither away. The resource-based perspective has traditionally ignored this dependence of capabilities on the external environment, instead emphasizing strategic variations from within firms and the resulting diversity across firms. Ironically, this emphasis on internal adaptation and organizational diversity, which is so foreign to traditional economics, has much in common with traditional sociology (Selznick, 1948; Thompson, 1967, Pfeffer and Salancik, 1978). In contrast, this study emphasizes that shared institutional environments push firms based therein towards a significant homogeneity, a view most often associated with newer, neo-institutional perspectives in sociology (DiMaggio and Powell, 1983, 1991; Davis and Powell, 1992).

If this homogeneity exists, then core attributes of the environment predict core capabilities of firms based therein. Put simply, *markets define and organize rather than merely aggregate transactions*, and the idiosyncracies of any particular organization powerfully affect the firm. So long as the firm has a certain specific form of relationship with capital providers, with labor, with science, with consumers, and with suppliers, the firm will perform in a particular way. It is not free to alter itself in isolation, and indeed *the firm is its relationships* with these local transactors. And in one given location, changes of the local environment will predictably lead over time to changes in corporate capabilities. Put differently, the domestic ecosystem is a key resource (non-transferable, non-imitable, valuable) for firms based therein (Kogut, 1993).

In the end, the debate over industrial policy at its core reduces to the magnitude of spillovers among members of the domestic ecosystem. If these spillovers are generally minor, the traditional economics model of firms and industries holds. There is then only a minimal role for appropriate industrial policy. In contrast, if spillovers are large and frequent, and in particular if the constitutive and constructive aspects of inter-actor ties are important, the economics model is simply wrong and sociology models of firms and industries hold true. Here, to the great consternation of conservative economists, industrial policy is inescapable.

This discussion of theories of the firm and the industry may be summarized by highlighting three key points. First, from the sociology-based perspective outlined above, firms may have durable competitive advantages. High-skilled firms will outperform others, and low-skilled firms will under-perform the industry. Because these internal skills may be quite difficult to imitate, the resulting competitive advantages and disadvantages can be quite durable over time. Further, because skills are accumulated in specific competitive environments, imitation of needed skills may mean reshaping not only the firm itself but also other important actors in the environment. The complexity of this task will further impede imitation. Second, corporate strategies and skills are environment-dependent. Because corporate skills are acquired in a specific environment, they will match the very different institutions in various nations. The strategies followed by firms will be significantly enabled and constrained by their existing collection of skills, formed in a particular environment. Thus firms will have distinct national identities based on differing constituting institutions, industrial skills, and corporate strategies. Third, appropriate government industrial policy focuses on the accumulation and application of corporate skills needed for superior performance. Static competition is based on utilization of a given set of technologies and skills (the production function of neoclassical analysis). Dynamic competition focuses on acquisition and maintenance of these skills themselves. The best competitive environment provides the nurturing and discipline that encourages formation of new corporate skills.

From these three points on firm constitution and conduct, the role of industrial policy follows directly. Appropriate industrial policy structures the national network to encourage rapid accumulation of appropriate corporate skills. Government plays a pervasive and inescapable role in *constructing* national competitive advantage. The perspective of conservative economics is quite different. Firms have no sustained competitive advantage, no environmental dependence, no national identity, no dynamic competition, and no need for nurturing. Critics of the conservative perspective would point out that these features are absent from traditional economics analysis because they are brazenly assumed away, and with these features goes any semblance of the modern firm and realistic corporate strategy. Only for these reasons is there little for industrial policy in the traditional model other than correction of expectedly rare and isolated market failures.

In the end, the debate over industrial policy, the theory of the firm, and the theory of industry will be resolved on an empirical basis. Systematic studies of specific firms and industries will indicate which theories best predict the strategies and performances of individual firms and the patterns of national success and failure across industries.

THE SOCIAL CONSTRUCTION OF INDUSTRIES

The goal of appropriate industrial policy is the social construction of industry to nurture corporate capabilities. To provide a greater perspective on this process, we stress three features of such social construction: first, it is fundamentally based on innovation; second, it is achieved primarily through implicit means; and third, the impact of social construction is pervasive. These three points are examined in turn below.

It has been widely recognized that firm capabilities and local networks take on greater importance under circumstances of rapid and extensive innovation (Porter, 1990; Thomas, 1996). This argument is unsurprising, on the basis of the discussion above as to the importance of spillovers. Innovation at its heart generates innumerable spillovers, from the innovator to imitators, from firms to consumers and back, from firms to suppliers and back, and so on.

The literature on innovation has identified several important sources of spillovers among members of a domestic ecosystem. Foremost among these features are *regimes of appropriation*, or mechanisms by which a firm obtains its share of the benefits from innovation (Levin, *et al.*, 1985; Teece, 1986; Levin, *et al.*, 1987). Firms with strong regimes of appropriation can afford to reinvest in continued research and development generating new innovations, and thus succeed in the long-run process of dynamic competition. In contrast, firms with weak regimes of appropriation are unable to afford continued innovation, and are forced to leave their industry.

Studies of the economics of innovation have established a vital point: the most important regimes of appropriation usually do not arise from formal policies of government explicitly designed to encourage innovation (like patents or copyrights). Rather, the most important regimes occur through day-to-day interactions of firms with other members of their competitive environment, often completely inadvertently. It is precisely through this process of shaping regimes of appropriation that the local competitive environment has so strong an impact on firms. For example, in the pharmaceutical industry, there are many regimes of appropriation that trace the expected product life cycle and net profit of drug innovations. While patents actually matter in pharmaceuticals (unlike most other industries), we must realize that they are hardly the only regime of appropriation in this industry. It is relatively straightforward for drug firms to invent molecules comparable to any new pathbreaking drug. These molecules will carry their own separate patents, and will directly compete with each other – a process quite visible in the United States with recent extensive advertising of the variety of anti-ulcer drugs: Tagamet, Zantac, Pepcid, Axid, and so on. The relative rewards to innovators and imitators in the pharmaceutical industry are thus shaped not only by patents, but also by such diverse factors as doctor behavior (how quickly innovative products are adopted and how much brand loyalty exists after adoption), safety regulation (how easily various molecules obtain market access), antitrust (how drugs firms relate vertically to retailers and wholesalers in sale of molecules), and pricing systems (how high prices are set for various molecules and how these prices trend over time). As a result, regimes of appropriation for pharmaceutical firms are determined through an uncoordinated and implicit process throughout the entire competitive environment, not just through the neoclassical presumption of formal policies of government.

Two other features of the external network of a firm affect its innovation: *technological opportunity* and *industry challenge*. There is considerable variance across industries and firms in their opportunity for innovation. Much of the scholarly literature treats such varying technological opportunity as some exogenous factor for firms (usually called 'science'). But an important stream of work has documented the importance for technological opportunity of the immediate transactors in the network surrounding firms, such as consumers, suppliers, universities, and government agencies (Jewkes, *et al.*, 1958; von Hippel, 1988; Klevorick, *et al.*, 1993). A general finding of these works is that existing transactors with firms provide much greater facilitation with innovation than do 'distant' or indirect sources such as 'science' in general. As the networks surrounding firms and the relations within these networks vary significantly across nations, technological opportunity varies, and thus the nature and patterns of firm innovations will vary correspondingly. Finally, it has long been argued that intense rivalry within an industry pushes firms to innovate more rapidly and more profoundly (Arrow, 1962; Scherer and Ross, 1990). We must recognize, however, that rivalry is only one form of industry challenge pushing firms to innovate. Sophisticated consumers, aggressive suppliers, and stringent regulators provide alternative and perhaps even more important sources of challenge. Again, as the networks surrounding firms vary significantly across nations, industry challenge varies and thus corporate innovations vary.

Because regimes of appropriation, technological opportunity, and industry challenge will vary significantly across different domestic ecosystems, the paths of innovation will take fundamentally different trajectories among various nations. The trajectory that is actually chosen is thus *socially constructed*. Innovation frequently leads to multiple possible outcomes when only one outcome is viable. Examples of required technological choice are provided by the conflict between VHS and Betamax for videocassette recorders, and by MS-DOS or Macintosh for personal computer operating systems. Under these technological circumstances, the ultimate outcome will be determined by the ecosystem, especially by the capabilities of ecosystem members and the political interactions among them. An important example of the social construction of technology, known to every international traveler, is electrical power. The advent of large-scale electrical systems offered two fundamental choices: alternating current (AC) that easily spanned long distances and direct current (DC) that efficiently served densely populated urban areas. Additional choices were offered by voltage levels and connection equipment. The electricity industry in each nation was socially constructed by economic and political conflict, often between rural and urban factions. In the USA, adoption of AC technology was achieved by the triumph of Thomas Edison over Westinghouse and its DC technology (Hughes, 1983).

This review of aspects of innovation immediately suggests a second important feature of the new view of industrial policy: that industrial policy is not driven by explicit, formal, acts of government. This second point holds even in circumstances that do not at first glance appear to be centered on innovation. An important example can be seen from the motor vehicle industries of the USA and Japan, illustrated in Figure 2.3. In the USA, automobile firms such as General Motors have traditionally operated in an ecosystem characterized by arm's-length, formal/legalistic, and often adversarial ties with other transactors (such as the United Auto Workers union) in a highly fluid and unstructured environment. A key resource of US firms resulting from this ecosystem is the capability to innovate new product categories, such as the minivans and sport-utility vehicles pioneered by Chrysler. In Japan, automobile firms such as Toyota have traditionally operated in a very different ecosystem of integrated, informal, cooperative relations with other transactors (such as vertically linked suppliers in the *keiretsu* system). A key resource of Japanese firms based in this ecosystem is continuous improvement of process technology resulting in higher quality and productivity. Note that both traditional ecosystems create corporate valuable, if different, capabilities. And both sets of capabilities ultimately center on innovation.

From the perspective of this study, automobile firms do not and indeed cannot act in isolation. In traditional economics, a firm acts completely independently within anonymous markets. Comprehensive change in strategy can be implemented at any time by this isolated firm. In contrast, this study regards the firm as merely one element of a complex ecosystem. Fundamental changes to firm conduct require collective changes to the ecosystem – a difficult and time-consuming process. For example, the different ecosystems facing American and Japanese automobile makers have profound implications for quality and reliability. For some 25 years, the superior quality of Japanese-made cars and trucks has been well established. American vehicle manufacturers have every incentive to close this quality gap. Yet, in the year 2000, quality ratings for vehicles sold in the USA continued to show severe differences across manufacturers, with emphatic national identity in quality patterns (Simison and White, 2000). The worst firms are the three American, while the Japanese are uniformly better. Why have American car makers not fully copied the production strategies of Toyota, Nissan, and Honda after 25 years? From the perspective of this study, the continuing lag is not surprising and is even

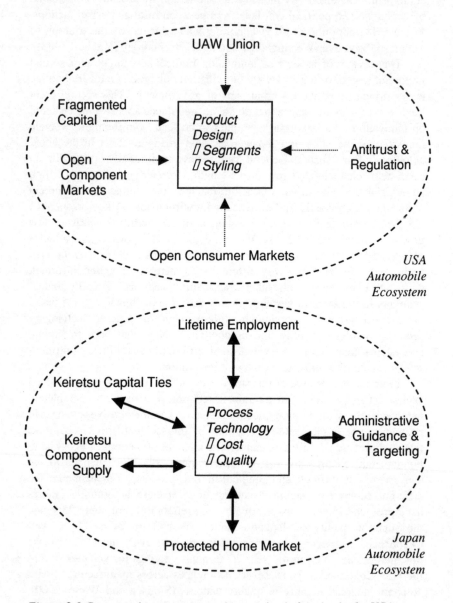

Figure 2.3 Comparative ecosystems: Automotive industries in the USA and Japan

expected. For US automobile firms to imitate Japanese firms successfully, they must do far more than merely reconfigure internal mixes of capital and labor. Rather they must completely change US industrial policy, including labor relations (union law), supplier relations (antitrust law), capital relations (laws on banking, pensions, and securities), and government relations (regulation). General Motors, Ford, and Chrysler have of course imitated certain elements of Japanese strategy and today, for example, have closer relations with suppliers and unions than in the past. Yet the domestic ecosystem for US firms remains fundamentally different from that of Toyota, Nissan, Mitsubishi, and Honda. Hence the quality and productivity gaps persist. Fortunately, the American firms can draw on other, very different capabilities in their competition with Japanese vehicle manufacturers.

In traditional economics, only formally stated and deliberately intended programs are industrial policies. In the new approach, any activity that importantly affects the domestic ecosystem is an industrial policy, as it significantly shapes the conduct and performance of firms based in that ecosystem. The new approach is almost Freudian in insisting that unconscious effects, some originating long ago, are implicit industrial policies that are as real and important as explicit policies. For example, in 1957, the US Supreme Court, in a reinterpretation of a 1914 law, forced Dupont to divest its 40-year-old, 25-percent holding of General Motors common equity (Howard, 1983; Solomon, 1993). This decision, in practice, totally prohibited the Japanese *keiretsu* system of long-term vertical supplier ties and activist investors who could discipline company management, at exactly the time period when Japanese vehicle manufacturers were assembling their own *keiretsus*. Yet the result of this obscure antitrust ruling from the judicial system is as much industrial policy in the USA as if the American Congress and President had adopted explicit legislation to that end.

In traditional economics, only government acts are industrial policy. This approach presumes a sharp and clear break between government and the rest of society, almost as if government is some alien occupying force. The new approach does not regard this arm's-length separation between government and society as a useful depiction of reality. For example, post-1945 policies towards labor unions were determined only in part by law, but more importantly by precedent-setting strikes both in the USA against General Motors in 1948 (Kochan, *et al.*, 1986) and in Japan against Nissan in 1952 (Gibney, 1988; Hart, 1992). The very different settlements in each of these strikes comprehensively shaped and transformed national labor relations. In the USA, labor unions subsequently gave up any role or responsibility for setting strategy with management, with its overtones of socialism. Instead, US unions adopted the legalistic, hostile, arm's-length stance that defined post-1945 US labor relations. In Japan, the implicit contract of lifetime employment in exchange for passive company unions had similar pervasive implications for Japanese labor relations. In each case, one of many possible trajectories was chosen not by government, but by private actors, and diffused throughout the economy by imitation of other private actors. Similarly, the nature of consumer demand for automobiles in the USA was significantly changed in the 1980s by the rise of rating systems for quality and long-term customer satisfaction. The fact that these ratings were generated by a private firm rather than the US government matters far less than the simple fact that they existed at all.

The modern approach to industrial policy is a source of confusion for those who consider only explicit, intentional acts by government as industrial policy. May we be very clear that the most important reason why the old approach must be abandoned is that it really does not explain very much. For example, those who regard the nature of Japanese industrial policy towards the automobile industry as mere protectionism with targeted subsidies really miss the point. Protectionism and subsidies have been tried all over the world, from Argentina to India to Zaire. These isolated policies, placed in profoundly different ecosystems, have usually failed and most have failed disastrously. To the extent they succeeded in Japan, it is only because they were interjected into an ecosystem with company unions, *keiretsu* suppliers, *keiretsu* capital, and an autonomous and politically sheltered bureaucracy. Companies in this North East Asian institutional ecosystem do not seek to maximize profits, but rather have a pronounced bias towards growth (Thomas and Waring, 1999). Only because of the integrated workings of this entire ecosystem did Japanese firms utilize profits from protectionism and subsidy to reinvest in the firm, and build internal capabilities. An Anglo-Saxon firm facing protectionism or subsidy, but isolated from suppliers and labor and beholden to shareholders, would promptly pay out any new profits as dividends or use such profits to diversify outside the motor vehicle industry.

A third feature of social construction of industries is that it can be pervasive, affecting not just relative production quality capabilities, but even the nature and size of firms and the products they make. An important example of the social construction of industry is provided by semiconductors. Semiconductor technology offers an astonishing array of possibilities: how a given product is to be made, which products to make, the pace of technical change, and so on. Figure 2.4 traces the very different ecosystems for semiconductors in the Japan and the USA. In Japan, semiconductors are made in a tightly coupled network of long-standing relations. Leading Japanese semiconductor firms, such as

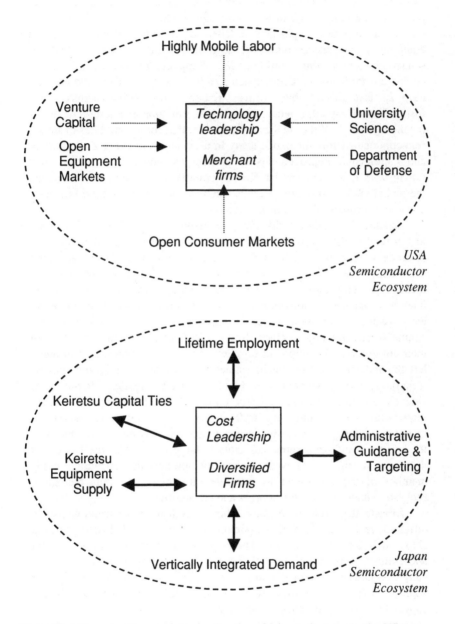

Figure 2.4 Comparative ecosystems: Semiconductor industries in the USA and Japan

Toshiba, NEC, and Hitachi, are enormous electronics conglomerates that purchase internally much of their own semiconductor output. These firms are among the most sophisticated sellers of consumer electronics, office equipment, and telecommunications in the world. Their demand for semiconductors is thus cutting-edge. Suppliers of key manufacturing equipment for semiconductors (such as silicon wafers makers and etchers) have *keiretsu* ties to these firms. Labor is not mobile across firms. Institutions of capital, science, and government support a long-term focus for the industry. Within this ecosystem, like that for automobiles in Japan, semiconductor firms focus on steady improvements of process technology and incremental improvements to product technology. Japanese firms (along with their very similar Korean counterparts) completely dominate the global market for memory chips (such as DRAMs) with their low costs and internal capabilities for process technologies.

Despite their original discovery of memory chips, US firms steadily lost ground in the 1980s to Japanese semiconductor firms. Internal efforts at process technology in the USA were hampered by the fluid and open ecosystem there. US semiconductor firms are merchant firms, being highly focused on semiconductors and related products. Unlike their vertically integrated Japanese competitors, US semiconductor firms have no long-term assurance for their sales. Equipment suppliers in the USA are similarly free-standing, focused firms. Without long-term support from their customers, US equipment suppliers were highly vulnerable and many left the industry. Corporate investments in worker training and process technology proved vulnerable to highly fluid labor markets of the USA. One US executive in this industry remarked that his company's recent innovations were doing very well, at five small companies down the interstate highway founded by former employees. Even the science base for basic research into semiconductors is largely public in the USA, and thus open to all. These weak regimes of appropriation encourage every member of the ecosystem to free-ride on others, and thus the entire ecosystem underinvests in resources and capabilities.

Despite their rout in memory chips, US firms have triumphed in a different, and arguably more important segment of the industry – logical chips, such as microprocessors. The very features of the US ecosystem that undermined performance by US firms in memory chips have facilitated their dominance in logical chips. In logical chips, the key regime of appropriation is speed to market, supplemented somewhat by software copyrights. US firms have a very narrow window of time within which they must launch and commercialize cutting-edge technology products. Towards the end of this window, imitators will drive down prices and sales, and the technology leader must come up with another, superior, generation of the product. The open and fluid nature of the US ecosystem, in which consumers, suppliers, capital, and labor move readily from one firm to the next, enable the best ideas and resources to coalesce swiftly with the best firm.

Note that the Japanese and US industries in semiconductors are entirely socially constructed. The firms are different: vertically integrated conglomerates in Japan versus merchant firms in the USA. The strategies are different: cost leadership in the Japan and technology leadership in the USA. The products are different, the suppliers are different, institutions of science are different, and so on.

Other nations have tried to imitate the US success in logical chips, but failed. It is important to recognize that each component of the US ecosystem for semiconductors represents a set of sophisticated institutions with their own highly evolved capabilities. Put differently, US semiconductor firms and their supporting transactors have *coevolved* over more than two decades, mutually developing each other's capabilities. The sophistication of capabilities for each component of the ecosystem very much depends on and evolves with that of other components. Consider, for example, the venture capital firms that have played so prominent a role in Silicon Valley. This unique institution serves multiple functions. Yes, it raises capital, but it is also a consulting firm (guiding the strategy of start-up firms), a personnel firm (providing links to key managers and technologists), a law firm (preparing corporate and financial documents), and an investment bank (serving on the board of directors for start-up firms). Each of these capabilities, let alone their distinctive mix, must be learned and refined over time in direct competition with more traditional financial institutions. Consider also the US tradition of job mobility for senior managers and scientists. Here again there is an evolving set of institutions and laws that balance the needs of existing firms to protect trade secrets against the advantages of moving promising individuals to positions where they will have greater impact. None of these institutions emerged overnight.

The pharmaceutical industry, like that of semiconductors, is highly socially constructed. As will be discussed at greater length in Chapters 4 and 9, there are many possible forms for individual innovations and the firms that create them. It is important to realize that the highly innovative pharmaceutical industry that we know in the USA exists in only a handful of nations, including Britain, Germany, Sweden, and Switzerland. There are entire regions of the world where pharmaceutical innovation as we know it is entirely absent, including the Anglo-Saxon nations Australia, Canada, and New Zealand. There is thus nothing at all inevitable about pharmaceutical innovation. An innovative pharmaceutical industry emerges through coevolution with sophisticated medical practice by doctors, sophisticated regulation by government, and sophisticated basic research by universities. Unfortunately for Japan, these basic prerequisites for an innovative pharmaceutical industry are largely absent in that country. The industry that has been socially constructed in Japan thus has severe pathologies, only one of which is the exclusion of foreign innovations.

ANTITRUST, TRADE POLICY, AND THE RULE OF REASON

Before we turn to a detailed examination of the Japanese domestic ecosystem for pharmaceuticals, and its limitations, we must specifically examine the issue of exclusion of foreign firms from a national market. There are actually two quite distinct literatures on the exclusion of competitors from established markets. The older literature is based on antitrust (for surveys, see Carlton and Perloff; 1990; Scherer, 1994; Scherer and Ross, 1990). The modern contributions to that literature focus on raising rivals' costs as the foundation of exclusion (Krattenmaker and Salop, 1986; Salop and Sheffman, 1983). The antitrust literature assumes firms of equal internal capability, and focuses on manipulations of the product market that increase the costs of market participation. Usually, such manipulations raise costs for all firms in an industry to some degree. But if costs rise asymmetrically, those firms suffering the higher cost increases may find it unprofitable to enter or remain in a market, and will thus be excluded. A diverse array of exclusionary mechanisms are iterated in the literature: brand proliferation (Schmalensee, 1978), capacity preemption (Ghemawat, 1984), factor pricing (Williamson, 1968), patent accumulation (Gilbert, 1981), product preannouncements (Farrell and Saloner, 1986), and safety and environmental regulations (Bartel and Thomas, 1987).

Put in terms of simple algebra, the decision to enter or remain in a given market is determined by the following inequality:

$$R_{all} \geq C_{all} + C_i \qquad \text{then enter}$$
$$R_{all} < C_{all} + C_i \qquad \text{then stay out}$$

R_{all} denotes the revenue for each firm, C_{all} denotes the similar costs borne by each firm, and C_i denotes the asymmetrically higher costs borne by the victim of exclusion. Note that, if the asymmetric costs are sufficiently high, firms bearing these costs will be excluded, even as other firms remain and perhaps thrive in the industry.

The traditional antitrust literature focused on external market positioning among identical firms. The new organizational economics offers a fundamental critique of this approach. Specifically, the new approach argues that many if not most asymmetric costs among firms exist not because of monopolistic market positions, but rather owing to internal differences in capabilities among firms. One firm may enter a market while a second firm does not because the first firm has lower costs (for example owing to superior process technology) or more attractive products (owing to superior marketing technology). The new approach stresses that many competitive acts that might initially look like exclusion merely reflect superior firm capabilities. Antitrust today must therefore draw an important distinction between superior capabilities that drive out inferior competitors and market manipulations that unfairly exclude worthy competitors. A quick perusal of the exclusionary mechanisms listed above suggests the vital importance of this distinction, as virtually every strategic act by firms is potentially exclusionary. A blanket prohibition of all these acts would simply shut down competition among firms, rather than promote it.

The first question, then, is whether or not specific corporate practices are capability-enhancing (hence pro-competitive) or are monopoly-promoting (hence anti-competitive). The second question is whether the specific capabilities or practices are desirable. Both questions turn on whether or not these capabilities and practices are welfare-enhancing for the economy as a whole. Traditionally, antitrust has focused on static competition and static efficiency, and the principal question has been whether consumer prices rise or fall with the corporate act in question. But, increasingly, attention is turning to dynamic competition and the rate of innovation in an industry as central issues for welfare. Consider, for example, Microsoft and the US software industry. Microsoft bundles some of its products (for example, combining its Internet browser with its Windows operating system) and engages in exclusive dealing with downstream firms (for example, prohibiting PC makers that preinstall Windows on their machines from also installing Netscape products). Traditional antitrust would examine the appropriateness of these practices by looking at their effects on current software prices. The new approach would examine their effect on the overall rate of innovation in the industry. This sort of analysis represents exercise of the so-called, rule of reason, trading off the public costs and benefits of strategic acts before ruling them exclusionary. Note that rule-of-reason analysis never focuses on exclusion, but rather concentrates on efficiency, and increasingly on dynamic efficiency (the rate and magnitude of innovation) rather than on static efficiency (price levels).

A second literature on exclusion examines industrial policy and strategic trade, notably in East Asia (Lincoln, 1990; Prestowitz, 1988; Tyson, 1992). This literature highlights protectionist actions that exclude foreign competitors, enabling domestic firms to use their home market as a profit sanctuary to attack foreign firms. Over the last few decades, this protectionism has moved from crude bans on imports and prohibitive tariffs towards more sophisticated non-tariff barriers to trade. In tandem, the locus of protectionism has moved from pure government acts to the cooperative interface between government and the protected domestic industry. Numerous examples of non-tariff barriers have been offered in this second literature: standard setting (Tyson, 1992), systems of public R&D support (Anchordoguy, 1989), vertical ties to distributors (Kodak, 1997), tax audits (Clifford, 1994), weak protection of intellectual property, and corporate governance systems (Gerlach, 1992; Lawrence, 1991).

Recent work in the industrial policy literature has begun to stress that many activities that initially appear to be non-tariff barriers are merely differences in institutional systems across nations (Jackson, 1989; Reich, 1990). For example, many East Asian economies have institutions that facilitate cooperation among firms in an industry. Commentators in the USA have often been quick to label these institutions as 'cartels', presuming that they are welfare-destructive. Yet closer study of industry cooperative institutions in Japan has indicated that there are often economic benefits to them, offsetting anti-competitive social costs and perhaps exceeding them. Similar revisionist studies have found comparable social benefits in the *keiretsu* structure of corporate control (Aoki and Dore, 1994; Kester, 1991), the informal and less legalistic joint setting of standards by industry and government (Badaracco, 1985; Vogel, 1992), and other hallmarks of the Japanese economy. If the domestic ecosystems of two nations are very different, we would expect that the social construction of firms and their internal capabilities in the two nations will be very different. Firms from two such nations will inevitably have difficulties in each other's markets, owing to the differing internal capabilities necessary for success.

Like the approach now common in antitrust, the new analyses of non-tariff trade barriers require us to exercise great care before condemning different industrial practices across nations as 'exclusionary' and deserving of attack by international trade mechanisms. Thus, an international rule of reason is called for. Like new analyses of antitrust, the principal issue in such inquiries should be whether the practices in question promote or retard innovation and dynamic efficiency. As we will see clearly in Chapter 4, exclusion of foreign firms from the Japanese pharmaceutical market does not remotely pass the rule-of-reason test. Indeed, the very factors that lead to exclusion of foreign drug firms from Japan have multiple destructive consequences, most of which are profoundly anti-innovative. Before we trace these pathologies of the Japanese domestic ecosystem for pharmaceuticals in Chapter 4, we must first describe that ecosystem in Chapter 3.

The domestic Japanese ecosystem for pharmaceuticals

To explain the new drug lag in Japan, we must examine the evolution of the domestic Japanese pharmaceutical industry since 1981. This evolution was catalyzed by 'reforms' to pricing regulations adopted in that year by MHW, and was then jolted in 1992 with reforms to clinical trial regulations. The impacts of both pricing and clinical trial regulations of MHW are powerfully affected by the entire Japanese domestic ecosystem for pharmaceuticals. To understand the impact of the regulatory changes, we must therfore consider the entire ecosystem. Let us examine in turn the three main components of this ecosystem.

DOCTORS AND PHARMACEUTICAL DEMAND

As would be expected with a nation dominated by a conservative party (the LDP), the health care system in Japan is largely privately owned. Figure 3.1 reports the number of doctors working in Japan in 1960 and 1990, and their distribution across health care establishments. The JMA has always been dominated by private practitioners (*kaigyo-i*) who own their own small hospitals or clinics (Mikitaka and Campbell, 1996). Given the political prominence of the JMA in health care policy in Japan, it is no surprise that MHW regulations have historically sharply tilted in favor of the private practitioners and against doctors employed at larger institutions (*kinmu-i*). Unfortunately for the JMA, the proportion of Japanese doctors in private practice has fallen (see Figure 3.1). The political support for and influence of the JMA have correspondingly declined as well. The average age of self-employed clinic doctors is now almost 60 (Yoshikawa, 1993).

Insurance schedules for medical care are directly regulated by MHW. The average annual income for a clinic doctor approaches $300,000 (¥ 36 million), while the average annual salary of physicians employed in ordinary hospitals is only $81,000 or ¥ 9.8 million (Yoshikawa, 1993). This distribution of income is the reverse of that in the USA, where hospital-based specialists earn far more than general practitioners. Given the

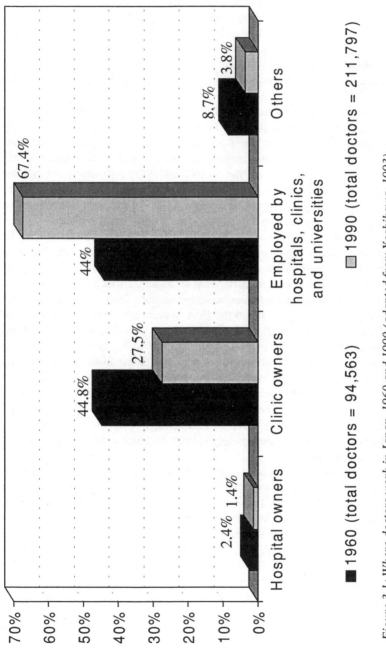

Figure 3.1: Where doctors work in Japan, 1960 and 1990 (adapted from Yoshikawa, 1993). Owners of hospitals and clinics are kaigyo-i. Doctors employed by institutions are kinmu-i.

financial constraints and pressures on MHW, it is clear that the JMA has traditionally acted to redistribute income in Japan from hospital-based physicians to private practitioners (Mikitaka and Campbell, 1996). Like the dual state itself, the overcompensated private practitioner sector (*kaigyo-i*) and the undercompensated large hospital sector (*kinmu-i*) make each other possible. Overpayments to JMA supporters are financially feasible because the JMA vigorously obstructs political voice for non-self-employed physicians, while it provides political cover for MHW to underpay that sector.

Two key mechanisms have been traditionally employed by MHW to boost incomes for clinic owners. First, MHW fee schedules are historically fee-for-service, and reward brief consultations between patients and doctors. The average visit time for patients in small clinics is five minutes (not including waiting time to see the doctor), while the comparable average for patients in large hospitals is 17 minutes (Yoshikawa, 1993). MHW fees do not correspondingly compensate hospital doctors for the greater time spent with patients. Private clinic doctors see an average of 50 patients a day; 13 percent of these doctors see in excess of 100 patients (Akira, 1993). An important consequence of these medical arrangements is that Japanese consumers of health care are quite ignorant of their conditions and options for care. This outcome is partly due to Japanese medical traditions, but since MHW payment schemes discourage doctors from spending time with patients, doctors in general and the JMA in particular have a strong stake in maintenance of this tradition. Japanese patients generally have no idea what drugs are prescribed for them, or what biomedical function these drugs are to serve. The multiple prescriptions they take home from their physicians are not even labeled for identification. A particularly egregious instance of this problem is that most Japanese cancer patients are not even informed they have cancer. Because of this lack of information, clinical trials of certain drugs in Japan are accepted outside Japan only with great difficulty, as foreign regulatory bodies usually require informed consent of patients for any trials submitted.

A second mechanism employed to boost incomes of private practitioners is *bungyo*, the combination of prescription and dispensing, so ardently defended by the JMA over the years. In large part because doctors are under compensated for their time spent with patients, they must offset their low fees by over prescribing and over supplying materials, especially pharmaceuticals. Doctors purchase drugs from wholesalers, who sell them at a discount from MHW-established retail prices. Yet the MHW reimburses doctors for all drugs they prescribe and dispense at the official retail price. The 'doctor's margin' is thus pure income for the prescribing physician. Doctors and hospitals therefore have a strong incentive to prescribe/dispense the most expensive drugs (Ikegami, Ikeda, and Kawai, 1997). They also have a powerful incentive to overprescribe products.

> The Japanese spend more on drugs that anybody else in the world: $228 per person per year, compared with $169 in western Germany, the second most-prolific pill-popper. ... Doctors have now become the butt of much criticism for their excessive prescribing habits – whose effects are jokingly referred to as *kusurizuke*, or pickled in drugs... (*Economist*, 1993)

The distortions of pharmaceutical consumption caused by JMA political pressure are not limited to massive overconsumption of drugs. In one case, they actually involve underconsumption. Japan is one of the very few countries in the world to outlaw contraceptive pills, used by women for birth control. Up to the present time, Japan banned 'the pill' despite its safe and effective usage by some 80 million women throughout the world.

> Japanese women's groups have no doubts as to why their demand for a change in the [ban has been] resisted. Easy access to [contraceptive] pills would free Japanese women from turning to abortion as the principal means of birth control. At present an estimated ¥100 billion a year is spent on abortions. A newspaper survey in 1994 ... discovered that 13% of Japanese women would use the pill if it were made available. This nearly matches the 15% of women of childbearing age in other rich countries who say they use the pill. ... Officials say that 345,000 abortions are performed each year in Japan. But that excludes abortions carried out by doctors but described as other operations, or the backstreet abortions which typically cost ¥100,000 a time (and are rarely reported to the tax authorities). For the medical profession, abortion represents a major source of income which it is not prepared to give up without a fight. A study by the Asia-Pacific Research Centre finds that abortions were under-reported in Japan by a factor of at least three. This suggests that half of all pregnancies in Japan end in abortion. (*Economist*, 1997b; also see Maruyama, *et al.*, 1996)

The nature of doctor demand for pharmaceuticals in Japan creates enormous economic inefficiencies and problems for public health. Yet this demand endures as a political equilibrium, or truce among key political actors. While it would seem 'obvious' and 'easy' to eliminate the doctor's margin for pharmaceuticals and raise fees for time spent with patients, this reform fundamentally threatens the interests of the JMA. Higher fees for doctor time threaten to reallocate resources not only from pharmaceuticals to doctor service, but also away from private practitioners to hospitals. Once the political logjam is broken and interests of doctors in the hospital sector are given voice, overall costs in the medical sector may rise, threatening interests of insurance providers and the MOF. Thus the truce, and its attendant inefficiencies, endure.

THE CLINICAL TRIAL SYSTEM

Legislation adopted by the Diet in 1967 requires premarket approval (registration) for all new drugs in Japan. This legislation incorporated the unusual requirement that pre-market testing, both preclinical (animal) and clinical (human), be conducted in Japan prior to MHW registration. Foreign firms then had to reproduce, significantly if not totally, new drug studies inside Japan in order to register their product and gain market access. Foreign firms lacking Japanese research facilities were put at a particular disadvantage by this barrier. MHW has in principle been willing to accept some foreign data since 1976, and recommitted itself in 1986 to accept such data. The nature of the MHW registration process, however, has meant in practical terms that only very recently has any foreign data been accepted, and then often grudgingly. As this registration process is described below, it is important to note that the non-acceptability of foreign data is largely an implicit outcome of acts by private parties, rather than an explicit act of government.

The clinical trial system in Japan is completely distinctive from that of other nations. Japan's clinical trial system has its own internal logic and own traditions that operate analogously to the internal operating system of a personal computer. For personal computers, there are of course multiple operating systems: Microsoft Windows, Apple Macintosh, IMB OS/2, AT&T Unix, and the NEC system, among others. These systems each have various strengths and weaknesses, and there are debates as to which is best. Ironically, many regard the Apple Macintosh system as technologically the best, even though it is installed on only a tiny minority of PCs sold each year. On one issue, however, there is no debate and that is that Microsoft Windows is the dominant operating system in the world, and most personal computer software is written for Windows. Yet, until 1996, most personal computers sold in Japan relied on the NEC operating system, used by vitually no one else in the world. Japanese personal computer makers were at a strong disadvantage in external markets because they had to export Windows-based machines without any direct experience in their home market.

With regard to clinical trials for pharmaceuticals, the US Food and Drug Administration (FDA) occupies a position comparable to that of Microsoft in PC operating systems. FDA views on acceptable levels of side-effects, how efficacy is measured, due process for clinical trials, and so on are the foundations of a worldwide consensus. Clinical trials acceptable to the FDA have wide global acceptance. In contrast, MHW occupies a position with regard to clinical trials comparable to that of NEC in PC operating systems. Just as virtually no one outside Japan wants a PC with an NEC operating system, so Japanese clinical trials are accepted virtually nowhere else in the world.

There are several profound differences between the globalized FDA approach to clinical trials and the MHW approach unique to Japan. The first difference is the structure of authority among participants. Clinical trials in Japan are conducted under what is often called 'The Old Professor System'. The core of this system is the Drug Review Committee (or 'expert committee') for the MHW, traditionally comprising senior university professors who serve on the committee in their spare time. A second component is the primary investigator, another senior university professor who designs and executes clinical trials for new drugs in Japan. Until recently, drug companies in Japan did not have legal authority to conduct clinical trials – only primary investigators could do so. The primary investigator assembles colleagues at diverse institutions to provide human subjects for testing. Oddly, patients for clinical trials most often came from many small hospitals and clinics run by private practitioners, and only rarely from the large university hospitals with which the senior professors are nominally associated. The medical outcome of these strange assemblages is often quite counterproductive.

> Yataka Mizushima, a past member of the MHW's Drug Review Committee and currently an Upper House Parliament Councilor is trying to initiate changes in the system. He has noted that there are too many investigators at too many sites with too few cases at each site, and many of the investigators do not have sufficient knowledge or experience to perform drug trials ... In addition, because different investigators at different sites each have their own way of carrying out a study, the standardization of outcome measures is difficult ... Flaws in drug trial methodology seem to have resulted in the inability of Buspar (buspirone, Bristol-Myers Squibb) to be approved [in Japan]. Buspar, an non-benzodiazepine anxiolytic that has been shown to be effective and has been available in a number of countries since the 1980s [a global product for this study], was determined to be no more effective than placebo by two multicenter double-blind trials in Japan. However, close scrutiny of these studies shows that too few patients at too many centers led to inter-site variation ... Similar protocol designs in Japan were not even sensitive enough to find benzodiazepines (that is, Valium) superior to placebo for anxiety in five or six multicenter placebo-controlled studies, even though studies performed outside Japan have concluded overwhelmingly anxiolytics are more effective than placebo. (Berger and Fukunishi, 1996)

These doctors and institutions are assembled for clinical trials on the personal authority and stature of the primary investigator in Japan.

> One has to understand the unhealthily close relationship that exists between doctors, pharmaceutical companies, and the MHW. Data presented to the MHW for approval are mainly in the form of unpublished results or of reports published in Japanese in company-financed or company-related journals. Those in charge of clinical trials often set up their own foundations, funded by the [Japanese] pharmaceutical companies, for which they organize clinical trials. And often some heads of clinical trials also belong to the Drug Review Committee. Thus a data-producing mechanism by the company for the company is inherent in the system. (Fukushima, 1989)

A critical component of the personal ties that hold together this system are the estimated 100 former highly ranked MHW officials who have retired from the ministry to executive positions in Japanese drug firms (Ross, 1996). This well-established ministerial career path is commonly labeled 'descent from heaven' or *amakudari*.

The 'Old Professor System' is extremely hierarchical, formal, and non-transparent. In every developed nation, the clinical trial system has three main actors: drug companies, regulatory authorities, and university investigators. In almost all developed nations, authority in the system is weighted towards regulators and drug companies. Not in Japan. There the principal investigator has clear supremacy of influence. This influence goes beyond the legal formality of his sponsorship of the trials. It is bolstered by the profound hierarchy and bureaucracy of Japanese universities (Sunao, 1988). It is even tainted by the '50 years war' between the JMA and the MHW, with overtones of the JMA obsession with autonomy from regulators and its contempt for MHW bureaucrats. Further, in almost all developed nations, the three main actors deal with each other in a consultative and cooperative manner. Again, not so in Japan. No advance consultations are possible. Drug companies are not allowed to attend Drug Review Committee meetings, or to contact members of the committees directly. Rather, MHW representatives attend the meeting and subsequently meet with the drug company. MHW officials convey to the drug firm their (not always fully correct) understanding of what the distinguished professors on the expert committee intend. One pharmaceutical executive described relations among senior professors, MHW officials, and pharmaceutical executives as 'like a bad marriage; they don't talk to each other; they don't respect each other; they don't understand each other.' These details make clear that the MHW has vastly less control over its clinical trials than does the FDA.

This first difference between the FDA and MHW systems has at its core a difference in the formality of relations among participants. The Japanese clinical trial system is highly formal and structured. To senior professors in Japan, the more casual system employed by the FDA offers severe risks of corruption, comparable to allowing defendants in criminal trials to negotiate directly and privately with their judges. American critics of Japanese clinical trials must remember that many administrative processes in the USA are even more highly formalized (Badaracco, 1985). Further, much of the relative flexibility of the FDA has emerged precisely because it has been politically bludgeoned steadily over 20 years for being too slow and bureaucratic in its approval of new drugs. The FDA has become more cooperative with industry and US university professors largely because it has been forced to do so.

A second key difference between the FDA and MHW systems is the extremely passive role of Japanese patients. US clinical trials emphatically require the informed consent of all participating patients. In contrast, before 1994, patients in clinical trials in Japan would only rarely be made aware of their consumption of experimental drugs, their participation in clinical trials being driven by the financial self-interest of the private clinic owner and his personal ties with a senior university professor. Another widespread and still current difference is the presence of 'protocol violations' in Japanese clinical trials. It is not uncommon for one-third of patients enrolled in Japanese clinical trials to be ultimately thrown out of data analyses, because they were improperly included in the first place or were treated in a manner other than that called for in the clinical trial protocol. Examples of common protocol violations are inclusion of patients who suffer from multiple medical problems and are under treatment for these other problems (the presence of other treatments confounds isolation of effects for the experimental drug under study), failure to adhere to dosage regimes as given in the clinical protocol, and failure to report medical outcomes tracked by the protocol. In most developed nations, including the USA, if even 5 percent of enrolled patients were inevaluable in a clinical trial, this failure would call into question not only the entire clinical trial itself, but the very competence of the primary investigator and the pharmaceutical firm that retained him. Not so in Japan. From a Western perspective, protocol violations are not only inefficient, they are completely unethical. The research protocol for an experiment drugs is seen as a formal if implicit contract between regulators and investigators. Regulators allow experimentation on human beings, but only if investigators follow the approved protocol. In contrast, senior professors in Japan have regarded clinical trial protocols as something much more informal, more as recommendations to be adapted over the course of clinical trials.

A third, and critical, difference between the US and Japanese systems of clinical trials is how they are paid for. In the USA, the company sponsoring the new drug pays most costs associated with drug testing, a process the Japanese consider 'corrupt'. In Japan, the government pays basic costs of clinical trials, as part of normal public sponsored medical service – an ostensibly purer approach. Yet, ironically, conflicts of interest are arguably more severe in Japan than in the USA. Over the last decade, there have been several instances where the 'data-producing mechanism for the company by the company' has led to patient death and political scandal in Japan. In 1988, MHW approached three Japanese drug firms (including the large firms Takeda and Tanabe) and encouraged each of them to pool their best vaccine. The new triple vaccine would compete with the MMR (measles, mumps, and rubella) vaccine marketed worldwide by Merck (a US firm) and taken by over 100 million children. MMR was not approved for sale in Japan, however. The Japanese triple vaccine was speeded through clinical trials in one year, and when marketed in spring 1989 was required in compulsory national immunization programs for schoolchildren. The shabby clinical trials for the Japanese vaccine predicted side-effects entirely by reference to the extensive experience of the Merck product, assuming the two products were effectively identical. Unfortunately, within six months, the actual instance of side-effects of the Japanese product was found to be 100 times greater. The most frequent severe side-effect for vaccinated children was meningitis. Contemptibly, MHW did nothing to withdraw the Japanese vaccine or to approve the Merck product for Japan. Instead, it made the vaccine voluntary rather than mandatory. Two years later, it allowed the three Japanese firms to sell their own distinctive version of the triple vaccine, which did little to reduce side-effects (Helm, 1993).

An even greater scandal occurred with Factor VIII, a clotting agent for blood, given to hemophiliacs. Factor VIII was introduced worldwide by Baxter (a US firm) in 1978, but was not approved in Japan by MHW until 1983. By that time, three Japanese firms were also approved to sell versions of Factor VIII. Since products of Baxter and the Japanese firms went on sale at the same time, the Japanese firms were able to dominate sales because of their superior distribution (Goozner, 1995). The largest Japanese sales were garnered by the domestic firm Green Cross. Both the Baxter and the Japanese versions of Factor VIII were made from blood collected in the USA from thousands of donors, some of whom were infected with the AIDS virus. To address the large risk of HIV transmission to hemophiliacs, Baxter launched in 1983 a heat-treated version of Factor VIII. The heat treatment was designed by Baxter to kill hepatitis viruses in donated blood, and fortunately killed HIV as well. Mid-level MHW officials promptly met Baxter executives and promised on an 'emergency basis' to speed the heat-treated product through clinical trials and thereby curtail the risk of AIDS transmission to Japanese hemophiliacs. A senior university professor from Teikyo University, Takeshi Abe, led the clinical trials for the imported Baxter product. Unfortunately, both Dr. Abe and senior MHW officials had strong ties to Green Cross. Since Green Cross could not make the heat-treated version of Factor VIII, it stood to suffer significant financial losses from MHW approval of the heat-treated Baxter import. In mid-1983, Green Cross donated $90,000 to a new hemophiliac foundation to be run by Dr. Abe (Hamilton, 1996). Subsequent donations from Green Cross and four other Japanese firms selling competing products totaled over ¥43 million (Ross, 1996), while several former senior MHW officials had retired from the ministry and were at that time senior executives at Green Cross (Hamilton, 1996). Suddenly, MHW ceased discussions with Baxter and Dr. Abe's committee not only dropped consideration of the Baxter product but engineered a cover-up of Japan's first AIDS death - a hemophiliac who died at Teikyo University hospital. It was not until 1984 that Baxter was allowed to conduct Japanese clinical trials for its heat-treated product. The trials were administered by Dr. Abe, along with those of four Japanese firms. Despite a four-month headstart by Baxter in Japan, and a year of global experience by that firm, all five firms in Japan received MHW approval on the same day in mid-1985, over two years after FDA approval (*ibid.*). Even after approval of its new heat-treated product, Green Cross continued for two years in Japan to sell down its inventory of non-heat-treated products (Ross, 1996). Over 400 hemophiliacs in Japan have died from AIDS, and over 1800 are infected with HIV, about one-third of all hemophiliacs in Japan (Ross, 1996).

A fourth and final difference between the US and Japanese clinical trial systems concerns the trade-offs between safety and efficacy. This trade-off pervades even the most basic logistics of clinical trials. For example, a fundamental task of any clinical trial is determination of appropriate dose for new medicines (for example, 5 mg per day, or 50 mg per day). In the West, this dose is determined by sequential dosing from low levels until appropriate effects are achieved. In Japan, sequential dosing leads to levels where side-effects occur, with much less attention to effect. A second example lies in measurement of effect. In the West, effectiveness of a drug must be empirically demonstrated with well-controlled (double-blind) studies. In Japan, the 'overall physician evaluation,' a formal if impressionistic component of the Japanese clinical trial process, has historically been sufficient to achieve approval for a new drug. In other words, the judgement of some doctor that 'the product seems to work well', wholly apart from any real evidence, is adequate for registration of a drug in Japan. Even the measurement system for recording side-effects in clinical trials (so-called 'adverse event scoring') is different in Japan. Japanese clinical trials record only those side-effects that the doctor (with his wisdom, and with his financial ties to the drug company) deems to be truly caused by the drug. In the West, all adverse events (headache, drowsiness, death, and so on) must be recorded for patients in clinical trials. Subsequent statistical analysis, in comparison with a control group, appropriately determines whether these adverse events are legitimately associated with the experimental drug or not.

The Japanese system thus displays an acute concern for safety, with a disregard for efficacy that in the USA and the UK is regarded as cavalier. We should note, however, that other advanced nations (such as France and Italy) have historically maintained a comparably relaxed attitude towards drug efficacy. Furthermore, even some Americans wonder if US doctors do not go too far in valuing efficacy relative to safety. Some cancer treatment specialists in the US are derided as 'chemo cowboys' using extremely high dosage levels of anti-cancer treatments to 'zap' malignant growths in their patients. Regardless of these concerns, we must recognize that the FDA approach to safety-efficacy tradeoffs is the world standard for clinical trials.

An important consequence of the historic disregard for drug efficacy in Japan is provided by the many products and even entire therapeutic categories of drugs sold only in that country. For several years in the mid-1980s, the best-selling drug in Japan was Krestin, a mushroom derivative similar to Laetrile and sold as an anti-cancer product. Krestin has not been approved for use in any other advanced market, and would clearly never be approved by the FDA for launch in the USA. Total sales of Krestin and comparable ineffective anti-cancer products reached $1 billion a year in Japan (Fukushima, 1989). Whole categories of ineffectives exist in Japan, including tonics, hepatics, various enzymes, cerebral stimulants, folk medicines, and vasotherapies. The mix of ineffectives sold in Japan has also shifted over time in response to price cuts from the MHW. But new categories of ineffective products have steadily emerged. Over 10 percent of the total demand in Japan falls into therapeutic categories for which there is no analogue in the USA or UK, amounting to almost ¥1 trillion a year that from an Anglo-American perspective is simply thrown away.

As a consequence of these four differences, results of the Japanese clinical trial system are acceptable and respected almost nowhere else in the world. From the dominant Anglo-American perspective, Japanese clinical trials very much resemble those of the USA in the 1950s and seem disconnected from four decades of advances in biomedical science. Indeed, part of the problem with the Japanese clinical trial system is that the science base of biomedical research in Japan is weak relative to other nations. A common measure of the strength of the research base of a nation is the number of global citations in academic journals of scientific papers originating from that nation. If we examine the number of citations in clinical medicine per capita for those nations with innovative pharmaceutical industries in 1990, Japan is at the bottom roughly tied with Italy. Germany and France have 50 percent greater citation rates per capita than Japan, while rates for Britain, Canada, the Netherlands, Sweden, Switzerland, and the USA are two to four times that of Japan. Figure 3.2 (at top) specifically compares the Japanese and British share of world citations in clinical medicine. Given that Japan has twice the population of the UK, we can readily calculate that per capita Japanese citations are still less than half those of the UK. The Japanese share, however, has steadily risen and is now over twice what it was 15 years ago. It might be argued that the low Japanese share of global citations is due to the inability of non-Japanese to read the Japanese language. Yet if we examine the Japanese and British share of scientific citations in chemicals in Figure 3.2 (at bottom), we find Japan has almost twice the share of the UK in that science, making for roughly comparable per capita citation rates. It is far more likely that the distinctive politics, science, and regulation described above for the clinical trial system in Japan explain its low level of international citations for Japanese biomedical research.

The Japanese clinical trial system is again part of a larger political equilibrium, in the interests of senior university professors, domestic Japanese pharmaceutical firms, and MHW bureaucrats – and no one else. That political equilibrium was initially disturbed in 1981, with 'reforms' to the pricing system, and again in 1992 with reforms to the clinical trial system.

PRICE REGULATION AND 'REFORM'

By 1981, pharmaceutical sales in Japan had been growing at over 10 percent a year for decades, meaning that industry sales doubled every six to seven years. The initial postwar growth of the industry represented catching up, as Japanese standards of living approached those of Western nations. Yet pharmaceutical demand showed no signs of slowing down, and indeed drug expenditures as a share of total health care expenses remained two to three times the shares of other advanced nations. At that point, MHW attacked drug consumption through 'reforms' to its system of price regulations.

Maximum prices for ethical drugs in Japan are set in a Reimbursement Fee Schedule (RFS). This schedule is technically determined by the Central Council (*Chuikyo*), which again is an advisory council comprising

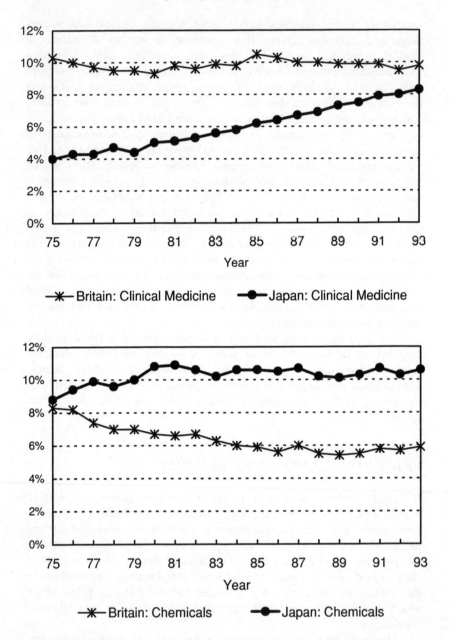

Figure 3.2 National shares of scientific citations in clinical medicine (at top) and chemicals (at bottom), 1975–93, Britain and Japan

representatives of health insurance payers, medical providers, and the public interest. MHW however closely supervises this council, and the Ministry of Finance (MOF) has important influence on price setting as MOF determines the overall health care budget for MHW. Pharmaceuticals in Japan are sold by wholesalers to hospitals, doctors, and retail pharmacies, who then distribute them to patients. The actual price paid by dispensers varies enormously and is determined by a complex set of discounts from the MHW-determined RFS. When the bargaining power of dispensers is strong, as might occur for products with ready substitutes, the discounts obtained from wholesalers are of course larger.

Before 1981, RFS prices for drugs were essentially set and reduced later only occasionally by small percentage amounts. Beginning in 1981, however, MHW steadily lowered the RFS price for drugs, with a sharp initial drop of 18 percent in that year. The average price cuts imposed by MHW are listed in Table 3.1. Note that, since the onset of this new system, drug prices have fallen by roughly 5 percent a year on a steady basis. In addition to broad reductions in prices, MHW in some years has also targeted specific products that it regards as excessively consumed.

For those products selected for price reductions, fall-off in demand was severe. For example, between 1986 and 1996, prices for cephalosporins (an advanced antibiotic) fell by an average of 13 percent a year. The effects on Japanese consumption can be traced in Figure 3.3. In the mid-1980s, Japanese patients were grossly overprescribed cephalosporins, so much so that these drugs accounted for almost 14 percent of prescription value in Japan (against less than 2 percent in the USA). By 1996, prices for individual cephalosporin products were on average only 27 percent of their 1986 price level and total consumption of cephalosporins had fallen to around 5 percent of prescription value. Two points should be noted. First, US consumption of cephalosporins exhibits none of these gyrations over time. Second, while Japanese consumption of cephalosporins has indeed fallen from the mid-1980s to the mid-1990s, actual consumption did not fall as much as prices. In terms of the yen value of cephalosporins consumed, the fall was only 50 percent. In terms of the share of overall drug consumption, the decline was from almost 15 percent to over 5 percent (a fall of 55 percent). The source of this difference is new products by Japanese firms. To counter the effects of MHW price cuts for specific products, Japanese firms continuously introduced distinct new cephalosporin molecules at higher prices.

The ability of Japanese firms to innovate around MHW price regulations is hardly confined to established product categories. Japanese firms have created entire new categories of often completely dubious

Table 3.1 Price decreases for Japanese pharmaceuticals imposed by MHW (Ministry of Health and Welfare) since 1981

Year	Average Percentage Price Decrease Imposed by MHW	Repricings of Specific Products as Share of Total Drug Sales	
1981	-18.6%		
1982	-4.9%		
1983	-16.6%		
1984	-6.0%		
1985			
1986	-5.1%		
1987			
1988	-10.2%		
1989	+2.4%[‡]		
1990	-9.2%		
1991			
1992	-8.1%		
1993			
1994	-6.6%	-0.8%	7 products
1995			
1996	-6.8%	-1.7%	20 products

Note: ‡ compensation for introduction of 3% consumption tax in 1989.
Source: Ikegami, Ikeda, and Kawai (1997).

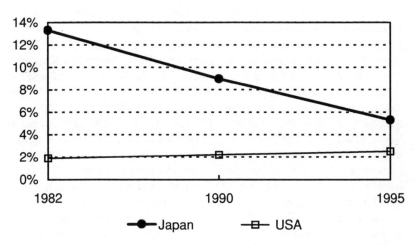

Figure 3.3 Cephalosporins as a percentage of total pharmaceutical sales, Japan and the USA

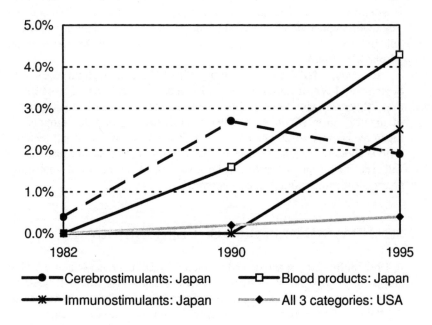

Figure 3.4 Three new therapeutic categories as percentage of total pharmaceutical sales, Japan and the USA

products, sped them through the domestic clinical trial system, and sold them to doctors desperate to make up for income lost owing to MHW price cuts. Consider for example, cerebrostimulants, a category of wholly ineffective drugs that does not even exist in the USA. These products in the mid-1990s accounted for almost 2 percent of total pharmaceutical sales in Japan, up from almost nothing in 1982 (see Figure 3.4). Additional drug categories that did not even exist in 1982 include platelet inhibitors, anti-anaemics, and immunostimulants. Products in these three new categories now account for almost 7 percent of drug sales in Japan, well over ten times their comparable percentage in the USA where they are only rarely prescribed. Again, note that the gyrations in sales in Figure 3.4 have no basis in biomedical reality and are complete artifacts of price controls in Japan, in the context of the entire domestic ecosystem.

By the early 1990s, the failure of price cuts to control overconsumption of drugs was apparent. In 1994, MHW imposed capitation for certain medical conditions in geriatric hospitals: doctors who treated certain conditions in the elderly received a flat fee per patient out of which they paid for all services and drugs. Somewhat over 10 percent of hospitals were affected by this mandate, and the effects were immediate and dramatic. In cases with imposition of capitated payments, hospital consumption of drugs fell by 83 percent, and out-patient consumption fell by 60 percent (*Economist*, 1996).

Recently, MHW has gone further in a drive to restrain costs. In September, 1997, it raised medical insurance fees for salaried workers by over 70 percent, and doubled copayments for patients from 10 to 20 percent of medical costs (*Economist*, 1997a). Pharmaceutical sales dropped in Japan by as much as 20 percent. After 50 years, MHW has at last become serious about restraining excessive consumption of pharmaceuticals. As we will see below in Chapter 9, however, there is more to managing pharmaceutical demand than cost control.

SCANDAL AND REFORM OF CLINICAL TRIALS

In 1992, buffeted by scandals and pressured by US trade negotiators, MHW proposed Good Clinical Practice (GCP) standards that would henceforth guide clinical trials in Japan. These standards were a radical departure from the 'Old Professor System'. Responsibility for execution of clinical trials was transferred from primary investigators (senior university professors) to pharmaceutical firms. Informed consent was now required of all patients participating in clinical trials. And Institutional Review Boards (IRBs) were to monitor and ensure compliance with research protocols during clinical trials. These proposed changes offered a severe shock to the system, resulting in temporary greater delay and confusion in the clinical trial system, as documented in Chapter 6 below. In effect, the GCP standards in Japan would put MHW through a process similar to that experienced by the US FDA in the 1960s and early 1970s. As discussed in Chapter 1, the US FDA took over a decade to assimilate higher standards for clinical trials to implement the 1962 Amendments to the Food, Drug, and Cosmetic Act, and to process new drug applications without excessive delay.

In 1994, a new scandal rocked MHW. Sorivudine, a drug marketed by the Japanese firm Nihon Shoji, led to 16 deaths from side effects. Re-examination of clinical trials for this drug uncovered the fact that three patient deaths occurred during the trials. Yet Nihon Shoji, in collaboration with its primary investigator, suppressed information about these deaths and obtained MHW approval for launch in Japan despite them. Even more egregiously, senior executives of Nihon Shoji engaged in insider trading, selling shares in their firm just before the public learned of the scandal.

In the same year, the GCP guidelines proposed in 1992 took effect. The combined impact of scandals and newly required standards have virtually paralyzed the clinical trial system in Japan, resulting in a near shutdown of approvals for new drugs. While this hiatus indeed spares Japanese patients from side effects of inappropriate new drugs, it deprives them of benefits of new medications as well.

THE DISTRIBUTION SYSTEM AND REFORM

The distribution system for pharmaceuticals in Japan is complex, highly fragmented, and grossly inefficient (see Figure 3.5). Over 90 percent of drugs in Japan are distributed by wholesale firms, and the vast majority of these drugs are directly dispensed by prescribing hospitals and doctors (GPs in Figure 3.5). The driving force behind the distribution system is the doctor's margin, and the fact that doctors and hospitals derive significant proportions of their income from dispensing drugs. This powerful self-interest continuously shapes the distribution system, and gives it several distinctive features. First, because individual doctors directly dispense drugs to patients, they must themselves have access to adequate inventory. Yet inventory carrying costs are expensive, particularly in Japan where high land prices make doctor's offices small. This fragmentation of distribution creates the need for a large army of distributors and salesmen to service doctor and hospital needs. Second, the doctor's margin pushes drug prices to become a far more powerful determinant of prescription patterns in Japan than in other developed nations. The retail price in Japan is set by MHW, but the wholesale price is negotiated directly between wholesalers and doctors. These continuous and highly fragmented negotiations of prices further increase the need for extensive distribution networks in Japan.

The resulting scale of distribution effort required in Japan dwarfs that of other nations. For example, 60 manufacturers' representatives (or detail men) are regarded as an appropriate scale for a pharmaceutical sales force to cover the entire United Kingdom. The ratio of detail men to doctors in Britain is thus small, at one to 34 (Howells and Neary, 1995). In contrast, 1400 representatives are needed for a drug firm to cover all of Japan, although only two Japanese firms can afford this large a distribution staff and only nine firms maintain a detailing staff of over 1000. The ratio of manufacturers' representatives to doctors in Japan is one to four, and this astonishing figure excludes the large detail staff of Japanese wholesale firms and contract sales representatives in private practice (*ibid.*).

The doctor's margin creates three other distinctive features of distribution in Japan. In order to minimize various costs (inventory, materials, doctor time, and so on), doctors in Japan dispense drugs to patients with minimal packaging and labeling. Patients thus often do not even know what drugs they have been given by their physician, let alone what biomedical function these drugs perform or what side-effects to watch for. Further, distribution of drugs in Japan is highly focused on patented medicines sold under prescription, leaving only a quite small over-the-counter (OTC) market where patients directly purchase their own drugs (like aspirin, cold medicines, or stomach remedies). Since doctors in Japan do not earn any income from OTC products, they have no incentive to suggest them to patients. This artificial reduction in demand for OTC products artificially reduces the demand for drugstores to stock such products, and the minimal presence of Japanese pharmacies then further encourages and reinforces direct physician dispensing of ethical drugs. Finally, because generic drugs (off-patent copies of originally patented ethical drugs) carry lower prices than patented medicines, generics have a strikingly minimal market share in Japan.

The Japanese distribution system is riddled with vertical linkages between domestic manufacturers and wholesalers. Many Japanese drug firms evolved out of wholesalers, retaining strong histories of cooperation, supplemented in some cases by cross-ownership of equity and personnel transfers. The drug wholesaling industry in Japan is highly fragmented, with no wholesaler providing complete national coverage. Pharmaceutical manufacturers must therefore stitch together a complex network of multiple wholesalers in order to approximate national distribution for their products. Because of traditional ties between various wholesalers and certain large Japanese drug manufacturers, other manufacturers (including small

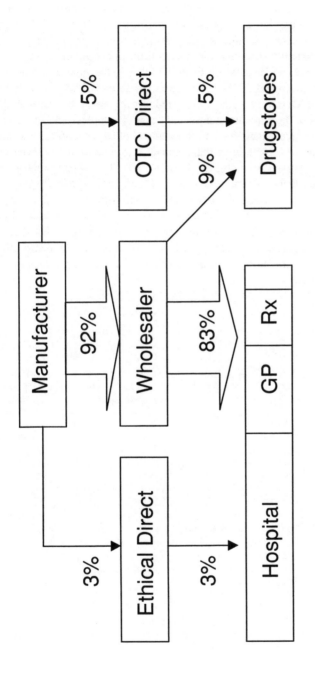

Figure 3.5 Distribution system for pharmaceutical products in Japan (adapted from Kimura, et al., 1993).

Japanese firms) suffer exclusion and gain access to doctors only at a disadvantage. Five large Japanese firms (Fujisawa, Sankyo, Shionogi, Takeda, and Tanabe) dominated the wholesale network in Japan and performed almost all distribution for foreign firms operating in Japan.

In early 1991, under pressure from the USA in the bilateral Structural Impediments Initiative of 1989–1990, the Japanese Fair Trade Commission (FTC) announced reforms that would reduce the force of vertical ties between Japanese drug manufacturers and Japanese wholesalers. A variety of vertical practices that had traditionally linked manufacturers and wholesalers (such as resale price maintenance, and rebates and allowances) were declared illegal. Actually, the Japanese FTC had already long since ruled that many vertical practices were anti-competitive and illegal, but Japanese firms just ignored the Commission (Howells and Neary, 1995). This time, with US trade negotiators watching, Japanese drug firms grudgingly complied. The resulting changes in Japanese distribution practices make it easier for foreign firms to gain access to the distribution system and offer the hope of rationalization and greater efficiency for Japanese wholesalers.

Pathologies of the
Japanese domestic ecosystem

When we combine these various features of the Japanese domestic ecosystem, we find several profound competitive pathologies. Many of these pathologies have grown in magnitude since 1981, even though MHW pricing regulations have been applied on a stable basis since that year. We should be clear, then, that it is the interaction over time of MHW pricing regulations with the Japanese system for pharmaceuticals that has produced these pathologies.

ULTRA-SHORT PRODUCT LIFE

A first pathology of the Japanese pharmaceutical industry is a product life in Japan that is significantly shorter than in other major markets since 1981. We can illustrate this pathology with the example of beta-blockers (cardiovascular products). The top panel of Figure 4.1 presents the aggregate market share for the first four successful products introduced into the beta-blocker therapeutic category in the United States and in Japan. Examining this figure, we find very different product life cycles. The trend for the USA is shown at the top, and we should note in passing that this trend is quite similar to that of Britain, Germany, and France. The first few products to be introduced lock up the market. Thus there is a strong disincentive to imitation in the USA, since late entrants have minimal demand. As the lower two panels of Figure 4.1 make clear, there is minimal successful late entry in the USA, and as a consequence almost no exit. In contrast, in Japan the first four products succeed initially, but then rapidly lose market share. There are waves of imitative beta-blocker products that come and go. Over 30 distinct products achieve a 1 percent market share of this segment at one time or another, though half of these products subsequently fail. Note that these products are distinct molecules that have the same biomedical function, each with its own patent.

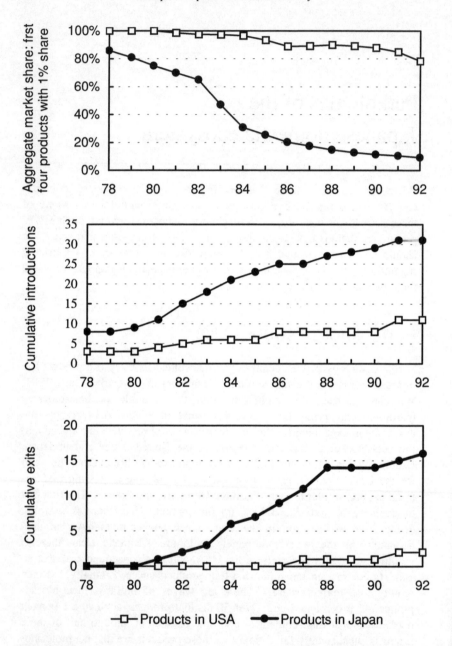

Figure 4.1 Comparative product lives for beta-blocker drugs in Japan and the USA, 1978–92

PROLIFERATION OF MINOR PRODUCTS

A second, related pathology of the Japanese system is that Japanese firms are induced to proliferate numerous minor, imitative new drugs that have little likelihood of diffusion outside Japan. Consider each factor of the system, summarized at the bottom of Figure 4.2. Owing to MHW regulations, prices for established products drop rapidly on average. Due to the nature of doctor incentives and consumer ignorance, products will experience 'brand disloyalty,' as doctors will prescribe and dispense the latest and most expensive brand (Ikegami *et al.*, 1997). If a firm in Japan sticks with old products, it risks having a product line with pervasive declining sales. In terms of registration, it is vastly cheaper and easier to register many new products in Japan than in other major pharmaceutical markets. And university science for clinical medicine is comparatively weak. What incentives does this domestic ecosystem provide for a Japanese firm? The incentives are to fragment its R&D into numerous minor imitative products. A Japanese firm must constantly restock its pipeline in order to have new, more expensive products to sell. Sales to doctors will be driven by price and inventory service by wholesalers, not by the results of expensive clinical trials. And such trials will be difficult anyway, given the limited domestic base for clinical medicine. The Japanese system thus rewards streams of minor products, not individual major products.

It is useful to contrast the industry system in Britain, which has a globally successful pharmaceutical industry, with that of Japan. The domestic system for the pharmaceutical industry in the UK is represented at the top of Figure 4.2 (drawn from Thomas, 1994). Pricing regulations by the UK National Health Service are deliberately biased in favor of firms conducting R&D in the UK, regardless of the nationality of these firms. Firms with innovative products, including almost all major American and Swiss firms, get high prices. Firms of all nationalities, including British, that are not R&D-intensive and that therefore produce minor, imitative products, receive a low price. Doctor behavior is quite loyal, like that of the USA with the beta-blocker example above. Premarket regulation by the UK Committee on Safety of Medicines is quite stringent. Drug firms must conduct expensive, well-controlled clinical trials proving that their drugs are effective before product registration, though these trials need not be held in the UK. And the research base for clinical medicine in British universities is very strong. The per capita citation rate for UK research publications in clinical medicine is almost four times that of Japan.

What are the incentives for British pharmaceutical firms? They are to concentrate R&D expenditures on a handful of important products. With this strategy, a British firm obtains a high price. Its products enjoy a long

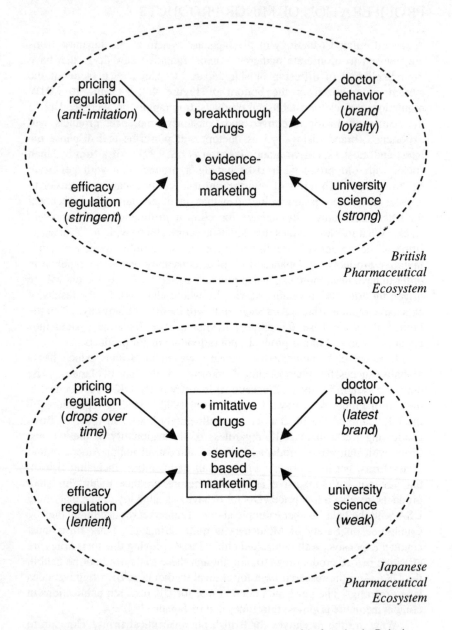

Figure 4.2 Comparative ecosystems: Pharmaceutical industries in Britain (at top) and Japan (at bottom)

life, with prominent university scientists providing clinical results documenting the excellence of these products. The British firm then uses this published information to sell the drug to doctors. With a high price and a long product life, the British firm can afford the extravagant cost of efficacy testing in Britain. What would happen if, in contrast, a British firm fragmented its R&D into many minor imitative products? If it followed this alternative strategy, it would receive low prices, doctors would not prescribe the second generation product anyway, university academics would denigrate the firm and its products, calling them 'derivative,' and the firm would suffer financial difficulties trying to get regulatory approval, constantly spending the high fixed R&D costs necessary to prove efficacy for numerous drugs. Clearly, British firms are forced to concentrate their strategy, resources, and organization on a few major blockbuster products because of the nature of their home environment.

As Japanese pharmaceutical firms have proliferated minor and imitative new drugs, the domestic industry in Japan has been steadily transformed since 1981, as can be seen in Figure 4.3. This figure contrasts the composition of launches onto the domestic markets of Japan and four other major markets, including Britain. What we see in Figure 4.3 for Japan is something unique in the developed world. The proportion of new drugs launched onto the home market that is *local products* increases over time. Local products are minor imitative drugs that sell in two or fewer nations. Some 60 percent of all drugs launched into Japan are local products, up from 30 percent in the 1970s. Further, and quite important, this deterioration in the quality of demand began in the early 1980s, precisely when MHW launched its regulations lowering prices over time. Note that in Britain the proportion of local products is less than 10 percent and has been stable since the early 1970s, when Britain gained its membership in the European Community.

UNCOMPETITIVE DOMESTIC FIRMS

A third pathology follows from the second. The post-1981 domestic system in Japan, created by MHW pricing regulations, has ensured that Japanese pharmaceutical firms are among the least competitive in the world (*Economist*, 1995, 1996). The strategies followed by British and Japanese firms are an immediate adaptation to their domestic systems. Japanese drug firms discovered five times as many new drugs as British firms during the decade 1985–94, despite the fact that Japanese firms only spent twice as much on pharmaceutical R&D. Unfortunately, only 10 percent of Japanese innovations were global products, while over 70 percent sold only in the

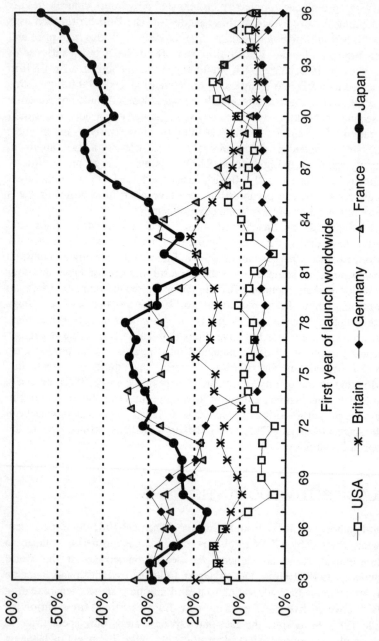

*Figure 4.3 Local products dominate the Japanese market, but not other leading markets;
percentages are three-year moving averages.*

Table 4.1 Average diffusion of innovations, British and Japanese firms, 1976–93

British Firms

Fisons	5.3	SmithKline Beecham	5.4
Glaxo	7.8	Wellcome	5.3
Reckitt	5.3	Zeneca	7.4

Japanese Firms

Ajinomoto	1.0	Nippon Kayaku	1.2
Chugai	2.1	Ono	1.7
Daiichi	1.8	Otsuka	2.7
Dainippon	2.8	Sankyo	3.2
Eisai	1.9	Shionogi	2.7
Fujisawa	3.1	Sumitomo	1.1
Green Cross	1.2	Taisho	3.2
Hokuriku	2.8	Takeda	3.1
Kanebo	1.0	Tanabe	1.5
Kyorin	3.2	Toyama	3.4
Kyowa Hakko	1.4	Toyo Jozo	1.7
Meiji	1.2	Yamanouchi	3.5
Mitsubishi	1.0	Yoshitomi	1.5
Mitsui	1.0		

Note: This table lists all British or Japanese firms that discovered three or more new molecules during 1976 to 1993. For each firm, the average number of countries into which its molecules diffuse is reported. Maximum diffusion measured for each molecule is 12 nations. Adapted from Thomas, 1999.

home market. In contrast, over half the British innovations were global products in this decade. Further, while British firms directly sell their own products in almost all major markets, Japanese firms must license their innovations to foreign firms in order to penetrate external markets. British and Japanese firms are mirror images of each other, but this mirroring arises because the domestic ecosystems are mirror images of each other. The British ecosystem rewards innovation and punishes imitation, and the Japanese ecosystem does the reverse. The powerful impacts of these local ecosystems can be seen in Table 4.1, which lists the average diffusion for innovations of British and Japanese firms over a 13-year period. All five British firms achieve widely diffused innovations. None of the Japanese firms does.

If we compare the seven major nations in the global pharmaceutical industry, we find a trade-off in the way firms based in these countries spend their R&D for innovation of new drugs. This trade-off is represented in Figure 4.4 as the 'innovation possibility frontier' (IPF). The IPF traces the possible innovative output of a given R&D expenditure. On the one hand, nations like Italy fragment their R&D budget by spending on numerous trivial products. Indeed, if we look only at the number of new drugs discovered per billion dollars of R&D during 1985–1993, the most productive country in the world was Italy. Italy discovered 33 new drugs for every billion dollars it spent. The problem is that virtually none of these drugs sold globally; almost all of them sold only in the local Italian market. At the opposite extreme is Switzerland. Swiss firms concentrated their R&D budgets on only a handful of major innovations, only about 11 new drugs per billion dollars of R&D. The benefit of this concentration is that over 60 percent of these Swiss innovations were global products that sold throughout the world.

The competitive consequences of strategic trade-offs made along the 'innovation possibility frontier' can be seen in Figure 4.5, which summarizes the ability of firms based in various nations to penetrate foreign markets. Most firms have advantage in their home market, so the real test of competitive prowess is the ability to sell in external markets. Hence, Figure 4.5 reports average external market share. Examining this figure, we find the most competitive firms in the pharmaceutical industry to be based in the USA, Britain, Switzerland, and Germany. Note that each of these nations ranked near the top left on the 'innovation possibility frontier' in Figure 4.4. The losers in the global pharmaceutical industry are France, Italy, and Japan. Note that these three nations are all towards the bottom right of the frontier.

To stress how important the domestic ecosystem is, consider the drug Zantac, an anti-ulcer drug which was a big success for Glaxo (which in recent years has merged to become Glaxo Wellcome, and now Glaxo SmithKline). Glaxo was second into the anti-ulcer market, and yet it quickly surpassed the first entrant despite the strong first-mover advantages already documented above for beta-blockers. How did Glaxo succeed with late entry? It took clinical trials from university doctors showing minor benefits of Zantac relative to the first entrant, Tagamet. Glaxo further took regulatory approvals which stamped and approved these minor benefits, and then marketed the drug to doctors on the basis of these clinical trials. Note that this is social construction of demand (for additional examples, see Carey, 1997; Narisetti, 1997; Weber, 1997). Just as personal computers and cellular phones are much more software than hardware, so in Britain and the USA the success of a drug has much more to do with clinical trials, public

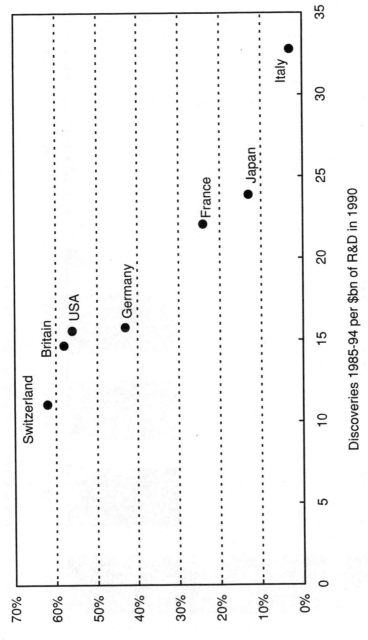

Figure 4.4 Innovation possibility frontier: Number versus significance of discoveries

71

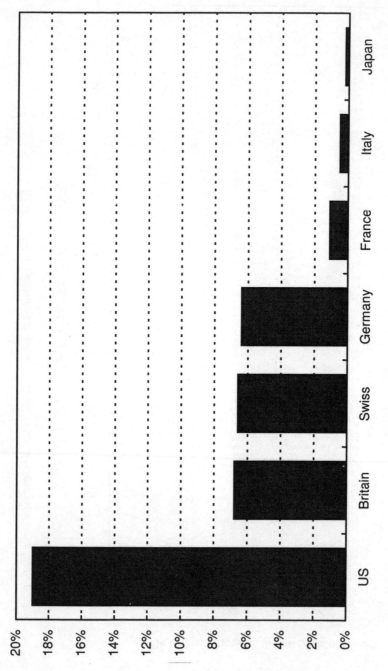

Figure 4.5 External sales share of firms based in major competitor countries

perceptions, and regulations than with molecular structure. Successful drugs are not just chemicals. With the rise of managed care and concerns over the cost-effectiveness of new drugs, the relative importance of the social construction (software) versus the chemical (hardware) is increasing. In a sense, Glaxo and other British firms focus on medical solutions, while Japanese firms focus on chemicals and on wholly idiosyncratic domestic issues such as inventory supply. Because Japanese firms fail to develop internal skills at producing and managing this social construction of demand, they lack the competence to penetrate foreign markets directly, even on the rare occasions when they have innovative products. For example, Pepcid is an anti-ulcer drug, similar to Zantac. Pepcid is sold in the USA by Merck, an American firm, but the chemical itself was discovered and patented by Yamanouchi in Japan. Note that the position of Yamanouchi in relation to Merck is similar to that of Japanese electronics firms providing LCD screens or CD-ROM drives for US makers of personal computers. Yamanouchi provides a component (the chemical) for a complex demand-articulated product (a medical solution based on extensive clinical trials of efficacy) created by Merck, in a way that Yamanouchi cannot master owing to the backwardness of its home environment.

There are many metrics that demonstrate the weak competitive position of Japanese pharmaceutical firms. In Figure 4.6, we see that the trade balance for Japan in pharmaceuticals is negative. For countries that are leading innovators of global products, this balance is positive. Japanese exports of drugs are a small share of total global exports, as we see in Figure 4.7, and this small share shows no signs of significant change over time. An interesting aside may be derived from Figure 4.7: US firms have steadily shifted production of pharmaceuticals outside the USA since 1983. Increased production from overseas subsidiaries of US firms has more than taken the place of falling US shares of exports. As a consequence, the external share for US firms in foreign markets has remained high (again, see Figure 4.5).

MASSIVE OVERCONSUMPTION

A fourth pathology of the Japanese domestic market, created by MHW regulations is that there is massive over consumption. Japanese doctors are strongly encouraged by the MHW pricing scheme to over prescribe. Japanese per capita drug consumption is the highest in the world: 40 percent greater per capita that in the USA and 80 percent greater than the in the UK. This over consumption is not uniform across all drugs, but rather is focused in specific therapeutic categories such as antibiotics, vitamins, cytostatics,

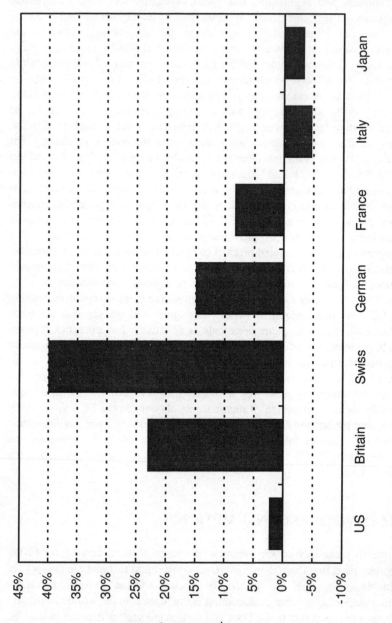

Figure 4.6 Weak domestic firms: Japan runs a negative trade balance in pharmaceuticals.

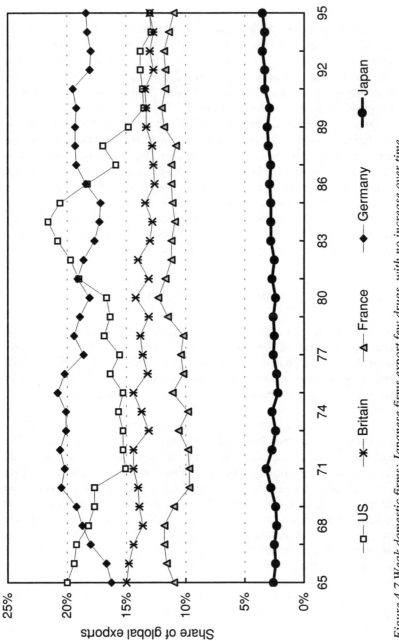

Figure 4.7 Weak domestic firms: Japanese firms export few drugs, with no increase over time

and immunostimulants. The mix of these categories has shifted over time, partly in response to MHW price cuts in categories of excessive consumption: as prices are dropped, the incentives for doctors to dispense is reduced. But Japanese over consumption is like an air-filled balloon – as one therapeutic category is pushed down, others expand elsewhere. For every therapeutic category where excess consumption is pushed down, others spring up to take its place. Japanese doctors and drug companies have proved very creative on this score.

Over consumption of drugs in Japan is not just large at a single point in time, but accounts for the vast bulk of cost increases for outpatient medical care in Japan (see Figure 4.8, adapted from Ikegami, Ikeda, and Kawai, 1997). Other segments of health care costs are well contained in Japan, but the perverse incentives for doctor prescription/dispensing in that country have led to steady increases in quantities of drugs consumed. And, as indicated above, the proliferation of trivial new local products has directly circumvented controls on price. In every other OECD nation, increased drug costs are historically a small part of increased health care costs.

EXCLUSION OF FOREIGN INNOVATION

The final pathology of the Japanese ecosystem for pharmaceuticals is the mounting exclusion of foreign products. In only a handful of quite rare instances, such as that discussed above of Baxter with its Factor VIII clotting agent, it is possible to document explicit bias by the Japanese against foreign pharmaceutical firms. How then is it that foreign firms are excluded?

The core source of exclusion is the fact that the Japanese ecosystem is so profoundly different from those of major innovating nations. This ecosystem creates and rewards very different and highly localized capabilities. Foreign firms, particularly those that do not directly participate in the Japanese market, do not possess these capabilities and are at an inherent disadvantage. To see how this exclusion plays out, we can examine a specific example, that of Taxol from Bristol-Myers Squibb. As we review this example, it is important to realize that Bristol-Myers Squibb (BMS) has extensive and long-standing operations in Japan, and thus is one of a handful of firms most likely to navigate well the Japanese ecosystem for pharmaceuticals.

Taxol (paclitaxel) is an anti-cancer agent derived naturally from yew trees. Initial research on this drug was performed throughout the 1970s by the National Cancer Institute (NCI) of the US National Institutes of Health.

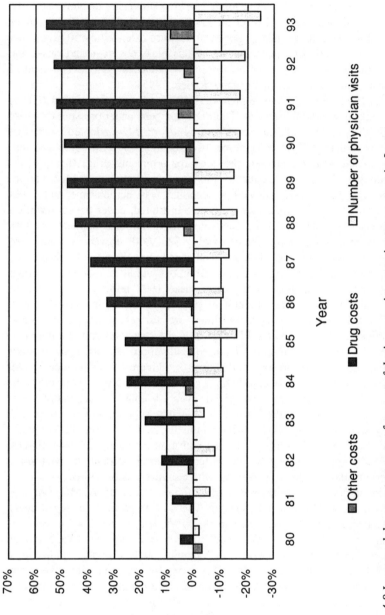

Figure 4.8 Increased drug costs account for most of the increase in outpatient care costs in Japan (adapted from Ikegami, Ikeda, and Kawai, 1997)

In 1989, clinical researchers at Johns Hopkins University demonstrated that paclitaxel shrank ovarian cancer tumors in one-third of women where other treatments had failed. Indeed, patient lives were extended by 50 percent on average. This finding generated enormous press coverage and raised the hopes of patient groups. The NCI promptly launched joint development of the drug with Bristol-Myers Squibb (Holden, 1993).

In 1992, the US FDA approved BMS's new drug application (NDA) after only five months' review. The FDA had been under pressure for years to speed its reviews of new drugs, and by this time had adopted a series of reforms to that end. In 1992 alone, two significant reforms were adopted. First, *accelerated review* was provided for promising drugs treating life-threatening illness. In exchange for some restrictions on distribution, innovating firms were allowed to conduct less burdensome and time-consuming tests. Second, *user fees* were instituted, under the Prescription Drug User Fee Act (PDUFA). Innovators filing new drug applications with FDA were now charged a fee of roughly $230,000. Revenues from these fees were used to expand FDA staff and speed reviews of NDAs. The FDA committed itself to acting on almost all NDAs within 12 months. Average NDA review times fell sharply after these 1992 reforms. The median approval time fell from 23 months in 1993 to 14 months in 1996 (Haffner, 1997). US regulatory approval times are further speeded by a new consultative approach by the FDA towards industry. Not only did the FDA approve Taxol in five months, it subsequently approved two supplementary NDAs, each in less than six months' time (see Figure 4.9). One such SNDA (in 1993) sought to use a slightly higher dose given in a three-hour infusion, rather than the original dose given over 24 hours as originally filed. Clinical experience with Taxol indicated that superior effectiveness and safety were achieved with a briefer infusion, and BMS sought to update regulatory approval to bring it in line with best practice. A second SNDA (in 1994) sought to replace the original natural product, derived from environmentally sensitive yew trees, with a semi-synthetic source.

In sharp contrast to the speed and efficiency of the FDA, MHW review of Taxol dragged on for 44 months. The need to replicate in Japan those clinical trials already conducted in the USA delayed NDA submission in Japan for two years. Japanese clinical trials were conducted at the National Cancer Center Hospital in Tokyo. Ultimately, the NDA submitted in Japan in 1994 was similar to that in the USA: a natural source product given with a 24-hour infusion. BMS, however, raised the dosage level somewhat to accord with worldwide clinical practice, including practice in the USA after FDA approval of the 1993 SNDA. Bristol-Myers also somewhat tested the boundaries for regulatory process in Japan by using a mix of Japanese and foreign clinical trials for its NDA in Japan, rather than the local norm of

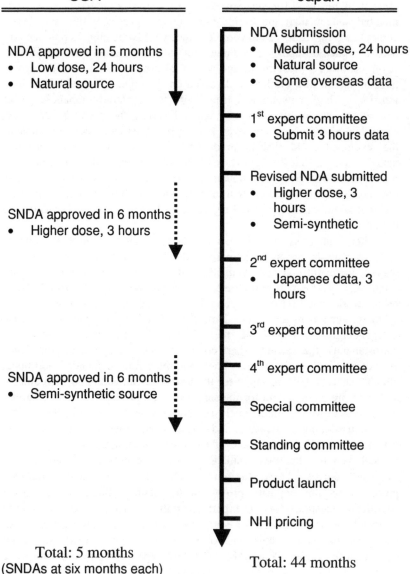

USA	Japan

NDA approved in 5 months
- Low dose, 24 hours
- Natural source

NDA submission
- Medium dose, 24 hours
- Natural source
- Some overseas data

1st expert committee
- Submit 3 hours data

SNDA approved in 6 months
- Higher dose, 3 hours

Revised NDA submitted
- Higher dose, 3 hours
- Semi-synthetic

2nd expert committee
- Japanese data, 3 hours

3rd expert committee

4th expert committee

SNDA approved in 6 months
- Semi-synthetic source

Special committee

Standing committee

Product launch

NHI pricing

Total: 5 months
(SNDAs at six months each)

Total: 44 months

Figure 4.9 Comparative approval times, USA and Japan, for Paclitaxel (Taxol)

purely Japanese trials. All the early Phase II and some of the late Phase II clinical studies used for the Japanese NDA were from abroad. After eight months (longer than the entire FDA review process), the first expert committee returned its initial verdict. Since worldwide clinical practice now used a higher dosage with a three-hour infusion, rather than the Bristol-Myers submitted medium dosage with a 24-hour infusion, the firm would have to submit new clinical trials based on the higher dose and three-hour infusion. These new clinical trials were to be entirely Japanese. This decision by the expert committee ignored several facts: that by this time, Taxol had already been approved for use by 75 nations, including most of the developed world; that the product had been safe and effective in these many countries; that the approvals for Taxol in most of these nations were for the lower dosage over 24 hours; that the higher dose and shorter infusion time resulted from actual clinical practice once the drug had been approved; and that additional delay would significantly harm Japanese patients denied use of this drug.

After eight more months, Bristol-Myers in 1995 submitted a revised NDA, raising the dosage to actual worldwide practice. Bristol-Myers also made a judgment call and changed the drug source from natural to semi-synthetic. The expert committee seemed to want the paclitaxel NDA to reflect worldwide best practice, and the FDA had already approved a semi-synthetic version in the USA. Note that Bristol-Myers made this change independently, and not at the request of the expert committee. Unfortunately, the second expert committee did not appreciate the firm's consideration of its interests. The committee now demanded additional clinical safety data from Japan for the three-hour infusion and both clinical and even pre-clinical data for the semi-synthetic product. To avoid further delay, Bristol-Myers immediately submitted a newly revised NDA. This revision used a mix of Japanese and overseas data drawn from trials the firm was already conducting on use of paclitaxel to treat breast cancer. Pre-clinical data for the semi-synthetic source were drawn exclusively from overseas sources. These foreign pre-clinical data created significant problems, as the impurity profile of the semi-synthetic source raised significant questions for the expert committee. While these issues were ultimately resolved in Bristol-Myers' favor, time and money were lost with questions and answers back and forth. Further delay resulted from a full docket for the Expert Committee. The third expert committee meeting was finally scheduled for review of paclitaxel after four months, but the chemistry expert for the committee was unable to attend, so the review was not conducted. Four months later, a fourth expert committee meeting finally approved paclitaxel. Over 34 months had passed since filing of the Japanese NDA, and over five years since FDA approval. But there was more. Over the next five months, the NDA was reviewed by routine Special, Standing, and Marketing Committees, and the drug was finally ready for market.

MHW then stunned Bristol-Myers by setting an NHI reimbursement price far below world market levels. MHW reasoning for its low price was absurd: paclitaxel was to be priced in reference to a generic version of cisplatin, a 15-year old inferior product with an appropriately low price. After three months of intense negotiation, Bristol-Myers took the almost unprecedented step of launching its product without NHI listing. Japanese patients using the drug would thus have to pay for it out of their own pockets, rather than from insurance. Two months later, MHW relented and listed the drug at an acceptable price

Several conclusions can be drawn from this example. First, there was no explicit bias against foreign products or even foreign clinical and preclinical data here. The expert committee for Taxol never rejected foreign clinical trials because they were foreign, but rather because they were different from established Japanese practice. The dosage level was wrong or the impurity profile raised questions. And ultimately the expert committee did accept much foreign data from BMS, but only at the cost of significant delay and questions back and forth. Pricing for Taxol did not discriminate against a foreign product, rather the price was simply too low relative to global practice. Second, the core source of resistance and delay for Taxol was not the MHW, but rather the ecosystem itself. Arguably, MHW was itself more open to use of foreign clinical data than the senior university professors that dominated the clinical trial system. Both sets of actors are far below world class in their performance, and their dysfunctional relationship compounds already severe problems. Nonetheless, if the entire FDA were flown in tomorrow from Rockville and installed in Tokyo to supervise the Japanese clinical trial system, that system would still be too slow and too exclusionary, because the academic base and the institutional capabilities necessary for world-class clinical trials are simply not now present in Japan. Third, Bristol-Myers Squibb was able to leverage its extensive presence and capabilities in Japan to succeed with Taxol. The acceptance of any foreign data by the expert committee was a significant accomplishment for BMS that demonstrated its capabilities in managing the clinical trial process. The credible launch of Taxol without MHW listing was a testament to the BMS marketing presence in Japan. Most foreign firms would not have either capability, and would not fare so well. They would have simply given up and never launched their products in Japan.

CORE HYPOTHESES

By now, the foundations of exclusion from Japan for foreign pharmaceutical innovations should be clear. Let us repeat the basic inequality for exclusion given at the end of Chapter 2:

$$R_{all} \geq C_{all} + C_i \qquad \text{then enter}$$
$$R_{all} < C_{all} + C_i \qquad \text{then stay out}$$

R_{all} denotes the revenue for each firm, C_{all} denotes the similar costs borne by each firm, and C_i denotes the asymmetrically higher costs borne by the victim of exclusion.

The core factor driving exclusion from Japan is the backwardness, provincialism, and self-reference of the clinical trial system in Japan. Because of the distinctive features of this system, foreign firms must almost completely replicate not only clinical trials for new drugs, but even at times pre-clinical trials as well. Further, their Japanese clinical trials will prove almost completely useless outside Japan. Because foreign firms must test their drugs twice to launch them in Japan, while Japanese firms must test them only once, they face a significant asymmetric cost, C_i. Thus, despite the very large pharmaceutical market in Japan, foreign firms may well refuse to launch their products in that country even though they are launched in every other major market. The core exclusion rate of 20 percent of global products for the last 35 years, shown in Figure 1.1, is predominantly caused by the redundancy and biomedical irrelevance of Japanese clinical trials.

A second factor driving exclusion is changes in MHW price control regulations since 1981. Revenues for new drugs have dropped in Japan owing to three mechanisms: lower MHW-set launch prices, the steady and large MHW-forced decreases in prices after launch, and sharp decreases in the life-cycle sales of new drugs launched into Japan (indirectly caused by MHW regulations). Thus the R_{all} term above has declined since 1981, and it is this decline that causes the observed greater exclusion since the mid-1980s. Note, then, that the increase in observed exclusion for new drugs from Japan in Figure 1.1 over the 20 percent historical base of exclusion is revenue-driven rather than cost-driven.

Third, the chaos at MHW caused by scandal and new clinical trial guidelines surely accounts for some of the observed exclusion since 1994. It will thus be necessary to segregate the effects on exclusion of pricing from those of the collapse of the registration process at MHW.

Fourth, and finally, firms in Japan should display differential capabilities for operating in that market. These capability differences might arise for three separate activities: (1) management of the clinical trial process in Japan, (2) management of the pricing process with MHW, and (3) the distribution and sales of new products in Japan. Specifically, Japanese firms should display far better understanding of their domestic system and have greater capability of operation there. Further, foreign firms with a long-term and large-scale presence in Japan should display greater capability than other foreign firms with minimal commitment to Japan (though presumably lesser capability than Japanese firms themselves).

The core hypotheses for this study are therefore the following:

1. For new molecules launched in Japan since 1981, the life cycle and thus cumulative sales of new drugs have steadily and significantly declined. Life cycles in other countries have remained stable or registered only moderate declines. Not only is the duration of product life now shorter in Japan, but the maximum level of sales attained is smaller there since 1981 owing to fragmentation of the market among many similar molecules.

2. Prior to 1981, launch prices for new molecules in Japan were higher than in most other countries. Today relative launch prices are lower. Further, prices after launch now decline over time in Japan as a result of repeated MHW-imposed price cuts.

3. Pre-market testing delays have significantly increased in Japan since 1992, because of the chaos caused by MHW scandals. These delays can be observed both between the initiation of clinical trials and filing time for MHW approval, and between the filing time and the time of actual MHW approval.

4. As the Japanese domestic pharmaceutical market has been transformed since 1981, the capabilities of firms to operate in this market have evolved. Firms with greatest participation in this market will achieve the greatest competitive capability for functioning in it. Evidence for this fourth hypothesis must be in the form of demonstrated differences among firms in their capabilities in either clinical trials, in pricing, and/or in sales in Japan.

5. Exclusion from Japan will not be uniform, as there will relatively greater exclusion of firms with weaker capabilities, hence higher asymmetric costs. Specifically, foreign firms will be relatively more excluded than Japanese firms. And among foreign

firms, those lacking long-term and extensive presence in Japan will be most excluded.

6. The domestic market share attained by Japanese firms will be artificially higher than those attained by foreign firms in their own home markets.

The next four chapters test each of these core hypotheses.

Evidence: Declining prices and life cycle sales in Japan

This chapter documents the downward shift of both prices and sales over the sharply declining life cycle for new drugs in Japan. It also provides evidence of clear differences in capabilities in Japan to price and market drugs in that nation. The datasets in this chapter comprise matched molecules, or drugs sold at the same time in two paired markets. To control for the varying medical and commercial attractiveness of the more than 600 molecules considered in this chapter, we examine the simultaneous sales and pricing of each drug in two countries. The experience of each drug in one country serves as a control for the experience in the other. Drugs in Japan are paired first with those in the United States, because prices in the US domestic pharmaceutical market are not regulated, and thus effectively serve as a statistical control to isolate effects of Japanese regulation. Britain is used as a second control. British industrial policy has been stunningly effective in promoting the competitive rise of pharmaceutical firms based in Britain (Thomas, 1994). Britain is thus employed as a different sort of statistical control, one that compares effective industrial policy and price regulations with those that prevail in Japan. Each observation in the datasets of this chapter thus concerns a molecule in a given calendar year, with a matched set of sales data in either Japan and the USA or Japan and Britain. Data are also collected for each molecule on the leading therapeutic category in Japan, and the leading manufacturing firm. These data are drawn from the IMS MIDAS system, are proprietary to IMS, and are used here with permission. Additionally, data on the launch dates of each drug in Japan and the USA are drawn from Thomas (1998).

In the analysis of this chapter, particular attention has been paid to three data issues: the computation of price, the extent of participation by the leading manufacturing firm in the Japanese market, and the therapeutic category of new drugs. Let us examine each of these data issues in turn, starting with the computation of prices. For each molecule, sales are registered in a very wide variety of dosage sizes (5 mg tablets versus 25 mg tablets), package sizes (ten 5 mg tablets versus one hundred 5 mg tablets), and so on. If we want to know the revenue generated by each molecule, we may simply add up sales recorded for each dosage/package group. To compute price, however, we must also add up 'units sold,' and then divide revenue by these 'units sold'. If the patterns of dosage size are the same for both the USA and Japan, then simple totals of number of pills would suffice for rough computation of 'price', though it should be clear that technically there are dozens of different prices depending on dosage form and package size. Unfortunately, there is a pronounced and systematic difference between consumption patterns of drugs in Japan and the USA: the Japanese use smaller dosage sizes. This difference derives in part from differences in medical culture and in part from the incentives for overconsumption given to Japanese doctors. As indicated above, Japanese doctors systematically overprescribe drug products. However, there is a strong ethic among the Japanese medical community to 'first do no harm' to patients. Smaller dosage sizes shield patients from possible damage due to overconsumption; again, safety is valued over efficacy.

To compare unit sales in Japan and the USA, this study chooses a 'base unit' for each molecule (for example, a 10 mg tablet). The number of recorded units in each nation is converted into the number of base units. Thus, if one million 5 mg tablets are sold and the base unit is 10 mg tablets, this data point would be converted to one-half million base unit tablets. Recorded unit sales of one million 25 mg tablets would be converted to 2.5 million base unit tablets. And so on. Prices in Japan and the USA are then computed as revenues for each molecule divided by the number of base units. This procedure is essentially equivalent to use of a 'price per kilogram weight', a common metric for such price comparisons.

A second data issue arises with the scale and nature of operations of foreign firms in Japan, and here we find a similar problem of diversity. At one extreme, seven foreign firms operate at a significant scale of operations in Japan, and have significant control over distribution of their products in that market. At the other extreme, most foreign firms have virtually no presence in Japan and must rely on *ad hoc* licensing of their products to Japanese firms to conduct clinical trials and to achieve distribution and sales in Japan. This study segregates foreign firms operating in Japan into three categories, listed in Table 5.1. *Large firms* distribute their own products in Japan, have operations in Japan that are directly controlled subsidiaries of the home corporation (not a joint venture with two parent firms), and registered sales in Japan of at least $200 million in 1990. Note that these cutoff points are a mix of scale and control, and foreign firms that are classified as 'large' have a very strong presence in the Japanese market. *Medium firms* have distributed their products in Japan either through a Japanese firm or through a joint venture with a Japanese firm since 1980, and registered sales in Japan of at least $50 million in 1990. All other

Table 5.1 Categories of pharmaceutical firms in Japan for this study

Large foreign firms

Bristol-Myers Squibb	Pfizer
Ciba-Geigy (Novartis)[†]	Roche
Hoechst	Schering AG
Merck/Banyu[‡]	

Medium foreign firms

(firms with formal joint ventures)

Abbott/Dainippon	Lederle/Takeda
Astra/Fujisawa	Organon (AKZO)/Sankyo
Bayer/Takeda	Rhone Poulenc/Chugai
Baxter/Sumitomo	Searle/Dainippon
Fisons/Fujisawa	Upjohn/Sumitomo
Glaxo (Glaxo Wellcome)	Wellcome/Sumitomo
Janssen/Kyowa	Zeneca (ICI)/Sumitomo

(self-owned firms allied with distributors)

Boehringer Ingelheim/Dainippon	Sandoz/Sankyo
Boehringer Mannheim/Yamanouchi	Warner Lambert/Sankyo
Novo Nordisk/Yamanouchi	

(self-owned self-distributing firm with 1990 sales below cutoff)
Schering Plough

Licensor foreign firms

all other foreign firms; examples include:

Amgen	Leo
Biogen	Lundbeck
Centecor	Pharmacia
Dupont	Serono
Lilly	Synthelabo

Traditional Japanese distributor firms

Fujisawa	Takeda
Sankyo	Tanabe
Shionogi	

Notes:[‡] before 1985, Merck was a 'medium' foreign firm in joint venture with Banyu;[†] before 1983, Ciba-Geigy was a 'medium' foreign firm in joint ventures with Fujisawa and Takeda.

foreign firms are *licensor firms* for this study, and have minimal or no presence in Japan.

A third data issue arises with therapeutic category, and again we must control for diversity. There are several pronounced differences in consumption patterns for drugs between Japan and the USA. A simple example is provided by the many recently launched antiviral products used to treat HIV infection. There is relatively little demand for these products in Japan, as that nation has been spared a significant HIV epidemic. All of these products were launched in the last decade. If we did not control for differences in national consumption due to the therapeutic category of products, we could falsely conclude that recently launched products had especially small sales in Japan, despite large sales in the USA and Europe.

MATCHED MOLECULES: USA, BRITAIN, AND JAPAN FOR 1975

This study argues that changes in MHW pricing regulations in 1981 set in motion a transformation of the domestic Japanese pharmaceutical industry. The Japanese market has become increasingly different since that time, and one implication of this difference is that foreign innovations have been excluded. To make this argument it is important to examine the Japanese market before 1981, and demonstrate that the life cycle in Japan at that time was quite similar to pharmaceutical life cycles in the US and UK markets.

Table 5.2 presents regression result for prices (revenues divided by number of base units) of products sold in both Japan and the USA in 1975. Note that there is a strong general similarity in prices between the two countries: drugs with high prices in one nation tend to have high prices in the other. Prices in Japan tend to be higher than those of the USA, by about 32 percent (take the exponent of the intercept term, or $\exp(0.28) = 1.32$). There are four sets of variations around this basic similarity. First, MHW seems to economize in pricing by setting lower prices for best-selling drugs in Japan and higher prices for drugs with minimal sales. An example of this behavior would seem to be offered by several recent antivirals used to treat HIV. Prices for these antivirals are quite high in Japan, though, as discussed above, the demand is quite low. To allow for this behavior, the logarithm of the ratio of maximum sales in Japan (during the period 1986 to 1996) to maximum sales in the USA (during the same period) is included in Table 5.2. The estimated coefficient on this variable indeed indicates that MHW gives lower prices to products with higher sales in Japan. Second, drugs sold by a Japanese firm in Japan might well be favored by MHW. In fact, this study finds no statistically significant bias for or against any set of

Table 5.2 Determinants of drug prices, Japan and USA, 1975

Independent variables	Dependent variables are logarithms of:		
	Japan prices	US prices	Japan/US ratio
Basic variables			
Intercept	.41 (.53)	-.18 (-.54)	.28 (.77)
log (US price)	.37 (4.11)		
log (Japan price)		.47 (3.84)	
log (Japan / US sales)	-.34 (-5.61)	.33 (4.74)	-.45 (-6.33)
Ownership/distribution binary variables			
Japanese firm	-.08 (-.38)	.13 (.89)	-.12 (-.78)
Therapeutic category binary variables			
Antibiotics	-.51 (-1.33)	.63 (1.40)	-.82 (-1.65)
Cardiovasculars	-.62 (-1.78)	1.15 (2.89)	-.43 (-2.92)
Cephalosporins	.48 (1.13)	-.08 (-.06)	.14 (.65)
Diabetes	-1.30 (-1.90)	2.19 (2.77)	-2.55 (-2.93)
Muscle relaxers	1.18 (1.69)	-.41 (-.53)	1.06 (1.27)
Nervous system	-.81 (-2.36)	1.14 (2.86)	-1.41 (-3.23)
Vertigo	1.80 (1.90)	-1.52 (-1.43)	2.33 (1.90)
Product life cycle			
Age in Japan	.001 (.05)	-.060 (-.61)	.047 (.40)
Age in USA	-.074 (-2.98)	080 (2.76)	-.107 (-3.42)
Summary statistics			
Observations	98	98	98
R^2 statistic	.36	.38	.40
F statistic	5.58	6.02	7.45

firms, by MHW, not only in Table 5.2 but throughout the analyses of this chapter. Zero-one binary variables for Japanese-owned firms are included and reported for all price regressions. Similar binary variables for the 'large' foreign firms listed in Table 5.1 are also included for estimation, but the estimated coefficients were not significant for the 1975 data and are not reported to save space in Tables 5.2 through 5.5. Third, there is some cross-national variation in prices due to therapeutic category, as mentioned above for the antivirals. Prices in Japan are lower for cardiovascular, diabetes, and nervous system drugs, and higher for anti-vertigo products. These therapeutic category variations might be indirectly exclusionary if Japanese innovations were concentrated in those categories with high prices, while foreign innovations were focused on categories with low prices. Fourth, Japanese prices are completely stable over the product life cycle due to fixed MHW regulations. Prices in the USA rise by an estimated 7.6 to 11.3 percent a year (calculated as $\exp(0.074)$ and $\exp(0.107)$). We must remember that these prices are nominal, or uncorrected for inflation. Part of the observed difference in price trends here is due to a slightly higher rate of inflation in general prices in the USA.

Table 5.3 presents regression result for units sold (number of base units) in Japan and the USA in 1975. Note that there is again a very strong general similarity in unit sales between Japan and the USA, though there is more cross-national variation in the sales of individual molecules than in pricing. Remember that multiple molecules can be introduced in the same therapeutic category (as illustrated in the beta-blocker example discussed above). Even if unit sales were identical in both nations for the therapeutic category as a whole, we would expect that various competing molecules might record the different successes in both nations.

There are three sets of potential variations around the basic similarity in units sold between Japan and the USA. First, there are again differences between the two nations due to therapeutic category, reflecting different incidence of disease and different methods of treatment. In fact, sales variations due to therapeutic category are much stronger than price variations between the two nations. Second, the ownership/distribution binary variable for Japanese firms remains insignificant, indicating that in 1975 Japanese firms had no real advantage over foreign firms to sell products in their home market. We must remember, however, that most foreign firms in 1975 participated in the Japanese market through joint ventures with local Japanese firms. This lack of difference in competence is thus perhaps not surprising, as most 'foreign' firms in Japan in 1975 were not really so foreign.

A final cause of variations in relative sales between the USA and Japan is the product life cycle in each country. Life cycle variables are of critical

Table 5.3 Determinants of unit sales for molecules, Japan and USA, 1975

Independent variables	Dependent variables are logarithms of:		
	Japan units	US units	Japan/US ratio
Basic variables			
Intercept	5.52 (4.76)	5.53 (4.14)	-.76 (-.98)
log (US units)	.42 (4.68)		
log (Japan units)		.52 (4.65)	
Ownership/distribution binary variables			
Japanese firm	.33 (1.52)	-.19 (-1.54)	.17 (.87)
Therapeutic category binary variables			
Antibiotics	1.72 (2.96)	-.62 (-.92)	1.51 (2.11)
Cardiovasculars	-.72 (-1. 04)	1.60 (2.78)	-1.63 (-2.56)
Cephalosporins	3.27 (5.42)	-2.32 (-2.95)	3.65 (4.92)
Diabetes	-.80 (-.77)	1.12 (.97)	-1.33 (-1.03)
Muscle relaxers	-.46 (-.41)	.54 (.45)	-.19 (-.17)
Nervous system	-.75 (-1.45)	.64 (1.07)	-.94 (-1.46)
Vertigo	2.25 (2.49)	-3.26 (-2.95)	3.80 (3.07)
Product life cycle			
Age in Japan	.48 (3.00)	-.38 (-2.49)	.58 (2.95)
Age in Japan squared	-.016 (-2.37)	.012 (2.01)	-.021 (-2.48)
Age in USA	-.20 (-2.54)	.21 (2.31)	-.28 (-2.86)
Age in USA squared	.007 (2.46)	-.008 (- 2.41)	.010 (2.88)
Summary statistics			
Observations	98	98	98
R^2 statistic	.55	.57	.42
F statistic	9.61	10.30	7.14

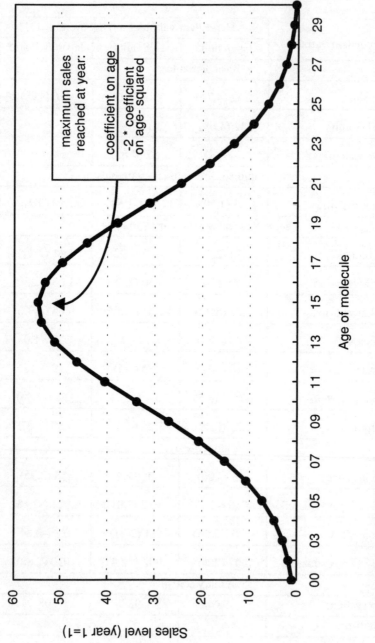

Figure 5.1 Estimated life cycle for unit sales, Japan, 1975 (calculated using estimated coefficients reported in left column of Table 5.3; coefficient on age variable is 0.48, and on age-squared variable is –0.016)

importance in this study, as the shrinking life cycle in Japan is the first and core hypothesis of this study. The estimated peak of the life cycle can be computed from Table 5.3 as the following ratio:

$$\frac{\text{coefficient on age variable}}{-2 * \text{coefficient on age-squared variable}}$$

Note from Table 5.3 (at right) that molecules in Japan have a life cycle peak at 13.8 years (calculated as 0.58/0.042), while molecules in the USA have a life cycle that peaks at a very similar 14.0 years (calculated as 0.28/0.02). The entire life-cycle is traced in Figure 5.1.

In summation, the differences we find both in prices and in sales between Japan and the USA in 1975 are rather what we would expect in comparing markets with very different medical cultures. There are pronounced differences in consumption in some therapeutic categories, and more minor differences in prices. But there is no evidence of bias against foreign firms in Japan despite the fact that all prices in the Japanese pharmaceutical market are directly set by government regulation, while prices are completely unregulated in the USA. Most important for our purposes here, drugs in 1975 have almost identical life cycles in the two countries, though prices rise over time in the USA while being held flat in Japan.

Tables 5.4 and 5.5 report comparable comparisons in 1975 of prices and units sold in Japan and Britain. Note that the sample for these two tables differs in minor ways from that of Tables 5.2 and 5.3, because some molecules sold in Japan and the USA are not sold in Britain, and vice versa. The regression results are sufficiently similar despite this difference in the samples to permit listing of the key findings without detailed discussion:

1. Drugs with high prices or unit sales in Japan tend to have high prices or sales in Britain.

2. There is no evidence at all for discrimination in price setting by MHW in favor of Japanese firms, and there is no evidence that Japanese firms had any greater capability in marketing drugs in Japan than the 'foreign' firms operating in that market in 1975.

3. There is minor variation in pricing and significant variation in units sold according to therapeutic category, as would be expected between two very different nations.

Table 5.4 Determinants of drug prices, Japan and Britain, 1975

Independent variables	Dependent variables are logarithms of:		
	Japan prices	UK prices	Japan/UK ratio
Basic variables			
Intercept	.89 (1.45)	.31 (1.03)	.62 (1.63)
log (UK price)	.42 (3.33)		
log (Japan price)		.37 (3.34)	
log (Japan / UK sales)	-.17 (-2.72)	.23 (5.11)	-.30 (-4.70)
Ownership/distribution binary variables			
Japanese firm	-.17 (-.93)	.04 (.23)	-.17 (-.80)
Therapeutic category binary variables			
Antibiotics	-.46 (-1.33)	.21 (.60)	-.52 (-1.09)
Cardiovasculars	-.22 (-1.78)	.56 (2.24)	-.56 (-1.62)
Cephalosporins	-.85 (-1.48)	.34 (.72)	-.92 (-1.45)
Diabetes	-.30 (-.40)	.22 (.42)	-.36 (-.48)
Muscle relaxers	1.00 (1.09)	-.53 (-.87)	1.42 (1.29)
Nervous system	-.22 (-.75)	.37 (1.50)	-.42 (-1.25)
Vertigo	.06 (.06)	.46 (.62)	-.25 (-.26)
Product life cycle			
Age in Japan	-.036 (-.95)	-.013 (-.45)	-.021 (-.53)
Age in UK	-.026 (-1.02)	-.080 (-1.51)	.004 (.13)
Summary statistics			
Observations	97	97	97
R^2 statistic	.42	.34	.30
F statistic	5.58	4.85	4.48

Table 5.5 Determinants of unit sales for molecules, Japan and Britain, 1975

Independent variables	Dependent variables are logarithms of:		
	Japan units	UK units	Japan/UK ratio
Basic variables			
Intercept	5.89 (8.45)	.91 (.72)	3.06 (4.36)
log (UK units)	.46 (5.75)		
log (Japan units)		.61 (5.75)	
Ownership/distribution binary variables			
Japanese firm	.11 (.39)	-.29 (-.88)	.17 (.87)
Therapeutic category binary variables			
Antibiotics	1.28 (2.04)	-.14 (-.29)	.59 (1.31)
Cardiovasculars	-.81 (-1. 79)	.91 (1.76)	-1.22 (-2.60)
Cephalosporins	4.29 (5.96)	-3.71 (-4.13)	5.10 (5.85)
Diabetes	.08 (.07)	-.46 (-.42)	.39 (.33)
Muscle relaxers	2.18 (2.25)	-3.08 (-1.96)	2.87 (2.35)
Nervous system	-1.34 (-3.13)	1.21 (2.42)	-1.63 (-3.13)
Vertigo	-.11 (-.08)	.55 (.35)	-.48 (-.29)
Product life cycle			
Age in Japan	.58 (3.00)	-.44 (-2.76)	.65 (4.03)
Age in Japan squared	-.029 (-2.37)	.021 (2.61)	-.031 (-3.53)
Age in UK	-.27 (-2.54)	.19 (2.28)	-.29 (-1.96)
Age in UK squared	.013 (2.46)	-.009 (- 1.88)	.014 (2.18)
Summary statistics			
Observations	97	97	97
R^2 statistic	.51	.48	.50
F statistic	8.34	7.30	8.41

4. There is no trend whatsoever in the regulated prices of either Japan or the UK. The estimated life cycle for unit sales in Japan reaches its peak at 10.6 years and in Britain at 10.4 years.

MATCHED MOLECULES: USA, BRITAIN, AND JAPAN FOR 1986–1996

More recent data for molecules sold simultaneously in Japan and either the USA or Britain are analyzed in this section. These data are fully comprehensive, covering every drug sold in either national pair launched since 1970. Both samples cover almost all matched molecules launched since 1960. Data are again from IMS, and are used with permission. The definition of variables and the setup of analyses are identical to that of the previous section, except that instead of data for a single year (1975), we now have data for 11 years (1986–96) in the USA and 10 years (1987–96) in Britain. Table 5.6 reports results for the analysis of prices for matched molecules sold in Japan and the USA. After our detailed discussion in the section above, we may proceed quickly to summarize central results.

1. Prices in Japan and the USA are highly correlated. Molecules with high prices in one nation tend to have high prices in the other nation. Note that over 85 percent of the variation in prices in one nation can be explained by using prices in the other nation, plus controls for ownership, therapeutic category, and product age.

2. Drugs with smaller sales in Japan than in the USA tend to have higher prices in Japan, and vice versa for drugs with larger sales in Japan. Again, this arrangement is a quirk of MHW price regulation designed to minimize expenditure on successful drugs.

3. To conserve space, the estimated effects of therapeutic category are not reported in Table 5.6. Nonetheless, there are again significant variations in prices between the two countries due to therapeutic category. In particular, anti-HIV products, cephalosporins, and diagnostics record much higher prices in Japan, while muscle relaxers and nervous system products are priced much lower there. Note that there are more therapeutic categories used in Table 5.6 (twelve) than in

Table 5.6 Determinants of drug prices, Japan and USA, 1986–96

Independent variables	Dependent variables are logarithms of:		
	Japan prices	US prices	Japan/US ratio
Basic variables			
Intercept	.01 (.32)	.26 (6.63)	-.01 (-.18)
log (US price)	.89 (110.56)		
log (Japan price)		.88 (110.57)	
[max (Japan units) / max (US units)]	-.11 (-12.07)	.12 (13.60)	-.13 (-13.77)
Ownership/distribution binary variables			
Japanese firm	.01 (.25)	-.06 (-1.74)	.04 (1.08)
Japanese innovation	-.04 (-.75)	.06 (1.06)	-.07 (-1.21)
Traditional distributor	.01 (.27)	.01 (.12)	.02 (.38)
Large foreign firm	.25 (5.77)	-.23 (-5.28)	.24 (5.68)
12 therapeutic category binaries estimated, though coefficients not reported here: antibiotics, antivirals, bile drugs, cardiovasculars, cephalosporins, diabetes, diagnostics, hormones, muscle relaxers, nervous system, respiratory, vertigo drugs			
Product life cycle			
Age in Japan	-.053 (-18.89)	.044 (13.60)	-.050 (-18.26)
Age in USA	.032 (12.37)	-.035 (-12.37)	.034 (13.24)
Summary statistics			
Observations	3282	3282	3282
R^2 statistic	.86	.85	.29
F statistic	855.27	785.55	58.22

Table 5.2 (seven) because there are many more drugs on the market by 1996 than in 1975.

4. We again find no statistically significant evidence that MHW favors Japanese firms in price setting. Rather those firms that directly benefit from MHW price regulations are the 'large' and highly innovative foreign firms identified in Table 5.1. These 'large' firms receive a price premia in Japan of roughly 24 percent. The finding of price premia in Japan for large foreign firms is statistically robust.

5. A second important difference between findings for 1975 in Table 5.2 and those for 1986–96 in Table 5.6 concerns product age. Prices now fall over time in both countries, around 5 percent a year in Japan (with estimated coefficients ranging from 4.4 to 5.3 percent) and about 3.5 percent a year in the USA (with estimated coefficient range of 3.2 to 3.5 percent). In Japan, these price declines are imposed by MHW regulation, as discussed in earlier chapters. In the USA, price declines are the result of generic competition for older drugs that lose patent protection. Both market features arise only during the 1980s, and are appropriately not found in Table 5.2.

Table 5.7 partitions these results according to the 'vintage' of molecule in Japan, where vintage denotes the year of launch in Japan. There is essentially no difference across these segmentations of the data. There is a strong positive coefficient for products of Japanese firms in the second period, 1980–1984, but this result is a statistical blip that is not repeated in other periods. In contrast, the most important findings of Table 5.6 (higher prices for 'large' foreign firms and a 5 percent average decline over time for all prices in Japan) are replicated in each period of Table 5.7. Prices for 'large' foreign firms are roughly 21 percent higher than those of Japanese firms for the oldest drugs in Japan, and 48 percent higher for the newest.

Table 5.8 presents regression results for units sold (measured as the number of base units, per our discussion above) in Japan and the US during 1986–96. Note that there is again a very strong general similarity in unit sales between Japan and the USA, though as expected there is more cross-national variation in the sales of individual molecules than in pricing, due to national differences in doctor-prescribing habits. Remember that multiple molecules can be introduced in the same therapeutic category (as illustrated in the beta-blocker example discussed above). Even if unit sales were identical in both countries for the therapeutic category as a whole, we would

Table 5.7 Determinants of drug prices, Japan and USA, 1986–96, partitioned by vintage of molecule (launch year in Japan)

Independent variables	Dependent variable is log (Japan price / US price) for drugs launched in Japan during these years:			
	1960–79	1980–84	1985–89	1990–96
Basic variables				
Intercept	.25 (-2.73)	.01 (.32)	.25 (3.09)	-.28 (-3.21)
[max (Japan) / max (US)]	-.11 (-8.46)	-.17 (-9.35)	-.14 (-5.76)	-.19 (-5.26)
Ownership/distribution binary variables				
Japanese firm	-.07 (-1.64)	.21 (3.04)	-.03 (-.54)	-.12 (1.13)
Japanese innovation	-.10 (-3.61)	.42 (4.12)	.37 (3.16)	-.39 (-2.10)
Traditional distributor	-.04 (-.57)	.14 (.99)	-.04 (-.61)	.21 (1.38)
Large foreign	.21 (2.74)	.31 (3.73)	.40 (3.82)	.48 (2.95)
12 therapeutic category binaries estimated, though coefficients not reported here: antibiotics, antivirals, bile drugs, cardiovasculars, cephalosporins, diabetes, diagnostics, hormones, muscle relaxers, nervous system, respiratory, vertigo drugs				
Product life cycle				
Age in Japan	-.051 (-11.20)	-.060 (-7.21)	-.104 (-7.97)	-.055 (-3.33)
Age in USA	.0008 (12.44)	.0004 (3.15)	.0022 (4.87)	.002 (4.76)
Summary statistics				
Observations	1636	765	646	235
R^2 statistic	.32	.30	.29	.31
F statistic	44.00	24.83	19.53	9.54

Table 5.8 Determinants of unit sales, Japan and USA, 1986–96

Independent variables	Dependent variables are logarithms of:		
	Japan units	US units	Japan/US ratio
Basic variables			
Intercept	1.56 (12.01)	2.02 (15.96)	-.25 (-2.40)
log (US units)	.79 (72.82)		
log (Japan units)		.80 (72.87)	
Ownership/distribution binary variables			
Japanese firm	.25 (3.62)	-.30 (-4.35)	.31 (4.18)
Japanese innovation	.94 (8.26)	-.88 (-7.76)	1.02 (8.47)
Traditional distributor	-.33 (-3.75)	.47 (5.39)	-.44 (-4.81)
Large foreign firm	.04 (.47)	-.27 (-2.95)	.18 (1.78)
12 therapeutic category binaries estimated, though coefficients not reported here: antibiotics, antivirals, bile drugs, cardiovasculars, cephalosporins, diabetes, diagnostics, hormones, muscle relaxers, nervous system, respiratory, vertigo drugs			
Product life cycle			
Age in Japan	.21 (14.08)	-.14 (-9.38)	.19 (12.48)
Age in Japan squared	-.0043 (-9.24)	.0030 (5.63)	-.0040 (-7.51)
Age in USA	-.19 (-16.23)	.163 (13.92)	-.20 (-16.00)
Age in USA squared	.0035 (12.45)	-.003 (- 9.48)	.0037 (11.56)
Summary statistics			
Observations	3282	3282	3282
R^2 statistic	.68	71	38
F statistic	333.66	370.32	92.78

still expect that various competing molecules might record different successes in both countries.

There are three sets of variations around the basic similarity in units sold between Japan and the USA. First, there are again differences between the two nations owing to therapeutic category, reflecting different incidence of disease and different methods of treatment. We again do not report estimated coefficients on therapeutic category binary variables in Table 5.8, to conserve space. Nonetheless, we find as expected that sales variations due to therapeutic category are much stronger than price variations. Second, the ownership/distribution binary variable for Japanese firms is now quite significant. Drugs sold by a Japanese-owned firm in Japan tend to have larger sales there, by roughly 31 percent. This significant difference in performance represents the greater capability of local firms to understand and respond to their immediate market – a market that is genuinely different from those in the West, as the discussions above should make clear. This difference in realized sales may also reflect nontariff barriers against foreign firms. Note the profound difference in these two interpretations: internal capabilities of firms as an explanation for performance differences versus artificially erected market barriers. The next set of findings, reported in Table 5.9, suggests that the internal capabilities explanation is the more valid one. Regressions in Table 5.9 again partition the sample by year of product launch in Japan. Here we find very stable superior sales performance by Japanese firms in their home market, with 55 percent higher sales (calculated as exp(0.44)) compared to most foreign firms. Note however that the performance of 'large' foreign firms sharply improves over time, so that in recent years their marketing performance in Japan approaches that of Japanese-owned firms. For the oldest drugs, large foreign firms under perform other foreign firms with sales in Japan only 54 percent of those attained in the USA (calculated as exp(-.60)). Clearly, before 1980, foreign firms did better in Japan by marketing their drugs through formal joint ventures or by licensing them to Japanese firms.

A final cause of variations in relative units sold between the USA and Japan is the product life cycle. The estimated peak of the life cycle in Table 5.8 and for each period in Table 5.9 can again be computed as the following ratio:

$$\frac{\text{coefficient on age variable}}{-2 * \text{coefficient on age-squared variable}}$$

Note from Table 5.8 (at right) that molecules in Japan have a life cycle peak at 22.9 years, while molecules in the USA have a life cycle peak at a very similar 26.9 years. When we examine Table 5.9, however, we see the

Table 5.9 Determinants of unit sales, Japan and USA, 1986–96, partitioned by vintage of molecule (launch year in Japan)

Independent variables	Dependent variable is log (Japan units / US units) for drugs launched in Japan during these years:			
	1960–1979	1980–1984	1985–89	1990–96
Basic variables				
Intercept	- .63 (-1.56)	.12 (.31)	-1.42 (-5.66)	-1.74 (-6.04)
Ownership/distribution binary variables				
Japanese firm	.03 (.36)	.32 (3.34)	.84 (8.37)	.78 (3.51)
Japanese innovation	.10 (1.07)	1.42 (6.63)	.72 (4.97)	.77 (1.85)
Traditional distributor	-.31 (-2.47)	-.80 (-4.93)	-.41 (-3.20)	-.56 (-1.95)
Large foreign	-.60 (-4.45)	.52 (2.90)	.71 (5.86)	.42 (4.36)
12 therapeutic category binaries estimated, though coefficients not reported here: antibiotics, antivirals, bile drugs, cardiovasculars, cephalosporins, diabetes, diagnostics, hormones, muscle relaxers, nervous system, respiratory, vertigo drugs				
Product life cycle				
Age in Japan	.151 (3.54)	.402 (4.75)	.319 (3.77)	1.10 (6.45)
Age in Japan squared	-.002 (-1.96)	-.012 (-2.72)	-.022 (-3.16)	-.135 (-4.11)
Age in USA	-.129 (-9.40)	-.392 (-9.06)	-.267 (-3.64)	-.328 (-6.13)
Age in USA squared	.0023 (6.65)	. 0094 (7.38)	.0066 (2.45)	.0105 (4.89)
Summary statistics				
Observations	1636	765	646	235
R^2 statistic	.42	.39	.51	.36
F statistic	67.68	36.99	48.32	13.82

very sharp reduction in product life for recently introduced drugs in Japan, declining from a peak of 38 years for pre-1980 drugs to a peak of under five years for post-1990 drugs. For these same time periods, the life cycle in the USA is much more stable.

To validate the statistical significance of trends seen in Table 5.9 for various vintages of molecules in Japan, we again use the entire sample of matched molecules for Japan and the USA for Table 5.10, as used earlier for Tables 5.6 and 5.8. Compared with these two earlier tables, independent variables are now added to formally test the statistical significance of trends over time for the capabilities of Japanese and 'large' foreign firms, and for the product life cycle in Japan. Note from Table 5.10 that these three trends are numerically large and are statistically significant. After 1980, Japanese firms outperform most foreign firms in Japan in terms of unit sales by 78 percent (calculated as exp(0.58)) and in terms of total sales by 109 percent (calculated as exp(0.74)). Before 1980, Japanese and foreign firms were at virtual parity in terms of sales achieved in Japan, though again, we must remember that before 1980 almost all foreign drugs were sold through joint ventures with Japanese firms. Large foreign firms also dramatically improved their sales capability in Japan after 1980, though from a initial position of pronounced weakness. Before 1980, large foreign firms were less competent than Japanese firms by half (calculated as exp(-0.65)) in selling pharmaceuticals in Japan. After 1980, stunningly enough, large foreign firms actually outperform local firms (calculated as [(1.47 − .065) > .58] and are 227 percent better than other foreign firms at unit sales in Japan (calculated as exp(1.47 − 0.65)).

The estimated life cycle peaks for various vintages of new drugs are shown in Figure 5.2 for the USA and Japan. These life cycle peaks are calculated from the estimates in Table 5.10 for Japan (denoted as Japan vs. USA) and for the USA. The estimated full trends from Table 5.10 of relative prices and relative units sold over the life-cycle are traced in Figures 5.3 and 5.4 respectively. In Figure 5.3, we see that the structure over time of relative prices in Japan and the USA has shifted down for newer drugs. Prices in Japan decline by an average of 6.2 percent a year, while prices for newly launched drugs in the USA actually increase over time, though by a statistically insignificant rate. Further, MHW has shifted down the entire price structure for drugs in Japan. New drugs launched in Japan between 1981 and 1985 suffer a downward shift of the entire price structure of roughly 19 percent, with an additional 14 percent downward shift after 1985 (for a total 34 percent decline compared to pre-1980 drugs). This is a large and severe decline in prices imposed by MHW on pharmaceutical firms operating in Japan, and acts as a powerful disincentive to launch new products in Japan. Examining Table 5.10, we

*Table 5.10 Determinants of unit sales, drug prices, and total sales,
Japan and USA, 1986–96*

Independent variables	Dependent variables, log (Japan/US ratio)		
	Units sold	Prices	Total sales
Basic variables			
[max (sales Japan)] / [max (sales USA)]		-.13 (-13.64)	
Intercept binary variables			
Intercept	-1.74 (-6.75)	.31 (3.68)	-1.18 (-4.75)
Product launch 1980–84 (binary)	.77 (5.01)	-.19 (-3.04)	.53 (3.39)
Product launch 1985–89 (binary)	1.00 (4.40)	-.34 (-4.59)	.46 (2.00)
Product launch 1990–96 (binary)	.72 (2.73)	-.34 (-4.63)	.18 (.66)
Ownership/distribution binary variables			
Japanese firm	-.03 (-.36)	-.01 (-3.89)	-.04 (-.42)
Japanese firm * [1 if launch year > 1980][†]	.58 (4.24)	.09 (1.51)	.74 (5.33)
Japanese innovation	.96 (8.11)	-.07 (-1.05)	.79 (6.55)
Traditional Japanese distributor	-.38 (-4.15)	.01 (.14)	-.40 (-4.24)
Large foreign firm	-.65 (-4.62)	.19 (2.90)	-.40 (-1.67)
Large foreign firm * [1 if launch > 1980][†]	1.47 (7.89)	.16 (1.79)	1.46 (7.68)

12 therapeutic category binaries estimated, though coefficients not reported here: antibiotics, antivirals, bile drugs, cardiovasculars, cephalosporins, diabetes, diagnostics, hormones, muscle relaxers, nervous system, respiratory, vertigo drugs

Table 5.10 continued on next page

Table 5.10 continued from previous page

Independent variables	Dependent variables, log (Japan/US ratio)		
	Units sold	Prices	Total sales
Product life cycle			
Age in Japan	.32 (12.27)	-.062 (-14.80)	.217 (8.37)
Age in Japan * [launch year - 1980][‡]	.012 (2.89)		.017 (2.75)
Age in Japan squared	-.0060 (-8.94)		-.0051 (-7.55)
Age in Japan squared * [launch year - 1980][‡]	-.0026 (-3.79)		-.0031 (-4.56)
Age in USA	-.194 (-16.23)	.008 (1.92)	-.161 (-13.04)
Age in USA squared	.0034 (12.45)	.0007 (5.49)	.0036 (12.07)
Summary statistics			
Observations	3282	3282	3282
R^2 statistic	.40	.30	.34
F statistic	114.95	63.50	65.62

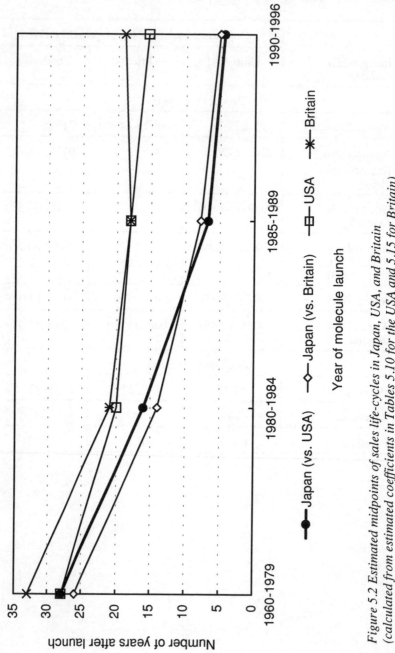

Figure 5.2 Estimated midpoints of sales life-cycles in Japan, USA, and Britain (calculated from estimated coefficients in Tables 5.10 for the USA and 5.15 for Britain)

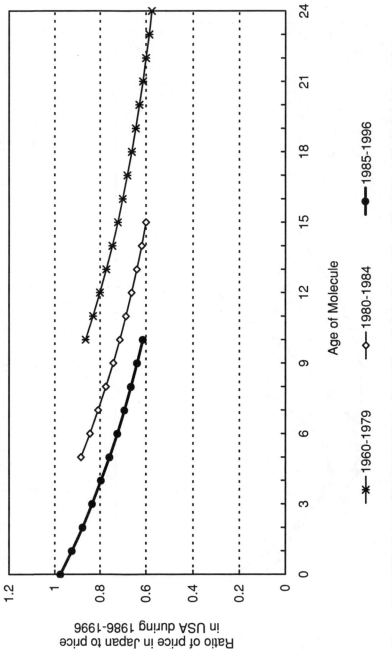

Figure 5.3 MHW pricing in Japan: Prices decline with molecule age and launch prices are lower for newer drugs

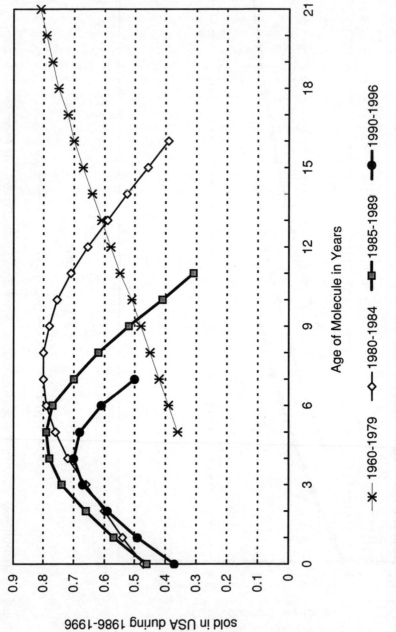

Figure 5.4 Estimated units sold over the life cycle: Recent drugs have much shorter lives in Japan

see that large foreign firms earn statistically significant price premia in Japan relative to other firms operating in that nation, of roughly 19 percent for products launched before 1980 and 35 percent afterwards (computed as 0.19 + 0.16). Note that these prices for large foreign firms still shift downward over time at the common rate of 6.2 percent a year, though the trend they follow remains above those of Japanese firms and of other foreign firms.

The pronounced shortening of product life for new drugs in Japan is traced in Figure 5.4. If per capita consumption of pharmaceuticals between Japan and the USA were precisely equal at each point over the entire life cycle, the trends drawn in Figure 5.4 would be flat lines at 50 percent (since the population of Japan is roughly half that of the USA). Instead, we see that new drugs launched in Japan break through to gain sales more rapidly there than in the USA. As a consequence of this faster market acceptance, the trends of relative units sold in Japan versus the USA are initially inclined upwards, and reach their peak at between 70 and 80 percent of those in the USA. Very quickly, however, unit sales growth in Japan slows, while unit sales in the USA continue to mount. Most importantly for the purposes of this study, the life cycle for new drugs in Japan has become systematically shorter since 1981, being compressed into a much narrower window of time. Per capita consumption of units in Japan returns to the 50 percent level against the USA after 14 years for drugs launched between 1980 and 1984 in Japan. The 50 percent level is attained after only nine years for drugs launched between 1985 and 1989, and after only seven years for drugs launched after 1990. This sharp reduction in sales in Japan is a powerful disincentive to launch of new products in that country.

Our goal in comparing prices and unit sales between Japan and the USA has been to isolate changes in the Japanese market, using the USA as a control. To ensure that our findings are not due instead to distinctive features of the US market, we conduct and report additional statistical tests using matched molecules in Britain and Japan. Tables 5.11 to 5.15 for Japan and Britain are the analogues of Tables 5.6 to 5.10 for Japan and the USA. There are slightly more observations for the Japan/Britain samples because the British market is relatively more open that that of the USA (consult Table 1.1, page 2). Thus, as we tabulate molecules sold at the same time in both Japan and Britain, we will find more such drugs than we found for Japan and the USA. Note that the Japan/Britain and Japan/USA samples are fundamentally different samples, not proper subsets of each other, as many molecules sold in Britain have never been launched in the USA, and vice versa.

Findings reported in Tables 5.11 to 5.14 using Britain as a control

Table 5.11 Determinants of drug prices, Japan and Britain, 1987–96

Independent variables	Dependent variables are logarithms of:		
	Japan prices	UK prices	Japan/UK ratio
Basic variables			
Intercept	-.79 (17.89)	-.55 (-12.23)	.72 (15.97)
log (UK price)	.89 (110.63)		
log (Japan price)		.88 (110.63)	
[max (Japan units) / max (UK units)]	-.09 (-13.61)	.10 (15.35)	-.10 (-14.91)
Ownership/distribution binary variables			
Japanese firm	.04 (1.44)	-.12 (-2.83)	.08 (2.43)
Japanese innovation	.02 (.29)	.02 (.41)	.00 (.04)
Traditional distributor	-.05 (-1.17)	.10 (2.65)	-.07 (-1.83)
Large foreign firm	.08 (2.06)	-.15 (-3.65)	.12 (2.75)
12 therapeutic category binaries estimated, though coefficients not reported here: antibiotics, antivirals, bile drugs, cardiovasculars, cephalosporins, diabetes, diagnostics, hormones, muscle relaxers, nervous system, respiratory, vertigo drugs			
Product life cycle			
Age in Japan	-.050 (-6.53)	.052 (4.22)	-.050 (-5.63)
Age in UK	.033 (1.04)	-.019 (-2.80)	.026 (2.04)
Summary statistics			
Observations	3451	3451	3282
R^2 statistic	.88	.87	.30
F statistic	872.46	843.66	68.22

Table 5.12 Determinants of drug prices, Japan and Britain, 1987–96, partitioned by vintage of molecule (launch year in Japan)

Independent variables	Dependent variable is log (Japan price / UK price) for drugs launched in Japan during these years:			
	1960–79	1980–84	1985–89	1990–96
Basic variables				
Intercept	.97 (9.87)	1.07 (8.40)	.47 (5.90)	.17 (1.14)
[max (Japan) / max (UK)]	- .12 (-10.41)	- .12 (-8.64)	- 08 (-4.96)	- .13 (-3.81)
Ownership/distribution binary variables				
Japanese firm	-.11 (-2.37)	.12 (1.71)	.32 (3.65)	.20 (1.79)
Japanese innovation	-.08 (-.62)	-.02 (-.18)	-.13 (-1.18)	-.06 (-.33)
Traditional distributor	-.02 (-.33)	-.09 (-1.07)	-.01 (-.06)	-.01 (-.10)
Large foreign	.19 (3.07)	.02 (.49)	.26 (2.89)	.43 (2.63)
12 therapeutic category binaries estimated, though coefficients not reported here: antibiotics, antivirals, bile drugs, cardiovasculars, cephalosporins, diabetes, diagnostics, hormones, muscle relaxers, nervous system, respiratory, vertigo drugs				
Product life cycle				
Age in Japan	-.047 (-4.51)	-.046 (-4.62)	-.044 (-2.37)	-.049 (-3.33)
Age in UK	.030 (2.04)	-.029 (-1.47)	.029 (1.88)	.060 (5.68)
Summary statistics				
Observations	1595	895	691	267
R^2 statistic	.22	.17	.30	.37
F statistic	24.53	13.08	21.10	13.18

Table 5.13 Determinants of unit sales, Japan and Britain, 1987–96

Independent variables	Dependent variables are logarithms of:		
	Japan units	UK units	Japan/UK ratio
Basic variables			
Intercept	4.62 (31.89)	.25 (1.41)	1.91 (13.73)
log (UK units)	.63 (57.72)		
log (Japan units)		.76 (56.63)	
Ownership/distribution binary variables			
Japanese firm	.46 (5.83)	-.38 (-4.54)	.47 (5.41)
Japanese innovation	.46 (3.55)	-.45 (-2.87)	.53 (3.20)
Traditional distributor	-.74 (-8.01)	65 (6.60)	-.80 (-7.67)
Large foreign firm	.09 (.99)	-.22 (-2.47)	.15 (1.45)
12 therapeutic category binaries estimated, though coefficients not reported here: antibiotics, antivirals, bile drugs, cardiovasculars, cephalosporins, diabetes, diagnostics, hormones, muscle relaxers, nervous system, respiratory, vertigo drugs			
Product life cycle			
Age in Japan	.222 (11.78)	-.175 (-8.37)	.226 (10447)
Age in Japan squared	-.006 (-10.93)	.0044 (6.90)	-.0058 (-8.73)
Age in UK	-.187 (-10.43)	.182 (9.27)	-.21 (-12.79)
Age in UK squared	.0034 (10.45)	-.003 (-5.55)	.0046 (8.66)
Summary statistics			
Observations	3451	3451	3451
R^2 statistic	.55	.55	.15
F statistic	182.86	181.08	31.62

Table 5.14 Determinants of unit sales, Japan and Britain, 1987–96,
partitioned by vintage of molecule (launch year in Japan)

Independent variables	Dependent variable is log (Japan units / UK units) for drugs launched in Japan during these years:			
	1960–79	1980–84	1985–89	1990–96
Basic variables				
Intercept	3.64 (6.76)	3.45 (5.60)	.53 (1.76)	.67 (2.09)
Ownership/distribution binary variables				
Japanese firm	.36 (2.88)	-.24 (-1.35)	.91 (4.44)	1.31 (5.50)
Japanese innovation	1.00 (3.14)	1.01 (3.22)	-.05 (-.07)	-.14 (-.36)
Traditional distributor	-.85 (-6.20)	-1.07 (-4.63)	-.60 (-1.73)	-.71 (3.36)
Large foreign	-.35 (-2.18)	-.54 (-2.47)	1.37 6.04)	1.10 (3.26)
12 therapeutic category binaries estimated, though coefficients not reported here: antibiotics, antivirals, bile drugs, cardiovasculars, cephalosporins, diabetes, diagnostics, hormones, muscle relaxers, nervous system, respiratory, vertigo drugs				
Product life cycle				
Age in Japan	.114 (2.02)	.423 (4.35)	.329 (3.28)	.622 (3.58)
Age in Japan squared	-.0022 (-1.27)	-.015 (-2.33)	-.021 (-2.56)	-.061 (-2.14)
Age in UK	-.28 (-6.44)	-.43 (-10.28)	-.01 (-2.63)	-.33 (-6.25)
Age in UK squared	.0042 (3.46)	.0103 (7.95)	.0028 (2.76)	.0087 (4.13)
Summary statistics				
Observations	1595	895	691	267
R^2 statistic	.28	.22	.39	.37
F statistic	30.60	16.80	25.38	11.65

confirm those reported earlier for Tables 5.6 to 5.9 using the USA. These findings may be summarized quickly.

1.   Prices in Japan and Britain are highly correlated. Molecules with high prices in one nation tend to have high prices in the other nation. Note that over 85 percent of the variation in prices in one nation can be explained by using prices in the other nation, plus controls for ownership, therapeutic category, and product age. These findings confirm those using the USA as a control.

2.   Drugs with smaller sales in Japan than in Britain tend to have higher prices in Japan, and vice versa for drugs with larger sales in Japan. This arrangement is a quirk of MHW price regulation designed to contain total expenditure on successful drugs. These findings again confirm those using the USA as a control

3.   In contrast to estimates using the USA as a control in Tables 5.6 and 5.7, those using Britain as a control find a modest domestic price premium granted to Japanese firms by MHW. For drugs of all vintages, the average premium is 8 in the rightmost specification of Table 5.11 percent and is statistically significant (the estimated premia range from 4 to 12 percent in other specifications). When we split the sample by vintage of drug in Japan (reported in Table 5.12), the domestic price premium becomes even larger for newer drugs. The estimated MHW price premium granted to 'large' foreign firms is smaller for the Japan/Britain sample than for the Japan/USA sample, and is no longer statistically significantly larger than that granted to domestic firms.

4.   Prices over time fall at roughly 3 percent a year in Britain, except for the most recent vintage of molecules. Prices in Japan trend downwards by roughly 5 percent a year. These findings for Japan are quite similar to those from the Japan/USA sample.

5.   Findings on the different capabilities of firms to sell drugs in Japan reported in Tables 5.13 and 5.14 for the Japan/Britain sample are similar to those found for the Japan/USA sample in Tables 5.9 and 5.10. Indeed, the capability differences reported earlier are even more pronounced now for the

Japan/Britain sample. Japanese firms sell 60 percent more units in Japan than do most foreign firms (calculated as exp(0.47)). This difference was estimated to be only roughly 31 percent using the Japan/USA sample. For recent vintages of molecules, 'large' foreign firms have gained significant competence to sell drugs in Japan. These foreign firms are now far ahead of other foreign firms in Japan, and have closed most of the gap between them and domestic Japanese firms.

6. The estimated product life cycles for Japan using the Japan/Britain sample are extremely similar to those using the Japan/USA sample. Drawing from Table 5.14, the estimated peaks for the product life cycle in Japan are 26 years for drugs launched in Japan before 1980, 14 years for drugs launched 1980–84, 8 years for drugs of vintage 1985–89, and 5 years for drugs after 1990. The comparable estimates using the Japan/ USA sample are 38, 17, 7, and 4 years, drawing from Table 5.9. Returning to Table 5.14, the estimated peaks for the British life cycle are 32, 21, 18, and 18 years, comparable to those for the US estimates reported in Table 5.9.

Tests for the statistical significance of trends over vintages of molecules in the Japan/Britain sample are reported in Table 5.15. This table is comparable to Table 5.10 above that employed the Japan/USA sample. Differences found between these two samples are minor and well within the realm of expected variation in two fundamentally different samples drawn to test common phenomena. The core findings in both samples are the same: minimal MHW discrimination against foreign firms, pronounced and predictable differences in the capabilities of firms to market drugs in Japan, dubious and penurious pricing policies by MHW, and a mounting abbreviation in the product life cycle for new drugs launched in Japan.

EXCLUSION, CAPABILITIES, AND THE RULE OF REASON

If we combine the downward shift in the price schedule directly imposed by MHW (visible in Figure 5.3) with the shortening of product life indirectly caused by MHW price regulations (visible in Figure 5.4), we attain a pronounced disincentive for foreign firms to launch new drugs in Japan. The rightmost columns of Tables 5.10 for the Japan/USA sample and 5.15

The Japanese pharmaceutical industry

Table 5.15 Determinants of relative unit sales, drug prices, and total sales, Japan and Britain, 1987–96

Independent variables	Dependent variables, log (Japan / Britain ratio)		
	Units sold	Prices	Total sales
Basic variables			
[Max (sales Japan)] / [max (sales Britain)]		-.10 (-14.17)	
Intercept and vintage binary variables			
Intercept	1.47 (4.56)	.31 (3.68)	2.47 (7.81)
Product launch 1980–1984 (binary)	.96 (5.61)	-.19 (-3.04)	.65 (3.88)
Product launch 1985–1989 (binary)	.07 (.23)	-.34 (-4.59)	-.69 (-2.45)
Product launch 1990–1996 (binary)	-.65 (-2.09)	-.34 (-4.63)	-1.27 (-3.94)
Ownership/distribution binary variables			
Japanese firm	.20 (1.87)	-.06 (-1.65)	.11 (1.12)
Japanese firm * [1 if launch year > 80]	.96 (5.32)	.52 (7.46)	1.36 (7.69)
Japanese innovation	.42 (2.55)	-.04 (-.57)	.42 (2.58)
Traditional Japanese distributor	-.67 (-6.53)	-.07 (-1.66)	-.63 (-6.30)
Large foreign firm	-.34 (-2.70)	.02 (.44)	-.27 (-2.17)
Large foreign firm * [1 if launch > 80]	1.66 (6.82)	.32 (3.45)	1.84 (7.37)

12 therapeutic category binaries estimated, though coefficients not reported here: antibiotics, antivirals, bile drugs, cardiovasculars, cephalosporins, diabetes, diagnostics, hormones, muscle relaxers, nervous system, respiratory, vertigo drugs

Table 5.15 continued on next page

Table 5.15 continued from previous page

Independent variables	Dependent variables, log (Japan / Britain ratio)		
	Units sold	Prices	Total sales
Product life cycle			
Age in Japan	.32 (12.27)	-.051 (-8.28)	.217 (8.37)
Age in Japan * [launch year - 80]	.012 (2.89)		.017 (2.75)
Age in Japan squared	-.0060 (-8.94)		-.005 (-7.55)
Age in Japan squared * [launch year - 80]	-.0026 (-3.79)		-.0031 (-4.56)
Age in Britain	-.219 (-10.63)	.035 (4.87)	-.159 (-7.80)
Age in Britain squared	.0033 (8.15)		.0023 (4.54)
Summary statistics			
Observations	3451	3451	3451
R^2 statistic	.26	.21	.25
F statistic	34.82	32.03	32.98

for the Japan/Britain sample document determinants of total sales for new drugs in Japan versus overseas markets. Total sales are the obvious product of prices and unit sales. Hence determinants of total sales combine the direct effects of changes in MHW pricing policies (vintaging and the downward shift for the price schedule) and the indirect effects (shortening product life and capability differences across firms). With these total sales estimates and some measure for cost of capital, we can compute the present discounted value of total sales for a new drug in Japan. Consider molecules with vintage in Japan before 1980 sold by most foreign firms. The rightmost estimates from Table 5.10 that apply under such conditions are the intercept term and Japan age variables. None of the coefficient estimates for the many binary variables apply for these specific molecules and firms. Take the cost of capital to be 15 percent, then for non-large foreign firms in Japan the present value of sales for molecules launched before 1980 is:

$$Present\,Value = \int_0^{40} \exp\left[-1.18 + .22 * Age - .005 * Age^2\right] \exp(-.15 * Age)\, dAge$$

For molecules launched in Japan after 1980, the coefficients in the bracketed term adjusts as per estimates in Tables 5.10 (or 5.15, for anglophilic readers). We may then readily compute four present values of sales in Japan for most foreign firms: (1) for molecules launched before 1980, as given immediately above, (2) for molecules launched during 1980–84, (3) for molecules launched during 1985–89, and (4) for molecules launched after 1990. The present values of sales for the first two vintages of molecules are almost identical. For molecules launched in Japan from 1985 to 1989, the present value of sales is roughly 74 percent of that for molecules launched before 1980. For molecules launched after 1990, the present value of sales is roughly 54 percent of that for molecules launched before 1980. The falloff in profits for new drugs launched in Japan will be even more than these 74 percent and 54 percent falloff in sales, because there are large fixed costs for registration, marketing, and distribution of any new drug that has not changed over time. Thus, for foreign firms without extensive presence in Japan, the falloff of profits from launching new drugs into Japan has decreased by more than half from the mid-1980s to the mid-1990s.

As should be clear from several points made in this chapter, the direct and indirect effects of MHW pricing regulations are much less severe for Japanese firms and for 'large' foreign firms with extensive presence in Japan. Both sets of firms have developed greater capabilities for selling and distributing their new products in Japan since 1980, so that a gap in distribution skills has opened and widened among firms in Japan. Indeed, as discussed above, 'large' foreign firms now register the greatest capability for sales in Japan of any firms operating in that country. Additionally, these 'large' foreign firms achieve the highest prices granted by MHW. Drawing on the estimates at the right of Table 5.10, domestic Japanese firms achieve sales that are 64 percent better than foreign firms lacking extensive presence in Japan. For Japanese firms, MHW-imposed changes in the domestic pharmaceutical industry have led to a fall after 1990 in the present value of sales of only 12 percent (calculated as [0.54 * exp(-0.038 + 0.53)]). For 'large' foreign firms, the higher prices granted by MHW and the greater capabilities of these firms for selling in Japan have actually led to an increase after 1990 in the present value of sales.

A common immediate reaction to these calculations is that 'markets work,' meaning that hardworking and capable firms succeed in Japan, while firms that fail to invest sufficiently in that market and acquire appropriate capabilities do not. Because 'markets work,' there is no justification for trade action by the USA against Japanese exclusion of foreign firms and foreign innovations. This reaction quite misses the point. Markets are not fixed and given entities, rather they are socially constructed. Thus the capabilities of firms in a specific market also are not given, but are also socially constructed. The relevant issue is not whether firms can adapt to whatever bizarre constructions Japan may use for its markets, but whether these social constructions are dynamically efficient. At issue then, is the 'rule of reason'. Whether exclusion is due to market manipulation or to differential capabilities, or indeed whether exclusion exists at all, are far less important issues than the dynamic efficiency of Japanese markets.

It is indeed clear that distinctive characteristics of the Japanese pharmaceutical market force large-scale and idiosyncratic investments in Japan in order to sell drugs successfully there. But these distinctive characteristics do not promote either static or dynamic efficiency, either in Japan or in the global pharmaceutical industry. The core of these distinctive Japanese characteristics is the doctor's margin, MHW price regulations (including both increasingly lower launch prices and price vintaging), and complex vertical ties between manufacturers and wholesalers. The first of these characteristics is profoundly corrupt and creates enormous inefficiencies in Japan, as described throughout this study. In the previous chapter, we found that MHW price regulations do not even control costs, and create severe market distortions.

Perhaps the most compelling argument here concerns not the exclusion of foreign firms from Japan, but rather of Japanese firms from overseas markets. The idiosyncratic marketing capabilities of Japanese firms are indeed essential for them to compete successfully in their home market. Yet, these capabilities (including the Japanese focus on inventory-distribution and individualized doctor price-fixing) are completely worthless outside the Japanese home market (again, see Figure 4.5). Indeed, it is clear that the weak global market capabilities of Japanese firms are their greatest barrier to international competition, far more than their product development capabilities. The distinctive practices and capabilities at issue in Japan are thus doubly exclusionary. It is quite time for these practices to end.

Evidence: Declining registrations in Japan

This chapter documents the mid-1990s breakdown of the registration process for new drugs in Japan, and adjusts launch data for this collapse in registration. These adjustments are designed to segregate the effects of changes in the registration process from changes in pricing and product life cycle.

We are able to make these adjustments in launch data because of the clear trail of data that new molecules leave as they pass through the clinical trial and registration systems. Like most developed nations, Japan requires that new drugs undergo testing for safety and effectiveness prior to launch. Initial tests of new molecules (preclinical trials) are performed on animals. Promising molecules are then given human testing (clinical trials). Because of the extremely high moral stakes for any experimentation on humans, the clinical trial process is highly regulated. New drugs must undergo general testing for safety (Phase 1 trials), tests for basic effectiveness in small populations of patients (Phase 2 trials), and expanded tests for both safety and effectiveness versus existing therapies (Phase 3 trials). On completion of clinical trials, a New Drug Application (NDA) is filed with the regulatory authority. Additional trials, both preclinical and clinical, may be requested by authorities as the NDA is processed, as we saw earlier with Taxol. In Japan, roughly 55 percent of molecules that begin Phase 1 trials ultimately receive filing for registration, and virtually all drugs with an NDA filing receive regulatory approval (JPMA, 1995). In contrast, in the more stringent regulatory environment of the United States, only 20 percent of molecules that begin clinical trials ultimately receive FDA approval (*ibid.*).

There are thus several well-defined markers in the process of drug development in a nation. Ideally, then, we could readily trace changes over time in the process of drug development by marking the transitions of new molecules from Phase 1 to Phase 2, from Phase 2 to Phase 3, and so on. At each step we could examine the probability of conversion from one phase to the next, and the time spent in each phase. Unfortunately, data on the drug development process are rather difficult to obtain. The research for this book was forced to focus on three key points in the development process for molecules in Japan: Phase 1 (start date for clinical trials in Japan), filing of the NDA in Japan, and MHW approval for marketing. Data for these key dates are in the form of month and year, and were compiled from *R&D Focus* by IMS, Inc, supplemented by direct inquiries to foreign firms operating in Japan. Owing to limitations in coverage of *R&D Focus*, data were collected only for global products and are complete only after 1985. Note that, while this approach is quite appropriate for this book, which focuses on exclusion of global products from Japan over the last decade, the resulting findings may well not apply to the proliferation of local products that are now launched in Japan by domestic firms.

BREAKDOWN OF THE REGISTRATION PROCESS IN JAPAN

Figure 6.1 reports the approval rate by MHW for all NDAs of global products filed in Japan after 1985. Each molecule is dated by the year of Japanese NDA filing. Examining the figure, we see that 96 percent of filings in Japan before 1992 were approved by MHW (confirming the JPMA data cited above). We also see the collapse of the registration process after that year, with only 40 percent of NDAs filed in 1993 and 1994 approved and virtually no products (except three anti-HIV drugs) approved after 1994. AIDS drugs were given speedier approval time as a matter of public policy by MHW. A more detailed analysis of the MHW approval process for global products is reported in the Table 6.1. The center column of that table gives a logistical regression of the decision by MHW to approve an NDA filing or not. Molecules that are diffused into many nations (a proxy for medical significance) are significantly more likely to be approved by MHW. There is no statistically significant difference among firms in the probability that MHW will approve their NDA filings. Japanese firms are estimated to have a 10 percent greater likelihood of approval, but again, that estimate is not statistically significant. And, as expected, the approval probability falls dramatically after 1992 and further after 1994.

Table 6.1 also explores the capabilities of different types of foreign firms to manage the MHW approval process. We again classify foreign firms operating in Japan as 'large', 'medium,' or licensor in terms of the scope of their operations in Japan. Note that with these classifications, we do not measure the global size of these foreign firms, but only their operations in Japan. In the table, we find no significant difference among any firm type for the probability of MHW approval.

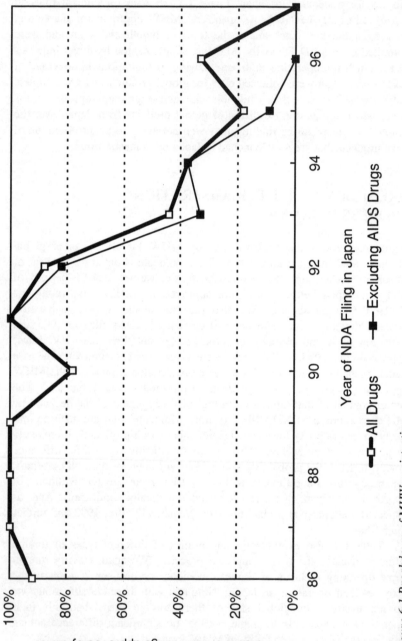

Figure 6.1 Breakdown of MHW registration process

Table 6.1: Determinants of MHW registration approval and delay

Independent variables	Dependent variables	
	MHW approval or not (binary variable)	Registration delay (logarithm of years)
Intercept	-2.29 (- 1.37)	.40 (1.82)
Molecule type		
Global diffusion[†]	.57 (3.01)	.01 (.72)
AIDS drug (binary)	1.87 (2.45)	-1.70 (-9.71)
Firm type binary variables[‡]		
Japanese firm	1.78 (1.40)	-.16 (-1.94)
Large foreign firm	-.26 (-.37)	-.12 (-1.75)
Medium foreign firm	-.35 (-.16)	.05 (.55)
Year of NDA filing in Japan (binary variables)		
Post-1992	-2.29 (-3.01)	
Post-1994	-2.87 (-3.58)	
Post-1989		.19 (2.67)
Summary statistics		
Number of observations	138	106
R^2 statistic		.48
F statistic		15.79
Pseudo-R^2 statistic	.51	
Chi^2 statistic	75.03	

Notes: † number of nations into which molecule was launched (range 6–12).
‡ originator of molecule; for foreign firm type, see Table 6.2.

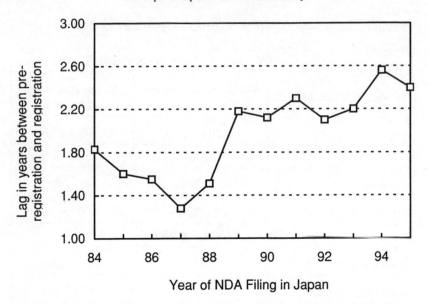

Figure 6.2 MHW registration delay is longer. Global products only; excludes AIDS drugs

Figure 6.2 reports the average delay in years between the month of NDA filing and the month of MHW approval in Japan for all global products since 1985. Data in the figure are of course only for those drugs actually approved. AIDS drugs are excluded, given the deliberate preferential treatment accorded them by MHW. Before the 1992 changes in the registration process, on average, NDAs were approved in roughly 1.6 years (19 months). After 1992, the average delay for NDA approval rose to 2.2 years and then after 1994 to 2.5 years. More detailed analysis of these delays is given in the right column of Table 6.1, with a regression analysis of registration delay. We find there that global products discovered by Japanese firms experience a 22 percent more rapid approval by MHW. This estimate is statistically significant. Interestingly, the average delay for MHW approval of NDA filings by 'large' foreign firms is comparably less than that of other foreign firms, and that difference is also statistically significant. Indeed, there is no statistically significant difference between registration delay achieved by large foreign firms and Japanese firms. Thus a firm like Bristol-Myers Squibb appears to be able to manage its NDA reviews in Japan almost as well as Japanese firms.

CLINICAL TRIALS IN JAPAN

Most studies of regulatory delay for pharmaceuticals examine only registration delay, or the time period between filing and approval for an NDA. Because this period is almost entirely controlled by regulatory authorities, it is obviously imposed by regulation. The time before NDA filing, however, is also powerfully controlled by regulation, since clinical trials are conducted in large part to gain regulatory approval. And the duration of the clinical trial process is over twice the length of the NDA review period. Therefore, we must also examine clinical trial delay as well as registration delay.

Figure 6.3 reports (in the bold line) the percentage of global products having Phase 1 clinical trials in Japan that have led to an NDA filing in that country. Before 1991, 80 percent of those global products that began Phase 1 clinical trials in Japan ultimately received filing with MHW for NDA approval. While this is a significantly higher percentage than reported by the JPMA for all drugs in Japan (55 percent, cited in the introduction to this chapter), it is plausible in view of the proven international success of global products. At the time this book was written, MHW recorded no NDA filings for non-AIDS global products with clinical trials beginning in 1993 or later. However, this absence of filings is not surprising. Examination of Figure 6.4 indicates that the average delay between the time a company begins clinical trials of its product in Japan (the start of Phase 1) and the time it files an NDA with MHW is about four and a half years. There is absolutely no trend over time in this average delay.

To get a better sense of post-1991 changes for clinical trials in Japan, we need to look beyond just the average for the distribution of clinical trial delays. Figure 6.5 gives the complete cumulative probability distribution for delays between start of Phase 1 trials and NDA filings in Japan. All global products with Phase 1 trials that began after 1982 and before 1992 are included. Again, we see that roughly 80 percent of global products that begin clinical trials ultimately receive NDA filing in Japan. And the median delay (at the 50 percent probability point) is indeed around four and a half years. We can use the data in Figure 6.5 to forecast the percentage of drugs with Phase 1 trials that would have received NDA filing had there been no changes in the clinical trial system in Japan after 1992. From Figure 6.5, we see that roughly 60 percent of drugs with clinical trials starting in 1993 should receive MHW filing by 1997. Comparably, 40 percent of drugs with clinical trials in 1993, 20 percent of drugs with clinical trials in 1994 and 5 percent of drugs with clinical trials in 1995 would have ultimately received NDA filing. These predictions are traced in Figure 6.3, and are in fact higher than actual experience.

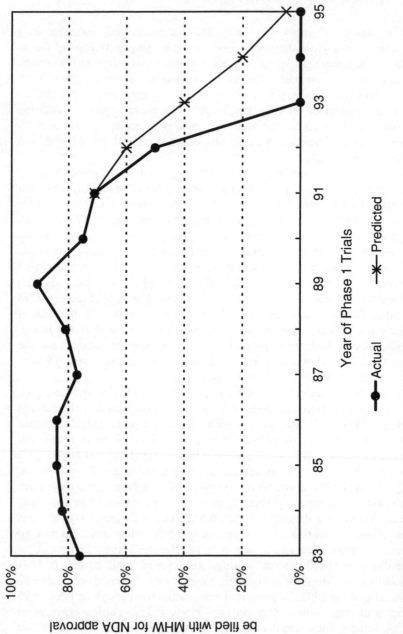

Figure 6.3 Filing probabilities decline after 1992: Global products only (excludes AIDS drugs)

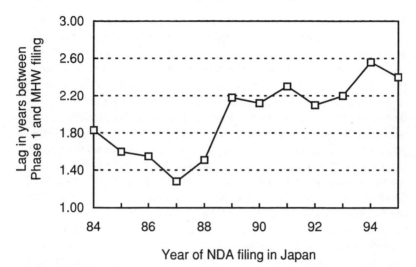

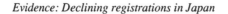

Figure 6.4 Clinical trial delays are stable over time (global products only; excludes AIDS drugs)

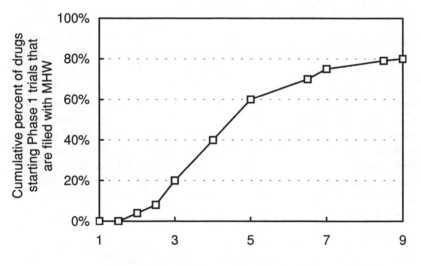

Figure 6.5 Pre-1992 distribution for filing delays (global products only; excludes AIDS drugs)

Detailed analysis of clinical trial delays is presented in Table 6.2. The results are quite similar to the comparable Table 6.1 for registration delays. In the center column of Table 6.2, we see that the probability that a drug beginning Phase 1 trials will ultimately lead to an NDA filing in Japan is positively associated with the global diffusion of that drug (similar to registration probability in the center of Table 6.1). If the drug was discovered by a Japanese firm, it has a 20 percent higher probability of achieving NDA filing, indicating the greater capabilities of Japans firms to navigate the clinical trial process in that country. There is no statistically significant difference among foreign firms in the probability that their product undergoing Japanese clinical trials will ultimately be given NDA filing in that country. In the right-hand column of Table 6.2, we see that the delay in years between start of Phase 1 trials and NDA filing is unrelated to the global diffusion of a drug (similar to registration delay in the right-hand column of Table 6.1). Japanese innovations enjoy almost one and a half years shorter clinical trial delay compared to innovations of foreign firms.

DECOMPOSITION OF EXCLUSION: REGISTRATION VERSUS PRICING

The estimates above allow us to 'rewrite history.' Consider NDAs filed in Japan after 1991. We know that there were no changes in the MHW registration process, that almost all of these NDAs would have been approved (again, see Figure 6.1). We also know that the average delay between filing and approval would have been 1.6 years (again, see Figure 6.2). We can then estimate the percentage of all global products that would have been launched in Japan before 1998 by treating every global product with an NDA filing with MHW as if it were actually launched in Japan 1.6 years after the date of that filing. Figure 6.6 reports this recomputation of the data, effectively rewriting history as if no changes in MHW registration process had occurred after 1992. The actual trend for access of global products into Japan is given for reference. Comparing the actual and 'rewritten' data trends, we find in both a pronounced drop for access of foreign products after 1984, from 80 percent to 66 percent. The access rate with 'history rewritten' is now stable at 66 percent until 1993, when it falls precipitously. Note that there is not much difference between the actual and historically rewritten trends.

We can add to our rewrite of history by including molecules that began Phase 1 trials in Japan after 1991, but have yet to file an NDA with MHW. Re-examination of Figure 6.3 suggests that some of these

Table 6.2: Determinants in Japan of NDA filing and clinical trial delay

Independent variables	Dependent Variables	
	NDA filing or not (binary variable)	Clinical trial delay (logarithm of years)
Intercept	-2.11 (-2.67)	1.72 (6.18)
Molecule type		
Global diffusion[†]	.37 (2.77)	-.09 (-2.36)
AIDS drug (binary)	-.52 (-.40)	-.09 (-9.71)
Firm type‡ (binary variables)		
Japanese firm	15.05 (2.49)	-.47 (-3.29)
Large foreign firm	.78 (1.14)	-.10 (-.53)
Medium foreign firm	-.05 (-.44)	-.06 (-.53)
Year of NDA filing in Japan (binary variables)		
Post - 1992	-3.72 (-3.18)	
Post - 1989		.02 (.18)
Summary statistics		
Number of observations	141	113
R^2 statistic		.18
F statistic		8.47
Pseudo-R^2 statistic	.29	
Chi^2 statistic	40.11	

Notes: † number of nations into which molecule was launched (range is 6 to 12).
‡ originator of molecule; for foreign firm type, see Table 6.2.

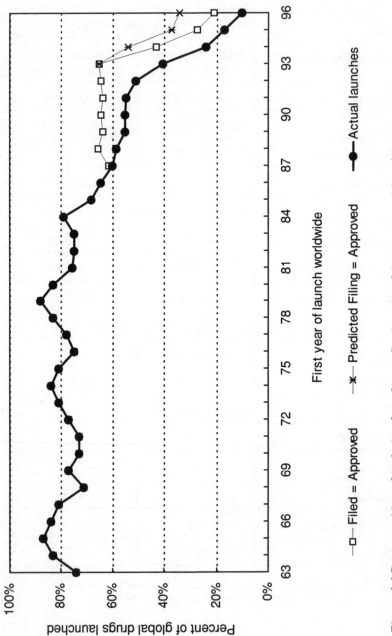

First year of launch worldwide

—□— Filed = Approved   —*— Predicted Filing = Approved   —●— Actual launches

Figure 6.6 Decomposition of exclusion from Japan: Registration-driven versus pricing-driven

molecules, particularly those with Phase 1 trials in 1993 and 1994, would have received NDA filing. We can then estimate the additional percentage of all global products that might have been launched in Japan before 1998 as follows. First, isolate those global products that had not received NDA filing but where Phase 1 clinical trials began after 1992. Second, estimate the probability that an NDA filing would have occurred for each such isolated molecule, and the year of that filing. Third, treat every global product with an estimated NDA as if it were actually launched in Japan 1.6 years after the date of that filing. Fourth, compute the expected number of additional molecules that would have been launched in Japan. These additional molecules are also included in Figure 6.6. There is even an even smaller impact of our second effort at rewriting history.

A key goal of this chapter has been to identify and isolate the impact of changes in the clinical trial and registrations systems in Japan since 1992. Once we identify registration-driven changes in the exclusion of global products from Japan, we may attribute the rest to pricing-driven changes. We are able to execute this segregation of registration-driven impacts because of the clear data trail from the clinical trial and registration processes in Japan (as in other countries). In this chapter we have traced the history of the various phases of clinical trails and registrations before 1992, and used this history to rewrite the post-1992 experience as if the clinical trial and registration processes were unchanged. The results of this revision are remarkable for their minor nature. When we recognize that only 70 percent of global products now receive even Phase 1 clinical trials in Japan, we should not be surprised by the minor nature of these changes. Even with no alterations whatsoever to the clinical trial and registration systems in Japan, at most 56 percent of current global products would ever be launched in Japan, with 70 percent of global products starting Phase 1 trials and 80 percent of those leading to NDA filing in Japan.

The findings of this revisionist exercise are straightforward. Before 1984, roughly 20 percent of global products were excluded from Japan, largely because of the provincial, backward, and anti-foreign nature of its clinical trial and registration systems. Between 1984 and 1987, the exclusion rate rose from 20 percent to 35 percent, with the 15 percent increment caused by the lowered prices and shorter product lives for new drugs resulting from MHW pricing 'reforms.' After 1993, continuing declines in product lives pushed the exclusion rate to 65 percent.

Evidence: Declining launches in Japan

This chapter documents the reduction in Japan of launches of registered new drugs, and breaks down the reduction by firm type. On the basis of discussions in earlier chapters, we would expect the greatest declines in launches to be concentrated in foreign firms lacking significant presence in Japan. These foreign firms receive lower prices from MHW, have weaker capabilities for sales and distribution in Japan, and experience significant delay with Japanese clinical trials. These firms have thus suffered particularly from the declining prices and shortened product life imposed by MHW, and are particularly likely to be excluded from Japan. In contrast, the handful of foreign firms with significant presence in Japan receive the highest prices granted by MHW (though they are still moderate by world standards), and have sales/distribution capabilities in Japan that exceed those of most Japanese firms. These few firms have suffered far less from the transformation of the Japanese pharmaceutical market since 1981, and are thus more likely to continue to launch their products in that nation.

LAUNCHES OF NEW MOLECULES IN JAPAN

Figures 7.1 and 7.2 trace recent launches into five major markets of new molecules from all sources. All new molecules are given in Figure 7.1, while Figure 7.2 counts only global products. Data for these figures are from Thomas (1998). Note that in 1989 there is a sharp downward ratcheting of introduction levels in Japan. This drop occurred three years before problems and scandals with the Japanese clinical trial system emerged in 1992, and thus cannot have been caused by changes in that system. After 1989, the total number of new drugs launched in Japan fell from an average of 43 per year to an average of 28 per year (see Figure 7.1). The number of global products launched in Japan fell from an average of 20 a year before 1989 to an average of 13 afterwards (see Figure 7.2). And virtually all the decline in new drugs launched into Japan has been concentrated in foreign products (see Figure 7.3). The number of foreign-discovered drugs launched in Japan has declined from an average of 28 per

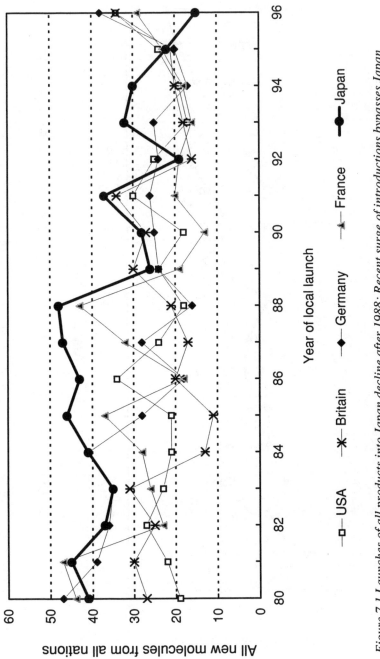

Figure 7.1 Launches of all products into Japan decline after 1988; Recent surge of introductions bypasses Japan

133

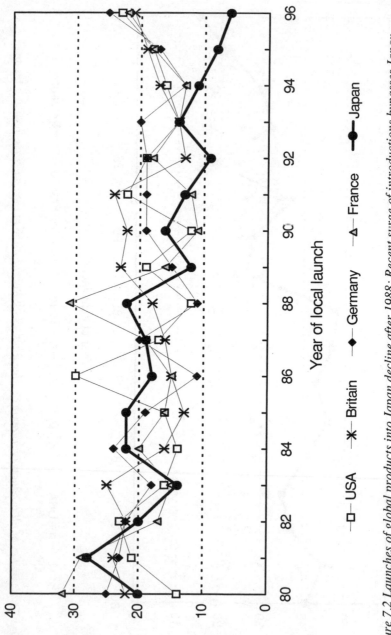

Figure 7.2 Launches of global products into Japan decline after 1988; Recent surge of introductions bypasses Japan

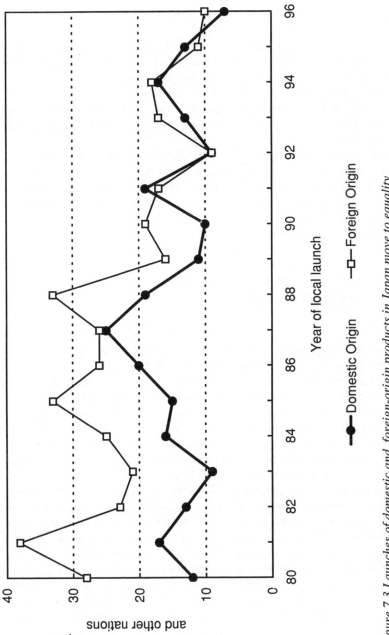

Figure 7.3 Launches of domestic and foreign-origin products in Japan move to equality

135

year to roughly 13 per year, while the number of Japanese-originated drugs has remained stable at roughly 15 a year.

The next section of this chapter will indicate that most of the exclusion of new drugs from Japan is concentrated in foreign firms lacking extensive presence in Japan. Specifically, then, the falloff in introductions visible in Figures 7.1, 7.2, and 7.3 represent the decisions by Japanese firms to reduce drastically their licensing of foreign innovations, and by foreign firms with formal joint ventures in Japan to bypass that nation when launching their new products globally.

In all three of these figures and for all types of introductions, there is a sharp one-time drop in 1992 and a downward trend after 1994. Both trends would be expected owing to the turmoil in the clinical trial system in Japan discussed in the previous chapter. This turmoil has caused the upsurge in pharmaceutical innovation since 1993, present in every other major market, to bypass Japan completely.

DECOMPOSITION OF EXCLUSION: CAPABILITIES AGAIN

This study has argued that exclusion of foreign innovations from the Japanese pharmaceutical market has been driven by declining life cycle revenues for new drugs in the Japanese market. As life cycle sales have declined, previously existing asymmetric costs have acquired greater salience and served to exclude firms burdened by these costs. Table 7.1 reports logistical regressions on the decision whether or not to launch a new drug in Japan, for all molecules launched in the world after 1970. The data for this analysis are again from Thomas (1998). Note with regard to the table that, before 1980, the principal determinant of product launch in Japan was the overall innovativeness and significance of the drug, where innovativeness can be proxied by the number of nations into which the drug diffuses – important drugs are widely diffused, while trivial drugs sell in only one or two markets. Prior to 1980, there was no statistically significant exclusion at all based on ownership of Japanese subsidiaries or direct control of Japanese distribution. Since 1980, however, the innovativeness of drugs has slowly ceased to determine whether or not they are launched in Japan, and firm type of the innovator has become the greatest determinant of the launch decision. Figure 7.4 sketches the shifting determinants of the launch decision for foreign new drugs in Japan, based on the estimates in Table 7.1.

If 'large' foreign pharmaceutical firms remain committed to launching their products in Japan, most of the new drug lag in that nation must be

Table 7.1 Determinants of whether or not a foreign-owned molecule is launched into Japan,1970-96, and by vintage of molecule

Independent variables	Dependent variable is launch in Japan (yes=1 and no=0)				
	All years	Molecules partitioned by year of first launch in world			
		1970-79	1980-84	1985-89	1990-96
Basic variables					
Intercept	-2.22 (-17.61)	-2.56 (-14.22)	-2.69 (-8.15)	-1.43 (-4.53)	-2.74 (-5.16)
Diffusion of molecule	.28 (15.30)	.45 (13.23)	.34 (7.12)	.13 (3.33)	.01 (.25)
Ownership/distribution binary variables					
Large foreign firm	.49 (2.40)	-.05 (-.14)	.13 (.21)	.66 (2.63)	2.33 (4.23)
Medium foreign firm	.54 (3.24)	.26 (1.40)	-.13 (-.30)	.46 (1.46)	1.43 (2.60)
Summary statistics					
Number of observations	1253	701	222	172	158
Pseudo-R^2 statistic	.22	.36	.28	.21	.24
Chi^2 statistic	357.62	343.17	76.12	38.82	42.22

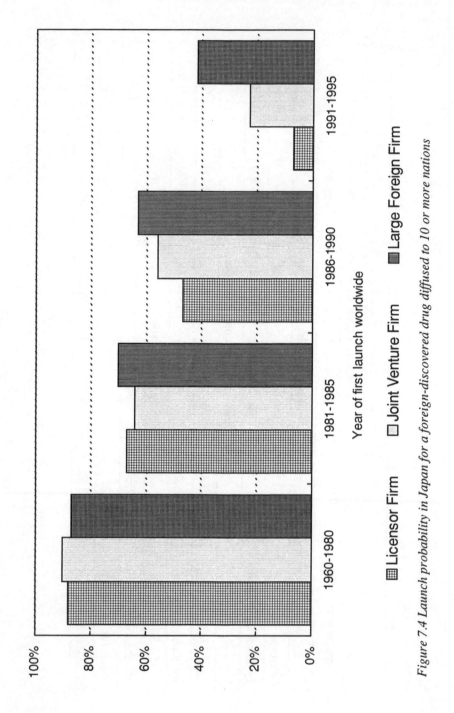

Figure 7.4 Launch probability in Japan for a foreign-discovered drug diffused to 10 or more nations

concentrated in the remaining foreign firms. We can split our analysis of excluded products by firm type to examine this hypothesis. Figure 7.5 examines the roughly 75 percent of global products innovated by non-Japanese firms lacking major presence in Japan, and thus lacking the associated capabilities to compete strongly in that market. This figure also 'rewrites history' using the methods of the last chapter to purge the effects of post-1992 turmoil in the clinical trial system. Because the vast majority of global products are innovated by the firms included in Figure 7.5, this figure is unsurprisingly similar to Figure 6.6 in the last chapter. Again, we see that exclusion from Japan went from 20 percent of global products before 1980, to 35 percent between 1981 and 1992, and to over 60 percent after 1992. The severe exclusion after 1992 for these foreign firms does not seem at·all driven or affected by the turmoil in the clinical trial system in Japan, even though it is contemporaneous with it.

Figure 7.6 performs exactly the same analysis, but restricted to the 24 percent of global products innovated either by Japanese firms or by the handful of foreign firms with extensive presence in Japan (again, see Table 5.1 for a listing of these firms). Confirming the findings of the logistic regressions in Table 7.1, there is no difference in the pre-1981 trends of Figure 7.5 for most foreign firms and those of Figure 7.6 for firms with large presence in Japan. After 1980, however, the trends are pronouncedly different. Firms with large presence in Japan continue to launch or plan to launch their innovations at roughly the same rate they have over the last 30 years. Most of the recorded decline in launches for these large foreign firms is an artifact of the changing clinical trial system in Japan. These large firms continue to conduct clinical trials in Japan on their innovations, and to file New Drug Applications with MHW. Most of their innovations will thus be launched in Japan, though with some delay after 1992. There is a sharp downward spike around 1990 for recorded launches. Examination of the raw data assures us that this not some statistical artifact. Large foreign firms operating in Japan apparently briefly entertained doubts about the strategic wisdom of their presence in Japan at that time. During that brief period, these firms either refused even to begin clinical trials for some products in Japan (as with acitretin by Roche or azelaic acid by Schering AG) or else halted clinical trials in Japan somewhat after the Phase 2 stage (as with buspirone by Bristol-Myers Squibb or ramipril by Hoechst Marion Roussel). Provocatively, this downward spike occurs at roughly the same time that total introductions into Japan plummeted (see Figure 7.1 above).

In summary, there are severe differences between firms lacking significant presence in Japan and those firms with such presence. The apparent exclusion of large foreign firms from Japan is mostly an artifact of delays caused by turmoil in the clinical trial system. The global products of

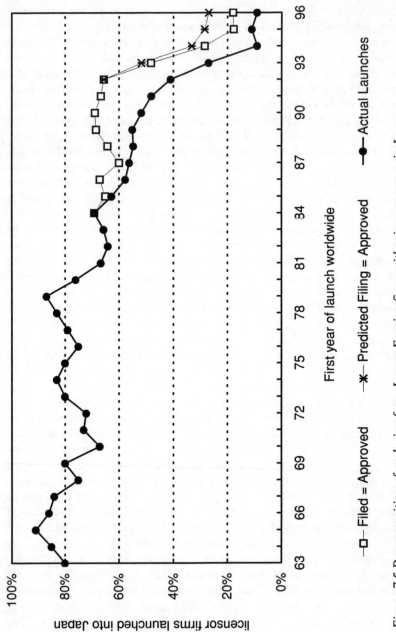

Figure 7.5 Decomposition of exclusion from Japan: Foreign firms with minor presence in Japan

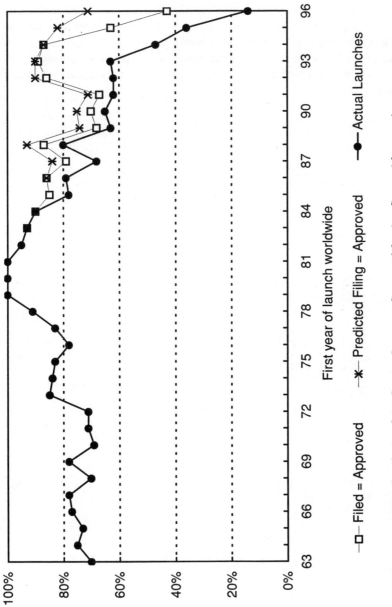

Figure 7.6 *Decomposition of exclusion from Japan: Japanese firms and foreign firms with extensive presence*

these firms are indeed undergoing clinical trials and with high probability will be launched in due course. In contrast, correction for clinical trial delays has little impact on predicted launch patterns for other foreign firms. The exclusion of these firms, which account for three-quarters of the global products of the pharmaceutical industry, is real and is not an artifact of delay.

Evidence: Inflated domestic market share in Japan

This chapter documents the distinctively high market share that Japanese firms hold in their domestic industry. This high share is particularly noteworthy in light of the poor global performance of Japanese pharmaceutical firms discussed earlier.

OPENNESS AND CLOSURE OF 12 NATIONAL MARKETS

The share that foreign firms collectively attain in an industry varies considerably across nations. Some markets are extremely 'open,' in that foreign firms collectively hold very large shares. Other markets are relatively 'closed,' in that domestic firms collectively keep extremely high shares. There are three basic determinants of the relative 'openness' or 'closure' of the home market to foreign firms, and we must control for these patterns to identify true exclusionary behavior. First, firms based in small home markets tend to have small domestic shares, while firms based in large markets tend to hold large shares. This pattern is purely an aggregation effect. For example, Danish firms currently hold less than 20 percent of their small home market. Yet if we aggregate firms and consider instead the Nordic share of the Danish market, we find a 49 percent share held collectively by Danish, Finnish, Norwegian, and Swedish drug firms. If we further aggregate, and consider the European share of the Danish market, we arrive at an 80 percent share, with almost all the remainder held by American firms. Conversely, were we to disaggregate the US pharmaceutical market, and break out firms from New Jersey, New York, Pennsylvania, and so on, then the market shares held by firms from these individual states would of course be smaller than those held by American firms all together. Note that, because Japan is the second largest pharmaceutical market in the world, we would expect Japanese firms to hold a relatively high share of their home market, merely because of aggregation.

143

A second pattern of market openness/closure is that the domestic share held by firms of a given nation tends to decline over time, owing to globalization. Figure 8.1 traces the steady trend towards openness in the five major markets for the world pharmaceutical industry. For almost all pharmaceutical markets, the domestic market share is higher in earlier years, and lower later. A third and final pattern is that more capable firms will hold a higher share of their domestic market, while weaker firms will hold a lower share. As we have seen in Chapter 4, Japanese firms are extremely weak global competitors and for this reason would be expected to hold a relatively smaller share of their domestic market.

Regression analyses reported in Table 8.1 formally measure the extent of market closure. Because tariffs on pharmaceuticals were not large during the period of this study, openness or closure of the home market is predominantly determined by nontariff trade barriers. The dataset for this empirical analysis is drawn from Thomas (1998). That study collected data on the domestic market shares of 12 nations: Belgium, Canada, Denmark, France, Germany, Italy, Japan, the Netherlands, Sweden, Switzerland, the United Kingdom, and the United States. Each observation for the statistical analysis is one country for one year during 1963 to 1994. The dependent variable for analysis is the share of the domestic market held by domestic firms. If national markets were comparably open, this internal market share should vary only with the size of the home market (owing to aggregation issues), the actual year (with a steady trend in more recent years to greater openness), and the capabilities of domestic firms (proxied by the external share achieved, the variable of Figure 4.5). Binary variables against the USA measure the deviation of national closure or openness from the predicted norm. Both linear and logarithmic specifications are estimated, with similar findings. By inspection, there is wide variation across nations in terms of the ease with which foreign firms penetrate domestic markets. In the Anglo-Saxon equity markets of Britain, Canada, and the USA, foreign acquisitions of domestic firms are easy and foreign shares of domestic sales are relatively high. In the less-fluid capital markets of Japan and continental Europe, foreign acquisitions are much more difficult and foreign firms attain lower shares. An extreme in Europe is Sweden, where domestic capital markets have ensured that the many acquirers of domestic drug firms have been almost completely restricted to other Swedish firms.

Both specifications in Table 8.1 imply that the domestic market share of Japanese firms should be roughly 30 percent, instead of the 80 percent that it is now (again, see Figure 8.1). Foreign firms would thus sell over two-thirds of all pharmaceuticals in Japan. To obtain this estimated domestic share in the absence of nontariff trade barriers, note from the linear specification on the left of Table 8.1 that the domestic share of Japanese firms is 47 percentage points above what it would be if the

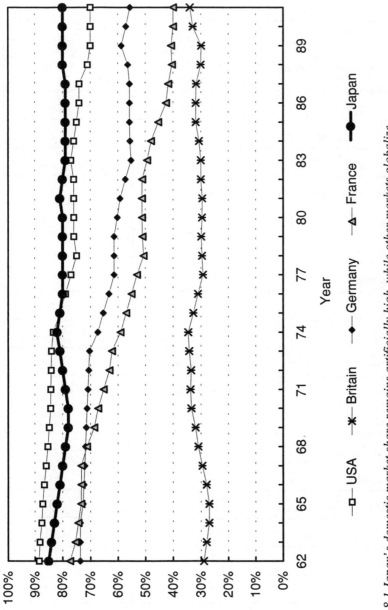

Figure 8.1 Japan's domestic market share remains artificially high, while other markets globalize

Table 8.1: Estimated domestic share held by domestic firms, 1961–94

Independent variables	Dependent variables	
	Domestic market share held by domestic firms	Logarithm of domestic market share
Intercept	.70 (23.30)	.85 (8.68)
Share of eternal markets	2.55 (9.51)	
log (external share)		.26 (5.60)
(home market size)	.51 (5.24)	
log (home market size)		.13 (4.18)
(year – 1961)	-.007 (-25.20)	
log (year – 1961)		-.21 (-20.70)
Japan	.47 (25.47)	.99 (5.96)
Sweden	.26 (7.63)	.75 (4.28)
Italy	.23 (7.85)	.53 (3.40)
France	.24 (10.04)	.40 (3.37)
Germany	.23 (9.82)	.23 (3.07)
Switzerland	.05 (1.05)	.10 (.90)
Denmark	-.03 (-.70)	-.02 (-.14)
Netherlands	.03 (.32)	-.06 (-.34)
United Kingdom	-.05 (-1.60)	-.25 (-2.34)
Belgium	-.11 (-3.32)	-.62 (-3.73)
Canada	-.13 (-4.06)	-.71 (-3.73)
Number of observations	384	384
R^2-statistic	.94	.95

Japanese domestic market functioned on average like the other 11 major markets. Subtracting, we obtain an estimate of 33 percent. Note from the logarithmic specification on the right of Table 8.1 that the domestic share of Japanese firms is exp(0.99) times what it would be if the Japanese domestic market functioned on average like the other 11 major markets. Dividing, we obtain an estimate of 27 percent as the predicted Japanese domestic share. Clearly, the domestic ecosystem for pharmaceuticals in Japan is extraordinarily exclusionary.

JAPANESE CORPORATE GOVERNANCE AND THE RULE OF REASON

To evaluate these findings, it is essential to remember the discussion at the conclusion of Chapter 2. There are many reasons why a market may be relatively 'open' or relatively 'closed.' Both the antitrust and trade literatures caution us to apply a 'rule of reason', and carefully diagnose why a particular market is open or closed before reaching conclusions. An important illustration of this need for caution is provided by Canada, the most 'open' nation of the 12 studied. Canadian firms hold only around 10 percent of their home market, against a predicted 20 to 23 percent. Yet this 'openness' of the Canadian pharmaceutical market to foreign firms results from the stunningly destructive industrial policies practiced by the Canadian government against its own pharmaceutical firms ('industrial genocide,' as one commentator has called it). For years, the government of Canada stripped pharmaceutical firms of their intellectual property rights, forcing them to license their innovations immediately to all other firms at rates failing to cover the upfront innovation costs. The practice of compulsory licensing destroyed the domestic pharmaceutical industry in Canada, and that nation ceased completely to innovate by the mid-1960s. The only Canadian-owned drug firms make generics.

This example of 'openness' is hardly an ideal for public policy. As is sketched in Figure 8.2, markets may be 'open' for both constructive and destructive reasons. The Canadian market is open for destructive reasons. In contrast, the British market is 'open' for constructive reasons, as detailed in Thomas (1994). British regulations of safety and pricing do not discriminate against foreign firms. Indeed, British pricing regulations actually reward with high prices those foreign firms that directly invest in Britain. In the 1950s, the very best foreign firms either bought or drove weak British firms out of the UK pharmaceutical industry, seizing over two-thirds of the British domestic market. While UK firms temporarily 'lost' the battle for their domestic market, the handful of British firms that

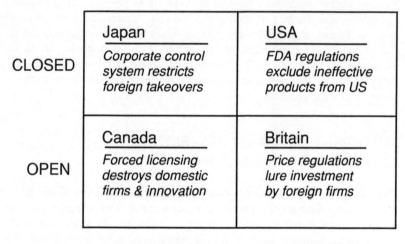

INEFFICIENT   EFFICIENT

Figure 8.2 Four examples of closure and dynamic efficiency for the domestic market, as illustration for the Rule of Reason

survived severe competition from their American and Swiss counterparts eventually emerged as extremely innovative and highly competitive. These British firms, notably Beecham, Glaxo, ICI (renamed Zeneca), and Wellcome, were forced to learn in their own home market the innovation and marketing of pharmaceuticals from the most capable firms in the world at the time, the large American and Swiss firms.

In a separate study, Thomas (1998) has demonstrated that the outcome of the pharmaceutical 'Battle of Britain' is not unique. Across nations, artificial exclusion of the sort documented for Japan in Table 8.1 is unambiguously damaging to the competitiveness of domestic firms. Firms shielded from foreign competition face less industry challenge, and are not forced to build internal capabilities that enable successful global competition. Furthermore, closure of the home market changes the character of the domestic environment and deprives local firms of the most effective form of organizational learning – immediate experience in the home market. Conversely, openness of the sort documented for the UK in Table 8.1 unambiguously promotes innovative and competitive excellence.

A comparison of Figures 4.5 and 8.1 is provocative in this regard. Throughout the last four decades, British and French firms each spent roughly the same total on pharmaceutical research and development expenses. Estimates in Table 8.1 indicate that the French market has been relatively closed. Indeed, Figure 8.1 indicates that foreign firms achieved only a 20 percent share of that market in the 1950s, a time when these firms had seized over 70 percent of the UK market. While British firms have never regained a majority of their home market, the capabilities they acquired through direct competition with American and Swiss firms has enabled them steadily to gain penetration of foreign markets (see Figure 4.5). French firms never acquired such capabilities, never achieved significant presence in foreign markets, and have ultimately lost share in their home market (Figure 8.1). Protectionism has thus been completely self-defeating for the French. Again, the informal and non-transparent nature of these vertical relations is a particular burden.

The complex system of corporate governance and control in Japan has long restricted foreign acquisition of domestic pharmaceutical firms. In the 1950s, foreign participation in the Japanese pharmaceutical industry was sharply restricted. Drug imports were regulated by quota. Licensing of foreign products to local firms was heavily regulated and subject to caps on royalty rates. And foreign direct investment was allowed only through joint venture with domestic firms, with foreign equity holding in the joint venture of no more than 50 percent. These severe nontariff barriers have faded with time, but other more subtle mechanisms sustain the difficulty foreign firms have with local acquisitions. Legislation and ministerial orders require approval of the board of directors of any Japanese drug firm for foreign stock purchases of more that 25 percent of outstanding equity. There is also an informal agreement among members of the industry that, should any Japanese pharmaceutical firm be sold, it will first be offered to other domestic firms before foreign buyers are considered.

Challenges to the dual state in Japan

In recent years, fundamental changes have transformed competition in many industries. This steady transformation profoundly threatens both segments of the dual state: the export sector led by MITI and the domestic sector governed by ministries such as MHW. This chapter traces the nature and implications of these competitive changes.

INDUSTRIAL POLICIES: SUPPLY AND DEMAND ARTICULATION

There are many generic industrial policies, but perhaps the two most important are supply articulation and demand articulation. Both are 'infant industry' policies designed to create durable competitive advantage where none existed previously. The first and older type is supply articulation, focusing on upstream transactors with the firm including capital providers, component suppliers, and workers (see the top of Figure 9.1). The goal of supply articulation policy is a sophisticated *architecture of supply*, with large production scale and efficient process technology yielding low costs. This method succeeds through the social construction of a local ecosystem that nurtures, challenges, and sustains the firm in ultra-efficient supply. Three critical outcomes of supply articulation include diversion of *cash* and other resources towards firms in the industry, accumulation of internal *skills* and capabilities at production, and social construction of *institutions* that formalize and shape relations with external transactors to support appropriate internal skills of the firm. To shelter infant firms while skills and institutions are attained, trade barriers and/or subsidies are usually employed. Supply articulation policy often exploits consumers because it leads to higher local prices, poor distribution, and slow diffusion for innovation originating outside the local ecosystem.

The example of the Japanese motor vehicle industry presented above in Figure 2.3 is one of successful supply articulation. Toyota triumphed in automobiles because it reshaped its local ecosystem, transforming the way cars are made. It constructed a *keiretsu*, or networked structure of long-term commitment and control with its 'lifetime suppliers.' It can thus depend on these suppliers for just-in-time inventory, co-development of

150

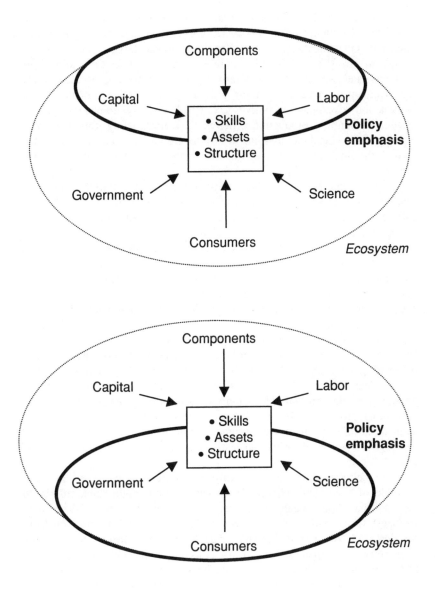

Figure 9.1 Generic industrial policies, supply articulation (at top) and demand articulation (at bottom), shape corporate capabilities

components, and high quality parts. Toyota also constructed lifetime employment with its most central workers. It is thereby able to justify intensive investments in worker training much larger than those of American firms facing highly mobile workers. The firm joins both suppliers and workers in cooperative pursuit of *kaizen*, or incremental improvement of process technology. Long-term capital, a protected home market, and government incentives to export have all combined to support a system of stunning production efficiency. Unfortunately, this ecosystem also produces local automobile prices for Japanese consumers that are among the highest in the world, with minimal penetration of foreign products.

The second type of industrial policy is quite different. Demand articulation also focuses on social construction of an architecture, but one of cutting-edge demand based on downstream transactors, such as exacting consumers, stringent government regulation, and sophisticated science (see the bottom of Figure 9.1). This type of policy focuses on the social construction of new products: how they are defined, what features they include, what standards are set, how they interact with other products. So demand articulation creates different skills and very different organizational designs for firms from supply articulation. The outcomes of demand articulation, however, are analytically surprisingly similar to those of supply articulation. These policies must shower a steady stream of *cash* on firms to encourage product development. The protection of infant firms is obtained, not through trade barriers, but rather through a window of delay before other nations act. These policies also enable and force continuous upgrading of the internal *skills* of firms. And to succeed in the long run, they must provide fluid coevolution of firms with local *institutions* of demand, such as regulators and science. Unless the cash from the window of delay is invested in skills and institutions, any initial advantage will be lost.

The cellular phone industry of the Nordic region is an important example of successful demand articulation. You might think this is an industry that Japan would dominate. You would be wrong. The three strongest firms in the world are Motorola from the USA, Ericsson from Sweden, and Nokia from Finland. The success of Nordic cellular phone firms over their Japanese competitors is as surprising and important today as the success of Japanese automobile firms over their US competitors 20 years ago. To understand this success, we must examine the domestic ecosystem for the local (regional) cellular phone industry (see Figure 9.2). The four Nordic nations (Denmark, Finland, Norway, and Sweden) aggressively and cooperatively promoted a regional standard for cellular technology: NMT, or Nordic Mobile Telephone. This standard subsequently became the most widely adopted in Europe. Because of

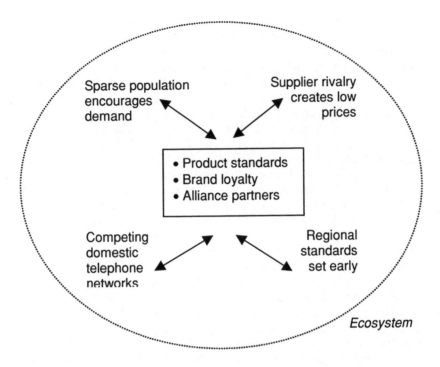

Sparse population encourages demand

Supplier rivalry creates low prices

- Product standards
- Brand loyalty
- Alliance partners

Competing domestic telephone networks

Regional standards set early

Ecosystem

Figure 9.2 Ecosystem for cellular telephone industry in Nordic countries

aggressive development by their home governments, Ericsson and Nokia entered this new industry almost a full decade ahead of other firms. Local sales were additionally spurred by two features of demand: competition instead of a national monopoly to provide regular telephone service, and competition among new providers of cellular service. For example, in Finland, almost 40 local networks compete with each other, a national security legacy of the Finnish-Russian struggle of 1914 when these local networks were used to coordinate defense against the Czarist army (Sachs, 1994). Local rivalry and market orientation led to lower prices, rapid diffusion, and higher demand. Finally, the sparse distribution of a wealthy and highly educated population in the Nordic countries encouraged demand for wireless service (Ibrahim, 1997). Note the differences between industrial policies that articulate supply and those that articulate demand. Demand articulation enlists the aid of sophisticated consumers to push the envelope of local demand; it encourages competition of suppliers in the local market; and it generates low local prices that are critical for encouragement of high demand intensity. Supply articulation relies on cartels and bureaucracy to restrict local demand (while promoting exports), creates local monopoly, and generates high local prices.

The result of the Nordic ecosystem for cellular phones is the most sophisticated and intense demand in the world (see the top of Figure 9.3). Cellular services were launched earlier in the Nordic region – almost five years before the UK and almost ten years before Germany. For the first decade of their operation, Nordic cellular networks were the largest in Europe (see the bottom of Figure 9.3), despite a comparatively small population. During this decade-long lead, Ericsson and Nokia were able to define the product functionally by writing and debugging software, creating prominent and respected brand names, and snapping up the most promising partners in other markets (including American distributors and small German manufacturers). Competitive positions created by demand articulation in the Nordic region have proved as durable and important as those created by supply articulation in Japan. Indeed, the Japanese market share of the European cellular phone market has been falling in some recent years, with that of Ericsson and Nokia rising (*Economist*, 1995).

Two features of cellular phone technology make likely the continued success of Ericsson and Nokia. First, cellular phones are as much software as hardware, containing elaborate computer protocols. The first-generation NMT standard has been succeeded by a second-generation Europe-wide standard, GSM. With the cooperation and speed of European action, GSM has become the leading standard in the world. Legal protections for innovation in software (copyrights) are more readily enforceable than legal protections for innovations in hardware (patents). Second, product technology in telephony continues to advance more rapidly than the process technology to make these products. Alongside wire-based and cellular systems, new PCS systems were launched in the mid-1990s. Cellular systems themselves migrated from analog to digital (from NMT to GSM). Third-generation standards that enable the 'wireless web' will be launched within the next few years. New features such as paging and e-mail, and new services such as continuous updates (sporting events, airline flights, financial markets) and payment systems (the 'online wallet') are becoming available. Questions are proliferating on how these multiple networks (wired, cellular, PCS, the mobile Internet) will interact and which priorities will be given to various features and services. These questions will be answered in the most sophisticated markets in the world (America and the Nordic countries), with those answers copied in nations with lagging demand.

It is provocative to note that Japan has always played a small but important role in cellular phone manufacturing: that of component supplier. For example, the mouthpiece of cellular phones contains ceramic filters, with 85 percent of the world supply made by the Japanese firm Murata

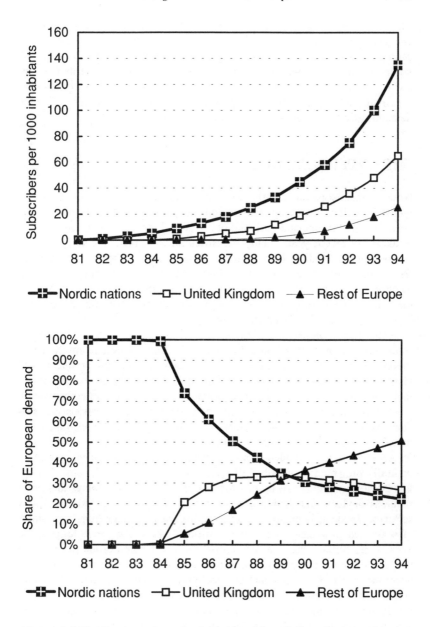

Figure 9.3 Nordic countries seize initial lead in cellular telephone demand, per capita usage (at top) and share of European demand (at bottom); adapted from ITU (1995) and Lipaski, et al. (1989)

Manufacturing (Pollack, 1994). The product technology for ceramic filters changes slowly, and Murata dominates this industry through entrenched economies of scale, experience, and scope.   Murata is based in Kyoto, home to many of the world's leading ceramic firms, and it benefits from the local supplier base. Thus, even in cellular phones, some key components are made in Japan through supply articulation and incorporated into demand-articulated American and Nordic products.

THE HYPERCOMPETITIVE SHIFT

Now we must confront a difficult reality for Japan. The basis for success in industrial policy is moving away from supply articulation, where Japan has been strong, to demand articulation, where Japan is historically vastly weaker. In recent years, many industries have witnessed a surge of new competitors (including firms entering from other nations or diversifying from other industries) and a proliferation of new products and new technologies.   The result is called *hypercompetition* (D'Aveni, 1994) and the shift from old to new forms of competition is called the *hypercompetitive shift* (Thomas, 1996).

The hypercompetitive shift is driven by three factors: improving technology, more sophisticated demand, and falling barriers to entry. These drivers enable the proliferation of new competitors and new products, with resultant *depreciation acceleration* for established strategic assets. Firms that once focused on intensive exploitation of a given strategic position must now transform and reorient their internal organizations towards continuous innovation of new strategic positions. Numerous examples can be offered of hypercompetitive shift. In telecommunications, service was for seven decades provided though underground coaxial cables, creating a naturally protected monopoly (AT&T in the USA, NTT in Japan). For the last 20 years, service can be provided through microwave relays and other wireless devices that enable a proliferation of new competitors and new services. In steel, vertically integrated mills used to create huge economies of scale and protected competitive positions. Now the technology of the electric arc furnace has enabled mini-mills to enter and erode positions of the larger firms. The banking industry in the USA is being transformed by telecommunications, information technology, and greater consumer sophistication. New products like credit cards, mutual funds, and corporate bonds have steadily increased the non-bank share of US savings and lending. Even the once formidable supercomputer industry has experienced hypercompetitive shift. Supercomputers used to contain proprietary, ultra-fast semiconductor chips and the ability to supply these chips was a central source of entrenched competitive advantage. Now, advances in parallel processing technology enable supercomputers to contain predominantly multiple off-the-shelf microprocessors, available in open markets. The source of competitive advantage in supercomputers has shifted from hardware to software, from mastery of supply conditions to mastery of demand.

For several reasons, a hypercompetitive shift in an industry moves the source of industrial success from supply articulation to demand articulation, as illustrated in Figure 9.4. First, a hypercompetitive shift depreciates entrenched positions of supply by facilitating rapid entry of new competitors and new products. Again, this process is called *depreciation acceleration*. Japanese positions in steel, television sets, and semiconductor chips have all suffered this fate as firms variously from Korea, Taiwan, and the ASEAN states have entered these industries. Second, a hypercompetitive shift raises the costs and reduces the benefits of upstream linkages with suppliers that are the foundation of supply articulation. The benefits of supplier linkages decline as new competitors provide merchant sources of formerly proprietary components. For example, US microcomputer firms Compaq and Dell now source from East Asia various components that once had to be produced internally or obtained from direct competitors out of Japan (Borrus, 1993). The costs of upstream linkages are increased because of the complexity and speed of technical change in upstream markets. As upstream markets themselves become more hypercompetitive, new suppliers with new technologies enter. A downstream firm tied too closely to a specific 'lifetime supplier' may find its has made a bad bet as regards the cost or technical sophistication of its components (Quinn, 1992). Third, the benefits of downstream linkages with consumers drastically increase with a hypercompetitive shift. As new products pour onto the market, the scale and speed of demand response become critical. New consumer products are increasingly protected by intellectual property rights. And as product technology moves faster than process technology, the basis of competitive success shifts from skill at making rapidly obsolescing old products to skill at defining rapidly evolving new ones.

The shift from supply articulation to demand articulation is a particular threat for Japan, precisely because it has relied so heavily on supply articulation in its industrial policies. Consider fiber optic cable, used in the telecommunications industry. The ecosystem for Japanese manufacturers of fiber optic cable in the 1970s is presented at the top of Figure 9.5. Here we see the power of successful supply articulation (drawn from Borrus *et al.*, 1985). In the early 1970s, the American firm Corning Glass applied to the Japanese Patent Office to register its patents on fiber optic cable. The Patent Office delayed granting these patents for a staggering ten years. During this period of protectionist delay, NTT (Nippon Telephone and

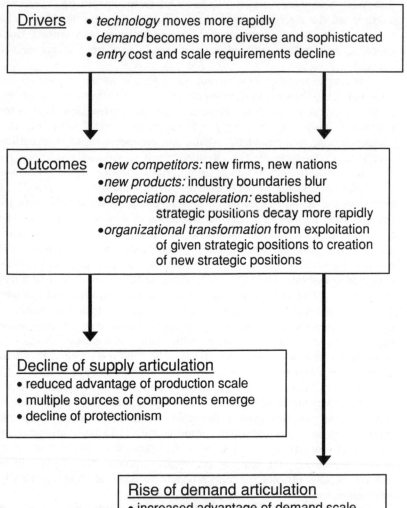

Figure 9.4 The hypercompetitive shift (adapted from Thomas, 1996)

Telegraph, the Japanese equivalent of the old AT&T monopoly in the USA) launched a crash development program with its vertically linked 'family of suppliers' for telephone cable. These firms, Sumitomo, Furakawa, and Fujikura, engaged with NTT in joint R&D to share the costs of copying Corning technology. NTT then purchased cable from this family of suppliers at prices three to four times those of the world market, and required these firms to build production capacity ten times the volume of Japanese demand. NTT purchased almost no fiber optic cable from foreign firms such as Corning, despite their lower prices. Because fixed costs of R&D and production were covered in the protected home market, Japanese suppliers could 'dump' or compete in external markets such as the USA with price near variable costs. It is absolutely critical to realize that supply articulation did not succeed here only because of the nurture of protection. These producers also faced a harsh challenge, forcing them to improve their internal skills aggressively. In this case, the demands of the ecosystem (NTT, *keiretsu* providers of capital, lifetime suppliers, and lifetime workers, as well as significant rivalry among the suppliers themselves) forced the firms to use the cash received during their ten-year window of opportunity to achieve economies of scale and experience, not to throw the cash away on excessive dividends or wages. When Corning finally received its Japanese patents in the early 1980s, Japanese makers of fiber optic cable were world-class producers and no longer needed protection.

Several features of the fiber optic cable industry indicate why supply articulation succeeded there, but fails in modern industries such as information technology. Note that product technology moves quite slowly in fiber optic cable, while rapid advances in process technology are possible. The opposite is true in information technology industries. Note that economies of scale in production are critical, while demand scale is unimportant as the product is a commodity. Again, the opposite is true in information technology. Most important, note that Japanese demand for fiber optic cable lags that of the rest of the world owing to high domestic prices and nontariff barriers to the import of superior foreign technology. In a commodity industry like fiber optic cable, this backwardness of domestic demand is no problem. In hypercompetitive industries of information technology, backward domestic demand destroys competitive advantage.

Next, consider the consumer electronics industry, where Japan has led for decades. If you look at Japanese consumer electronics firms, their product lines are very old. The major technologies went from radio to television to videocassette recorders (VCRs), and perhaps now to DVD players. Each of these three product segments was conquered through supply articulation. For example, the ecosystem for Japanese manufacturer of color televisions in the 1960s is presented at the bottom of Figure 9.5.

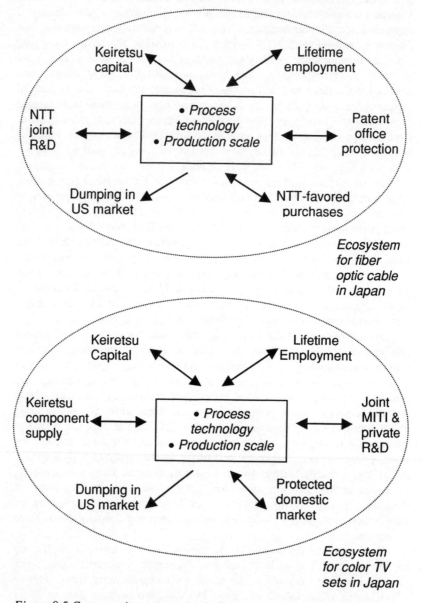

Figure 9.5 Comparative ecosystems in Japan: examples of traditional industrial policy through supply articulation: fiber optic cable (at top) and color television sets (at bottom)

The product technology for color televisions, of course, originated in the USA. A combination of industrial policies in the USA (a 1958 consent decree by RCA settling an antitrust suit) and in Japan (MITI led protectionism against US exports or direct manufacture in Japan) forced US firms to license their technology to Japanese firms. Additional barriers against US sales were provided by non-transparent import and certification procedures and by franchised vertical ties between Japanese manufacturers and distributors (Staelin, 1989). A joint government-industry research consortium, launched by MITI in 1966, enabled the Japanese industry to adopt solid-state technology rapidly (Millstein, 1983). With this new process technology, Japanese TV sets became simultaneously cheaper and much more reliable than US sets using the older multi-component process technology. Close ties between Japanese firms and their workers, investors, and component suppliers facilitated economies of experience and continued innovation of process technology. Finally, domestic and export cartels formed in 1963 set Japanese home market prices for color TV sets at two to three times those of exported sets to the USA (Staelin, 1989; Yamamura, 1982). Note again the critical features of successful supply articulation: excessive prices in the home market, accumulation of internal corporate skills (scale, experience, process technology), and the co-evolution of industry and supporting institutions (research consortia, cartels, component suppliers, distributor ties). Note also the non-hypercompetitive features of the market that allowed supply articulation to succeed (slow-moving product technology, rapid evolution of process technology, and vertically supplied components not available on open markets).

Yet, suddenly, the great industrial triumph of Japan in consumer electronics is very much at risk. What major product will come next in this industry, after radios, TVs, VCRs, and DVDs? The very high probability is that the next significant product will be some form of personal computer incorporating telecommunications, cable television, Internet services, and so on (Pollack, 1993 and 1996). Unfortunately, these areas of information technology are precisely where Japanese demand is very far behind. Figures 9.6 and 9.7 present the extent of per capita demand for four key products of information technology as of 1995. Japan is near the bottom among wealthy nations in the sophistication of its demand for these products. These lags have arisen precisely because of traditional Japanese industrial policies of supply articulation, with high domestic prices, regulatory barriers, and distribution bottlenecks. In cellular telephones, cozy cooperation between the Ministry of Posts and Telecommunications (MPT) and NTT stifled domestic consumption with the usual array of cartels, non-transparent regulations, exclusionary vertical ties, high domestic prices, and delayed diffusion of foreign technology (Tyson, 1992). Computer networks, including the Internet, have been suppressed by the

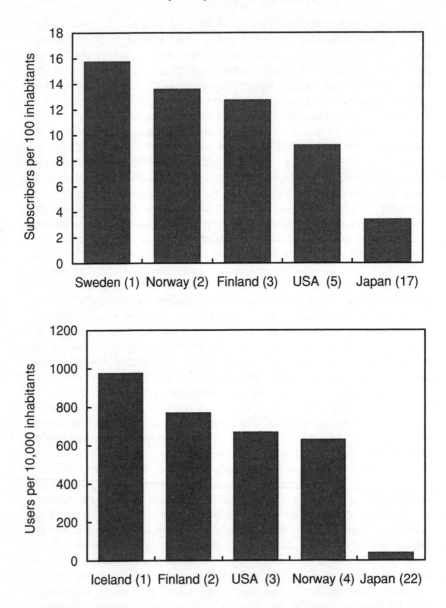

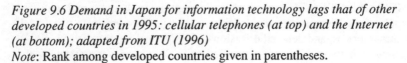

Figure 9.6 Demand in Japan for information technology lags that of other developed countries in 1995: cellular telephones (at top) and the Internet (at bottom); adapted from ITU (1996)
Note: Rank among developed countries given in parentheses.

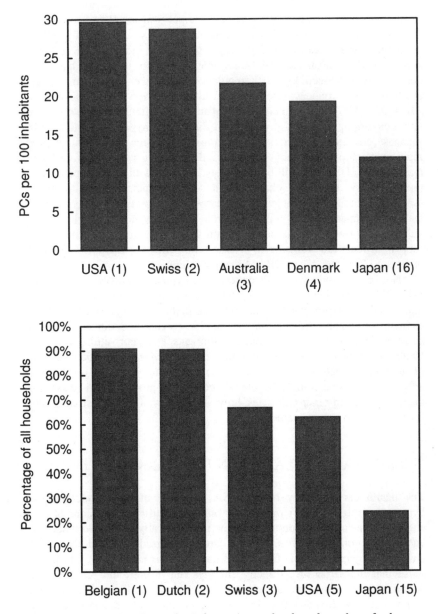

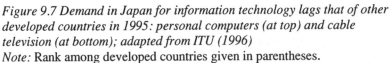

Figure 9.7 Demand in Japan for information technology lags that of other developed countries in 1995: personal computers (at top) and cable television (at bottom); adapted from ITU (1996)
Note: Rank among developed countries given in parentheses.

exorbitant prices charged by the NTT monopoly for telephone connection of computers (Salvaggio, 1994). Computer usage was slowed by NEC's dominant market position, high domestic prices, and incompatible software across vendors (Pollack, 1993). Cable television in Japan has been deliberately repressed by MPT regulation while the agency mistakenly targeted direct broadcast satellite as an alternative service (Pollack, 1993; Salvaggio, 1995). Unfortunately for Japan, these different technologies are now converging together in one grand digitalized hypercompetitive shift. Japanese consumer electronics giants must now focus on continuous and rapid redesign of multimedia computers, despite their very backward home market base. US firms will be intimately involved with this fast-paced and multi-industry technical change, and will compete by continuously redefining products assembled from the best components made anywhere in the world. Japanese firms will have a role in this new consumer electronics industry, but it will be a minor role – providing certain components where supply articulation remains a viable competitive strategy: CD-ROM players, LCD screens, and DRAM memory chips.

Not every industry will experience hypercompetitive shift. For example, the automobile industry will for the foreseeable future remain dominated by supply articulation. Yet even in this industry, we begin to see elements of demand articulation. Toyota has recently lost domestic market share to Honda, thanks to Honda's minivans and sport-utility vehicles. Honda was forced and facilitated in its innovation of these products because of its dependence on the American market, an example of demand articulation. In due course, Toyota will copy these products, and be safe for the meantime. In other industries, however, such wait-and-see strategies of imitation are no longer viable.

DEMAND ARTICULATION IN US PHARMACEUTICALS

The health care industry in the USA is at the moment undergoing a hypercompetitive shift in the pharmaceutical industry. The core of this change is the concentration of providers into vertically integrated units. So various functions (insurance, primary care, specialized care, and pharmacy) are all tied together in one firm. This integration is usually not full, in the sense that the same firm directly employs the insurer, the primary care doctor, the specialist, and the pharmacist. It is rather like the integration that we saw with Toyota in Figure 2.3, in that there are strategic ties between firms but not complete integration into one firm.

There are two expected effects of this vertical integration. One is promotion of *cost effectiveness*, or the requirement that medical products and services demonstrate benefits exceeding their prices. On the one hand, managers of the vertical provider promote cost effectiveness by restricting excess consumption. Expensive services like surgery must be approved by the vertical provider before doctors will be compensated. In pharmaceuticals, an increasingly common feature is a formulary of allowed products; prescriptions written by doctors must be for drugs contained in the formulary, or they will not be approved. On the other hand, vertical providers promote cost effectiveness through price reductions. Before doctors or pharmacies become affiliated to the vertical provider, they must accept price schedules offered by the vertical provider for their services. Pharmaceutical firms must offer acceptable prices, or their products will not be added to the formulary. Note that drug firms selling to vertical providers in the USA must now not only demonstrate safety and medical effectiveness to regulators, but they must also demonstrate cost effectiveness balancing price and medical effect.

Equal in importance to cost effectiveness, though, is *disease management*. The first step of disease management is broad collection of data: what symptoms are reported, what prescriptions are written, and, most important, what health outcomes are observed. The goal of this data analysis is internal innovation within the managed care provider to improve the health of patients without increasing costs. Disease management is a form of consumer *kaizen*, similar to the internal innovation of process technology at Toyota, except that now consumers rather than workers are the focus of invention. Consider a simple example. One managed care firm studied children with asthma, specifically why they were having so many attacks even though they had prophylactic treatment with inhalers. They discovered that children were using their prescribed inhalers improperly. As a consequence they were not actually getting the treatment they were supposed to, and later they would come down with severe conditions that would be expensive to treat. Armed with this analysis, the managed care company developed consumer literature and training regimes, then arranged for vertically affiliated nurses to train these children and their parents during home visits. This program reduced overall costs and improved health care (Montague *et al.* 1996). Note that disease management is a socially constructed system, with the patient now an integral part of demand articulation. And the vertically integrated provider coordinates patient activity, doctor monitoring, a database on patients, and training of both doctors and patients. Today, if you ask which of two drugs is more effective, you must look not only at the chemical, not only at clinical trials on efficacy from universities, but you must also look at the internal systems of the managed care organization and the ability of a pharmaceutical firm to interact with these systems: not just the hardware, but very much the software as well.

What are the likely effects of this hypercompetitive shift in US health care? The most critical effect is that it adds to the table, not just regulators and scientists who have been there since the 1960s, but now also integrated providers and informed consumers. Demand articulation will now be more complex and involve more actors. Pharmaceutical firms that cannot manage these relationships in terms of cost effectiveness and disease management will not be able to sell their products in the USA. As managed care spreads throughout the world, Japanese drug firms will fall even further behind. More and more, they will only supply components (chemical molecules) for the complex demand-articulated products sold by American and Northern European drug firms.

HYPERCOMPETITION AND JAPANESE INDUSTRIAL POLICY

The rise of demand articulation and the eclipse of supply articulation have profound implications for industrial policy. Nowhere are these implications more pronounced than in Japan, precisely because it has so extensively relied on supply articulation for its postwar economic rise. A long-hidden consequence of this supply articulation is the extreme backwardness of Japanese domestic demand. Considering the high levels of wealth, education, culture, and social cohesion in modern Japan, the passivity, ignorance, and technical inexpertness with which Japanese consumers approach their economy are especially striking. Backward demand will eradicate Japanese chances in industries of the future such as information technology and biotechnology. Even more frightening, this backward demand threatens already established Japanese prowess in industries such as consumer electronics.

The successes of the Nordic countries in cellular phones and the United States in pharmaceuticals offer important lessons on the future of industrial policies through demand articulation. Yet these lessons are a sharp contrast to those drawn by many from the Anglo-American political right. To listen to the conservative politicians, successful industrial policy requires 'getting government off the back of industry' and minimizing the role of collective action in an economy. Yet the basis of success for Nordic cellular firms lies precisely in collective action: joint regional adoption of the NMT standard, followed by joint continental adoption of the GSM standard, and high levels of public spending on education, infrastructure, and R&D. The renaissance of American firms in microcomputers and potentially consumer electronics rests powerfully on the rise of the Internet, government created and funded. The success of American pharmaceutical firms is a particular affront to the received wisdom of the right. FDA requirements for demonstrated efficacy and NIH multi-billion dollar funding of basic biomedical R&D have provided an essential foundation for the social construction of blockbuster drugs in the USA.

Contrary to the rhetoric of the right, the 'patron saint' of industrial policy after the hypercompetitive shift is not Adam Smith, but rather Joseph Schumpeter. The goal of public policy is not 'neutrality' to let existing markets clear, but rather the social construction of new markets in ways that encourage innovation. Successful industrial policy must simultaneously challenge firms to break down old ways of doing things and nurture them by rewarding appropriate innovation.

Quality is perhaps the most critical goal of the new industrial policy. Demand must be sophisticated, able to measure and respond promptly to legitimate features of innovations and to reward such features with appropriately high prices. The complexity of modern products requires appropriate institutions to promote consumer knowledge and education. In the case of extremely complex products, minimal quality must be assured through regulation. The pharmaceutical industry vividly illustrates the importance of quality regulation. In those markets where efficacy is not regulated (such as Japan or France), we find a proliferation of 'rubbish' products that have no demonstrable biomedical effect. The reward to Japanese and French firms of 'getting government off their backs' has been to render them largely incompetent to innovate and market efficacious products, and thus to deny them the opportunity to sell products directly in America or Northern Europe.

Cooperation must be a central mechanism for coordination of ecosystems to promote innovation. The definition of complex new products is an inherently collective activity. Some aspects of product definition are obviously collective, such as allocation of broadcast spectrum and construction of intellectual property rights. Other aspects are less obvious, such as consumer education and the extent of local competition. The rewards in new markets go to ecosystems that move early to define new products well.

Yet the USA does not excel at this sort of cooperation, while Japan does. Relations among members of an industrial ecosystem in the USA are arms-length, legalistic, and often adversarial (as at the top of Figure 2.3). These traits are deeply embedded into the US economic system. The American government is constitutionally fragmented into three divisions that question and undermine each other's actions, preventing serious commitment with industry. The ability of industry to share proprietary information with other parties is highly restricted by rules on antitrust (for competitors), administrative process (for judges and regulators), liability law (for consumers), and insider trading (for investors). In contrast, the typical relations within an ecosystem for a Japanese firm are informal (nonlegalistic) and cooperative, with a pronounced blurring of boundaries between a firm and its workers, suppliers, investors, and regulators.

We do not yet know how hypercompetition will play out in the global economy. By aggressively tearing down old industrial policies focused on supply articulation, the Anglo-American economies have clearly moved ahead. Yet this head start may prove to be transitional. The necessity of abandoning supply articulation is increasingly plain to all, while the complexities of building new policies of demand articulation are only beginning to be confronted. If Japan possesses the requisite economic vision and political will (a big 'if' for any nation), it could well adapt to hypercompetition as well as or better than the USA. Two items of evidence hold promise for Japan in the pharmaceutical industry. The first is the astonishing turnaround since 1995 in the Japanese domestic cellular telephone industry. The second is an emerging track record for discovery of significant drugs by Japanese firms (though still buried among the more numerous innovations of trivial products). We now examine each of these promising signs in turn.

DEMAND ARTICULATION IN JAPANESE CELLULAR TELEPHONES

In 1995, the domestic cellular telephone industry of Japan was one of the more backward among developed nations. Per capita subscriber demand was less than half that of the USA and less than one-third that of the Nordic countries (again see Figure 9.6 at top). This backward demand existed despite the fact the NTT launched mobile telephone service in the early 1970s, over a decade before most countries. Since 1995, however, consumer demand for mobile telephony has exploded in Japan and now exceeds that of the USA in per capita terms. More important, the growth of the Japanese mobile telephone industry has been driven by rapid and significant innovation. This newly vibrant domestic ecosystem offers the chance for Japanese firms to succeed in the global marketplace, not only for cellular telephone service, but for Japanese electronics firms such as Matsushita, Sony, and NEC with hardware and even newly emergent Japanese firms with software and consumer services.

Several factors lie behind the rapid and stunning transformation of the Japanese cellular telephone industry.

Trade Pressure

In 1994, the United States Trade Representative (USTR) threatened retaliation against Japan under the 'Super 301' clause of

US trade law. Under the 1989 Third Party Radio and Cellular Agreement with Japan (itself an outcome of earlier threats of trade war), the MPT in Japan committed itself to facilitate the emergence of Motorola's first-generation cellular telephone system in Japan, in competition with the NTT system (Smith, 1989; Tyson, 1992). The USTR forcefully argued that MPT, in collusion with NTT, had obstructed and unfairly restricted Motorola's competitive emergence in Japan. An agreement between MPT in Japan and the USTR in March of 1994 averted the threatened trade skirmish, and guaranteed Motorola entry into the large and lucrative markets of Tokyo and Nagoya (Friedland, 1994b).

Deregulation

To protect NTT from expanded competition from Motorola, MPT significantly deregulated the domestic cellular telephone industry in early 1994 (Friedland, 1994a). Before this deregulation, Japanese consumers were prohibited from direct ownership of cellular handsets, and instead were required to rent them from the literal handful of approved cellular providers, especially NTT. This leasing system not only dampened consumer demand, it also greatly favored handsets using the NTT's first-generation standard. In addition to the elimination of leasing, MPT expanded the choice of cellular providers from three to five with approval of entry of two new firms. And rates were slashed, through still set by MPT regulation.

Competition

In 1995, MPT allowed Kyocera to launch PHS (Personal Handyphone System) in competition with the three established and two new providers of cellular telephone service. PHS was the Japanese version of PCS, a cell-structured system but with lower power, shorter range, and different frequency than standard 'cellular' telephones. Kyocera is an applied ceramics manufacturer, based in Kyoto. It is firmly in the dynamic export sector of the Japanese economy, providing high-tech ceramic components for consumer and industrial electronics. Kyocera launched PHS through its majority-owned telecommunications firm, DDI, in conjunction with leading electronics firms, including Sanyo and Sharp, which provided the handsets. MPT initially resisted approval for PHS, fearing that it would 'damage' the market for cellular services – an old supply articulation perspective. Instead, competition between PHS and cellular ignited the market, by vastly lowering prices, expanding demand, and creating new affiliated markets – a demand articulation forecast. Within a year, mobile telephone connection fees had dropped by 45% and within two years, sign-up fees were eliminated (Fitzpatrick, 1997). The price for handsets dropped from $560 to virtually nothing.

Entrepreneurship

Japanese mobile telephone firms have adapted well to hypercompetition. They have focused on creation of new strategic assets, rather than protection of entrenched positions. The culture and structure of these firms has greatly contributed to their innovative orientation. As mentioned above, DDI is tied to Kyocera, a globally competitive and extremely successful manufacturing firm. In 1992, as part of continuing 'deregulation' of the Japanese telecommunications sector, NTT spun off its cellular telephone division into NTT DoCoMo, a separate firm two-thirds owned by NTT, with NTT itself still 60-percent owned by the Japanese government. Because NTT employees were afraid to move to the new firm, NTT DoCoMo readily broke with postwar Japanese tradition and hired many staff from outside.

Industrial Cooperation

The dominant position of NTT in the Japanese telecommunications section has enabled a degree of cooperation among Japanese firms that is almost unique in the world (with the distinct exception of South Korea). NTT has woven ties among firms that resemble those of the *keiretsu*, with parallel inter-linkages of equity ownership, cross-placement of executives, and near-exclusive trade. The obvious ties among MPT, NTT, and NTT DoCoMo have been supplemented with close working relationships with the two key handset manufacturers, NEC and Matsushita, who supply over 90 percent of NTT DoCoMo customer hardware. Unlike the arms-length relationships between cellular service providers and handset manufacturers in the USA, NTT DoCoMo, Matsushita and NEC have exercised a seamless partnership. Their close relations have enabled flows of information and coordination of technology and investment that are essential for rapid and widespread consumer acceptance of new technology (Yoon, 2001).

Government Cooperation

MPT, in conjunction with NTT and its family of suppliers has aggressively advanced standards for cellular telephones. By 1999, over 95 percent of Japanese cellular telephones used the second-generation digital network. In the USA, only 40 of cellular telephones were digital. Technological advance has been delayed in the USA by multiple, competing second-generation standards, against the unified standards within Japan and within Europe. These incompatible standards reduce geographic coverage, decrease service quality, and dampen consumer usage. Also, over half of Japanese cellular subscribers now use the wireless Internet. In the USA, such subscriber use is minimal. Japan expects to launch the third-generation or wideband digital network for cellular telephones in 2001, at least one year before Europe and several years before the USA. Rollout of third-generation networks in the USA will be even more contentious than the second-generation debacle, as overall limitations of spectrum require reallocation of frequencies already allocated, or 'encumbered', by competing uses, such as UHF television stations (*Economist*, 2000).

The post-1995 success of Japan in cellular telephones well represents the nature of contemporary industrial policy: a balance of challenge and nurturing for firms, a balance of individual firm initiative and cooperation throughout the domestic ecosystem. This success is striking because it is made possible by precisely the institutions of modern Japan that have been so thoroughly criticized in recent years, especially close cooperation between industry and government, and close cooperation among firms. Indeed the absence of such cooperation holds central responsibility for the lagging technology position of the USA in this industry.

While the institutions that make up the cellular telephone industry in Japan have not changed, what has changed is their purpose. This industry is now demand-driven, with NTT DoCoMo playing a central role as a clearing-house for information on rapidly changing consumer needs and tastes. Firms focus on innovation of new sources of competitive advantage, rather than preservation of established advantages.

Innovative foreign firms (such as Motorola) and the US government played an essential catalytic role in jump-starting hypercompetition in the Japanese cellular telephone industry. While the initial trade skirmishes seemed to involve only two actors (MPT and the USTR), in retrospect it is clear that the core struggle was between the 'two Japans' themselves: the dynamic export sector and the stagnant domestic sector. US pressure allied with and was in some senses used by innovative domestic firms (Kyocera, NTT DoCoMo, Matsushita) and forward-looking factions within MPT. In the end, the hypercompetitive shift benefited primarily these innovative Japanese firms, though global consumers stand to benefit as Japan pioneers third-generation cellular systems and the wireless Internet.

The stunningly rapid transformation of the cellular telephone industry in Japan has been facilitated by its closeness under strong MPT and NTT direction. In contrast, the pharmaceutical industry in Japan rests on three quite different and uncoordinated systems: medical care (where the JMA has historically been politically prominent), university research (under the Ministry of Education), and pharmaceutical firms (under MHW). A transformation comparable to that in cellular telephones would require the fundamentally new linkages of cooperation among these separate bureaucracies and interest groups. Formation of such linkages will be hampered by the absence of clear or historical dominance by any one organization.

THE PROMISE OF LEADING JAPANESE FIRMS

The domestic political actors with the greatest stake in a hypercompetitive shift for the pharmaceutical industry in Japan are its few truly innovative domestic firms. Table 9.1 lists the largest Japanese pharmaceutical firms in terms of R&D spending. Each of these firms now has launched at least one global drug, meaning a significant innovation that is widely diffused in world markets. Yet, in almost every case, these important products have been licensed to foreign firms for sale overseas, as indicated in the table. The income stream from these blockbuster products thus must be shared with overseas marketers. Further, this licensing prevents Japanese firms from learning about and mastering marketing for overseas industries. Each of the leading firms is slowly building the capability for direct marketing of their products overseas. But it will take over a decade of continued and committed overseas investment for these Japanese firms to be truly competent outside Japan. Remember the discussion and evidence in Chapter 5 on the abilities of 'large' foreign firms to market their drugs in Japan. These foreign firms were the worst in Japan at marketing their drugs in the late 1970s and early 1980s, as they fought to establish their own operations. Not until the 1990s did these firms attain rough parity with domestic Japanese firms in terms of marketing capability.

Table 9.1 Japanese pharmaceutical firms innovating global drugs and their key subsidiaries abroad
Note: dates of leading overseas acquisitions in parentheses

Leading Firm	Global Drugs 1985-98	Developers Abroad	Key Subsidiaries Abroad
Chugai	*Neutrogin*	Upjohn Rhone Poulenc Rorer	US: Gen-Probe (1992) EU: Chugai Pharma Europe
Daiichi	*Tarivid*	Johnson & Johnson Hoechst Marion Roussel	US: Daiichi Pharmaceutical EU: Daiichi Pharmaceutical Europe GbmH
Eisai	*Aricept*	Pfizer Sandoz	US: Eisai Inc EU: Eisai Europe Ltd. Eisai Sandoz GmbH
Fujisawa	*Prograf* *Cefzon*	Fujisawa Warner Lambert	US: Lyphomed (1989) EU: Klinge (1988)
Sankyo	*Mevalotin* *Banan*	Bristol-Myers Squibb Pharmacia & Upjohn Hoechst Marion Roussel	US: Sankyo Parke-Davis EU: Luitpold (1991)
Shionogi	*Seftem*	Schering Plough	US: capsule maker (1991) EU: Shionogi GmbH
Takeda	*Leuplin* *Takepron*	Takeda-Abbott (TAP) ventures with Roussel, Grunenthal, Cyanamid	US: Takeda Abbott (TAP) EU: ventures in France, Germany, and Italy
Yamanouchi	*Gaster* *Harnal* *Atock*	Merck Boehringer Ingelheim Novartis	US: Shaklee (1989) EU: Gist-Brocades (1991)

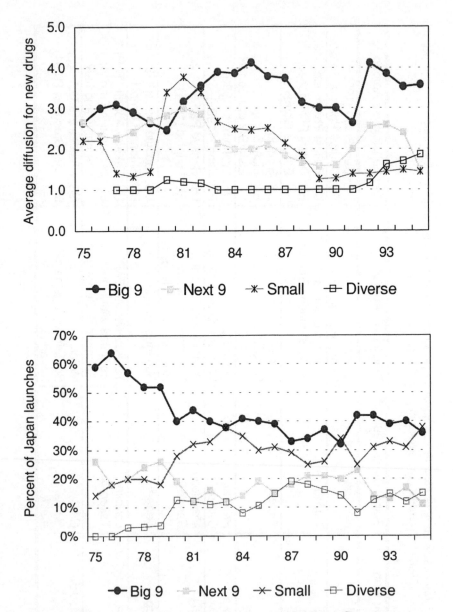

Figure 9.8 Average significance for new drugs of Japanese firms (at top) and the share of all new drugs launched in Japan for these firms (at bottom); 'small' refers to firms that rank below 18 in scale of R&D expense

While patient and committed investment will be required for the long-term success of these Japanese firms, an even more essential requirement is innovation of a broad portfolio of significant drugs. The most successful firms in the global pharmaceutical industry each distribute 20 or more global products. It is inconceivable that Japanese firms could afford or sustain the overhead for large-scale overseas distribution with only one or two significant drugs to sell. Indeed, nothing short of a complete merger of every existing Japanese drug firm into a monolith would yield a true competitor to foreign firms such as Merck or Glaxo. The core problem remains that Japanese firms are pushed by their domestic environment away from significant innovation towards proliferation of trivial products. Every firm in Table 9.1 innovates many more trivial drugs than significant ones (again see Table 4.1, page 69). Equally important, the domestic environment rewards many minor firms, and even diversified firms that entered the pharmaceutical industry during the bubble years of the 1980s. These diversified firms include makers of alcoholic beverages (Kirin, Kyorin, Suntory), petrochemical firms (Asahi, Mitsubishi, Mitsui, Sumitomo), textile firms (Kanebo, Teijin, Toray), food processors (Ajinomoto), and consumer products firms (Lion). Figure 9.8 at top demonstrates that these smaller and more diversified firms simply do not innovate significant products. The average global diffusion for such firms is essentially one nation, Japan itself. Only the nine largest firms in terms of annual R&D expense (denoted Big 9 in Figure 9.8) display any true significance for their innovations, measured as global diffusion, after 1990. Even the next nine largest firms in terms of R&D expense have fallen aside in terms of the significance of their innovations. Yet the Japanese domestic market does not focus its resources to reward these nine firms who are Japan's only hope of global success in pharmaceuticals. The bottom of Figure 9.8 demonstrates that the share of domestic launches by these nine large firms has fallen from 60 percent in the mid-1970s to only 40 percent by the mid-1990s. In contrast, the shares of small, imitative and diversified firms has risen.

Figure 9.8 describes the past. Table 9.1 suggests that the future might be profoundly different, in that several Japanese pharmaceutical firms have now established the capability to innovate important medicines. The final chapter examines options to make this optimistic possibility a reality.

Trade law and remedies
for market exclusion

The steady transformation of the Japanese pharmaceutical market over the last two decades represents an extraordinary failure of industrial policy. MHW has been systematically restrained by domestic politics from addressing the single most important problem facing the pharmaceutical industry in Japan: the dysfunctional nature of physician demand for pharmaceuticals. Instead of confronting this important problem, MHW has launched aggressive reductions of regulated prices that ought to be completely unnecessary given the large numbers of pharmaceutical firms that compete in Japan. Not only have MHW regulations failed to control costs, the market contortions introduced by these policies have undermined the global competitiveness of Japanese pharmaceutical firms, while excluding foreign firms from the Japanese market. One need not be an expert in Japanese political science to recognize here the subversion of public good by politically privileged special interests.

This series of outcomes is, of course, not unique to the pharmaceutical industry. Rather it is matched in numerous other sectors of the Japanese economy ranging from transport, to banking, telecommunications, agriculture, broadcasting, and so on. The political malfeasance and economic inefficiency of these domestic sectors provide a sharp contrast to the renowned innovativeness and competitiveness of the export sector of the Japanese economy. There are indeed 'two Japans.' The elimination of this self-induced dichotomy is in the strong interests of the USA, of the world economy and, most of all, of Japan itself.

This chapter examines the possibilities for US trade action against Japanese exclusion of foreign pharmaceutical innovations.

WHY INTERVENE AGAINST JAPANESE EXCLUSION?

There are two important reasons for US intervention against exclusion of foreign innovations from the Japanese pharmaceutical market. The more basic reason is that Japanese exclusion reduces innovation and raises prices for US consumers of drugs. Development of new drugs is an extremely expensive process, with an average cost per newly launched molecule estimated at $200 million ten years ago (Grabowski and Vernon, 1990; US Congress, OTA, 1993) and at almost $500 million more recently (Myers and Howe, 1997). Ethical drug firms compete with each other primarily through the continuous launch of new products over time, and the number of new products each firm develops depends on expected revenues. If revenues for new products can be earned through worldwide launch, greater R&D expenses can be recovered and more products will be investigated and ultimately launched. This study has demonstrated that between 50 and 90 percent of significant innovations in the global pharmaceutical market are now excluded from Japan. Because most Western drug firms can no longer recover their innovation costs in the second largest pharmaceutical market in the world, they will reduce the number of innovations planned. In Figure 10.1, the number of molecules discovered when revenues are earned from both the USA (R-US) and from Japan (R-Jap) is contrasted with the number of molecules discovered when revenues are derived only from the USA. Fewer innovations will mean higher prices in the US market, in part because of reduced competition in the domestic market and in part because of the need to cover the fixed costs of innovation predominantly in just the USA. Ironically, no small part of the reduced competition that the USA would face, should exclusion continue in Japan, would come from Japanese firms.

The impacts of Japanese exclusion will fall particularly heavily on newly emergent biotechnology companies in the USA. These firms entirely lack significant presence in Japan, and thus join the roster of firms that receive outcomes documented by this study: lower prices, lower sales, and longer clinical trial times in Japan. Biotechnology firms could, of course, license their products to an established foreign pharmaceutical firm in Japan, but such licensings of products impose significant *transactions costs* on innovative firms (Pisano, 1991). Perhaps the greatest transactions cost is the lost opportunity for building organizational capabilities. The experience of the foreign drug firms with significant scale in Japan demonstrates the powerful cumulative impact that actual experiences with distribution have on a firm.

The second reason why the USA should intervene against Japanese exclusion in pharmaceuticals is more long term, but quite important. This study has stressed that the entire pharmaceutical industry, including its products and firms, is socially constructed rather than some inevitable outcome of fixed technology. Further, this study has stressed that social construction of innovative industries is a political act. Innovation by its very nature requires investments now for future benefit. Politically, someone must pay the upfront costs rather than evading them. Further, innovation in a hypercompetitive environment by its nature requires

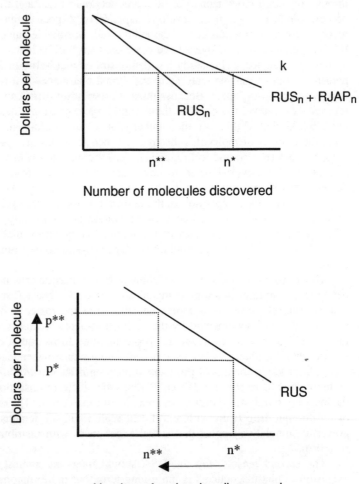

Figure 10.1 Exclusion from the Japanese market reduces
US innovation and raises US Prices

organizational change. Politically, organizational change is arguably even more difficult than cost assumption. There will always be advocates of lower taxes and lower prices, and there will always be opposition to organizational change. Persistent and significant innovation will occur only in those nations where an *innovation coalition* of political and economic actors that embrace new technology can dominate the political system

Accordingly, it is not surprising that only a handful of nations have pharmaceutical industries that are actively engaged in significant innovation. In the first tier of these nations, with firms that innovate global products, are only Britain, Denmark, Germany, the Netherlands, Sweden, Switzerland, and the USA (see Figure 4.4). These nations allow high prices for drugs and have sophisticated demand and regulation for new pharmaceuticals. As we have seen throughout this study, both high prices and sophisticated demand are political acts. Of the more than 1500 distinct new molecules that were launched worldwide between 1970 and 1996, 51 percent were discovered and developed in these seven first-tier nations. More important, of the more than 500 global products launched during that time period, more than 80 percent originated in these first-tier nations.

In a second tier of nations for pharmaceutical innovation, we have firms that indeed innovate, but whose innovations are predominantly minor, ineffective, or imitative products, mostly sold only in the home market. France, Italy, and Japan are the most notable members of this second tier (again see Figure 4.4). Second-tier innovating nations in pharmaceuticals are characterized by vastly less sophisticated regulation and demand for pharmaceuticals: per capita drug consumption is excessive; the tactic of 'poly-pharmacy', where patients receive many different prescriptions with a single doctor visit, is widespread; and completely ineffective products constitute a significant proportion of the market. As we have seen in detail for Japan, such unsophisticated demand is entirely socially constructed, and ultimately based on fundamental political realities. The most prominent of such political realities is the relative social and political standing of university medical faculty versus doctors and pharmacists who operate as independent businesses. Additionally, all second-tier nations, with the notable exception of Japan, set very low prices for new drugs, often at levels half that of first-tier nations (Thomas, 1998). For these nations, excessive domestic consumption and low prices reinforce each other, since healthcare budgets would explode were low prices raised without simultaneous reductions of demand. Second-tier nations account for 43 percent of all distinct new molecules since 1970, but only 17 percent of the global products.

Beyond the first and second tier of nations in pharmaceutical innovation, there is the rest of the world, where virtually no pharmaceutical innovation occurs. Several of these non-innovative nations have deliberately harvested and destroyed their domestic pharmaceutical industries, mostly by setting extremely low drug prices through regulation. The Anglo-Saxon nations of Australia, Canada, and New Zealand notably conducted 'industrial genocide' against their domestic pharmaceutical industries in the 1950s and 1960s, and as a consequence have discovered only three quite minor drugs in over 30 years. It is especially striking that a nation of the size and wealth of Canada, next door to the huge American market and the extreme sophistication of US biomedical sciences, should be so vastly out-innovated by the much smaller nations of Denmark, Sweden, and Switzerland. Canada offers an excellent example of a nation lacking an *innovation coalition* to foster and defend the innovation process.

Recent changes in Europe do not bode well for the continued social construction of innovative pharmaceuticals there. The European Union is gradually forcing integration of the very different pharmaceutical markets of northern and southern Europe. Most of the nations of northern Europe have historically been in the first tier of innovative. The nations of southern Europe have been at best in the second tier. The socialization of medicine throughout most of Europe artificially creates a very real dilemma that overlays and complicates this integration. As innovation advances, the share of national income devoted to pharmaceuticals should naturally increase. For example, the share of GDP devoted to telecommunications has gradually increased over time, from 4 percent to almost 10 percent in most nations, with the proliferation of new communications products and services. In telecommunications, consumers pay directly for innovations and themselves decide the pace and degree for greater expenditures. In health care, however, the socialization of medicine means that consumers mostly pay their doctors and pharmacists indirectly, through taxes and transfer payments. The governments of Europe have proved loath to raise taxes to pay for medical innovation, and indeed increasingly seem ready to sacrifice innovation in the name of 'cost control'. For Europe to continue innovation of significant new drugs, it must steadily increase expenditures on health care in the short run, and privatize its health care systems in the long run. These political decisions will not prove easy.

Should the nations of northern Europe sacrifice their pharmaceutical industries on the altar of socialized medicine, and should Japan fail to modernize its own industry, the USA will stand alone in fostering pharmaceutical innovation. It would surely be in the rational self-interest of American citizens to continue spending billions of dollars on basic medical research and high drug prices, even as the rest of the world parasitically benefits from US innovation and contributes nothing to defray its costs. Essentially, the rest of the world would behave towards the USA as Canada has for three decades, a situation that Americans have largely (but not entirely) ignored. Political realities, however, would make it difficult for

Americans to continue paying high prices and taxes when other nations do not. While it is quite difficult to imagine the disappearance of the pharmaceutical industry as we know it, it is arguably in the strong self-interest of supporters of innovation in the USA to push now for the modernization of the Japanese pharmaceutical industry, rather than risk innovative isolation.

APPROACHES TO US INTERVENTION AGAINST JAPANESE EXCLUSION

The nature of Japanese exclusion and the basis for countervailing US government action can be described from two fundamentally different perspectives. Readers should recognize that most scholars and policy-makers who study these issues usually fall pragmatically in between these pure perspectives. Readers will also recognize that this study leans strongly towards the second perspective, and argues that circumstances in the Japanese pharmaceutical industry best fit that perspective.

The traditional approach to exclusion and intervention posits exclusion as the result of formal, explicit, and artificial government intervention in otherwise competitive markets. Tariffs, import quotas, and explicitly discriminatory product standards are classic government mechanisms for excluding foreign firms. From this diagnosis of exclusion, trade traditionalists derive several implications for appropriate intervention against exclusion. First, intervention should take the form of rules against the specific practices in question. The goal of intervention should be removal of these practices and not numerical targets. 'Managed trade' that sets goals for US firms in Japanese markets is anathema to trade traditionalists. Second, should Japan fail to correct its exclusion, the USA should not retaliate by itself excluding Japanese products. From the traditional perspective, tariffs and quotas reduce welfare in Japan without significant harm to other nations. Japanese consumers pay higher prices and suffer reduced product variety as a result of Japanese exclusion. Retaliatory US tariffs against Japanese products such as automobiles, consumer electronics, or semiconductors would merely harm American consumers of these products. Third, multilateral action by many nations acting together is the only appropriate response to Japanese exclusion of American products. Since restrictions on trade are self-damaging, the only reason for US action against them is to assuage the economic ignorance of US voters. US special interests will exploit voter anger over Japanese imports and the 'lost jobs' associated with these imports into the USA to seek trade protection for domestic US firms. Any such protection will reduce the national income of the USA as a whole. The large costs of such protection, however, will diffuse throughout the economy, while the narrow benefits will be garnered by these special interests. Restriction of US intervention against Japan to multilateral forums like the World Trade Organization (WTO) is the most effective means of constraining domestic US special interests. Indeed, trade traditionalists can point to a 40-year history of successes through multilateral action in expanding global trade and promoting world prosperity, including recent sector-specific successes in agriculture, intellectual property rights, and service industries.

This study has argued for a new, organizational approach to exclusion and intervention. From this perspective, exclusion is the result of fundamentally different business practices in Japan that socially construct fundamentally different business ecosystems. Japanese exclusion is thus an implicit result of pervasive features inherent in the ecosystem, rather than a consciously intended result of isolated artificial interventions. The problem in Japan is the very construction of the market itself, not minor government intrusion into some technology-invariable market. From this quite different diagnosis of exclusion, we draw very different guidelines for intervention. First, intervention must take the form of rules in favor of specific outcomes. The USA must seek positive action from the Japanese government to reconstruct inappropriate business ecosystems, not the far easier cessation of existing interventions. In the pharmaceutical industry, significant political intervention is particularly needed with regard to doctor demand and university science. The required organizational change offers significant threats to entrenched actors in this ecosystem: *kaigyo-i* private practitioners who own their own small clinics, senior university professors who direct clinical trials, and senior MHW officials who would normally retire through *amakudari* to second-tier Japanese pharmaceutical firms or to *koeki hojin* special organizations. The degree of government intervention in these cases is large and highly politically charged. Necessary changes in doctor demand, such as elimination of the 'doctor's margin', have been rancorously debated for a full century.

Further, as the example of Bristol-Myers Squibb with Taxol makes clear, rules on practices are grossly insufficient to achieve requisite changes in the Japanese ecosystem. Japanese failure to accept foreign clinical data has been contested by the USA for over 20 years. Repeatedly, in 1976, in 1986, and again in 1993, the Japanese government has promised to accept foreign clinical data. Yet, for 38 months, the Japanese clinical trial system resisted not only foreign clinical data, but even foreign preclinical data, despite the fact that Taxol was already sold in 76 nations. Never once was the formal reason for rejection of foreign data on Taxol the mere fact that it was foreign. Rather, the dosage size was wrong, or the impurity profile raised questions. Clearly, explicit numerical targets are required for any meaningful change to occur.

A second difference between the traditional and the new perspectives is that US consumers are indeed harmed. The $500 million fixed costs for discovery of significant new drugs create enormous economies of scale that fundamentally violate the assumptions of traditional economics. If US pharmaceutical firms cannot cover these $500 million fixed costs through sales of their products at reasonable prices with reasonable product lives in Japan, then, as discussed above, US patients are harmed by reduced innovation and higher prices. Additionally, traditional economics regards an industry as a technologically fixed entity, with given 'demand' and 'supply'. Yet this study has stressed that the pharmaceutical industry is socially constructed, not given. Not only the rate of innovation, but the types of products innovated and even the organizational nature of firms themselves are determined by domestic ecosystems. Defense and maintenance of the US ecosystem is an important priority for future patients who will consume pharmaceutical innovations in the years ahead.

A third difference between traditional and new perspectives is that unilateral action is essential. Recent multilateral actions addressing 'structural impediments', or the pervasive features of business ecosystems, have largely failed. Recently, the WTO (the successor to GATT) rejected the case brought by the USA on behalf of Kodak. The Kodak case carefully and extensively documented the social construction of the domestic Japanese film industry so that foreign firms were excluded from that market. As a consequence, Japanese firms are able to use their domestic market as a profit sanctuary to fund competitive raids in other countries (such as the USA) against foreign firms (such as Kodak). The social construction of the Japanese film market was largely undertaken by private actors, including the Japanese film company Fuji, four key domestic distributors, several Japanese banks, and two Japanese interlocking conglomerates. The Kodak case, however, also documented the fact that this social construction was coordinated and encouraged by the Japanese government. Despite the strength of the Kodak case, the WTO declined to intervene against 'structural impediments' in Japan. With this decision, the WTO has chosen to interpret narrowly the treaties creating it, so that only formal government interventions into competitive markets will be actionable.

There is mounting evidence that multilateral negotiations to force the removal of structural impediments may be inherently less successful than the use of such negotiations to remove formal, explicit, isolated government interventions in competitive markets. Trade issues, both traditional and structural, have always been politicized (witness the parade of national debates over government agricultural price supports, stretching from the time of Adam Smith to today). But the degree of political consensus required to execute the social reconstruction of anti-innovative markets seems especially difficult to achieve through multilateral means. The current integration of the very different pharmaceutical industries of northern and southern Europe is not encouraging from this perspective. It is far easier politically to lower prices in the north, both directly through regulation and indirectly through parallèl imports, than to force higher prices on the south. The resistance to higher prices in southern Europe stems only in part from the pressures of cost control for socialized medicine. It also stems from core features of southern European pharmaceutical markets that mimic pathologies of the Japanese pharmaceutical ecosystem mentioned above: significant over-consumption, unsophisticated consumers, weak regulations of efficacy, and uncompetitive domestic firms. The failure of multilateral negotiations for European pharmaceuticals over very similar issues to those the USA confronts in Japan offers a very poor harbinger for multilateral solutions there.

Furthermore, US unilateral interventions in the Japanese pharmaceutical industry have already proved remarkably successful. From 1983 to 1986, Japanese pharmaceutical firms pushed MHW to provide some degree of patent restoration for new drugs launched in Japan. The time clock for patented medicines in Japan begins 15 years from the date of publication of the patent. But a significant portion of these 15 years is consumed by preclinical and clinical trials to prove safety and effectiveness for drugs. In the USA, the Waxman-Hatch Act of 1984 provided some extension of patent life to cover premarket testing times (in exchange for government encouragement of greater use of generic drugs once patents had expired). Yet Japanese firms had no success at all in convincing MHW to imitate some form of the Waxman-Hatch patent restoration in Japan. Then the ongoing Market-Oriented Sector-Selective (MOSS) bilateral US-Japan negotiations of 1985–86 raised the issue of intellectual property rights in Japan. Suddenly, MHW drafted patent restoration proposals in 1986 which were in due course adopted by the Diet in 1988 (Howells and Neary, 1995). Note the provocative suggestion that American trade negotiators have significantly more political clout in Japan than Japanese pharmaceutical firms. Additionally, the subsequent bilateral US-Japan negotiations in 1989–90 labeled the Structural Impediments Initiative (SII) achieved comparable success with distribution reform. As mentioned earlier in Chapter 3, the Japanese Federal Trade Commission (FTC) had already ruled in 1982 that the exclusionary vertical practices tying domestic pharmaceutical distributors to the historically dominant Japanese drug firms were illegal under Japanese law. The 1982 ruling was simply ignored by the Japanese pharmaceutical industry. But when the Japanese FTC issued a similar ruling in 1991, under US pressure from the SII talks, Japanese firms led by Takeda decided to radically reform their distribution practices (Howells and Neary, 1995). It is provocative and important to note that both patent restoration and distribution reform clearly promote innovation, and have greater immediate benefit for innovative Japanese firms than for foreign firms. This point will be stressed in the next section.

BEYOND *GAIATSU*: SPECIFICS FOR US TRADE ACTION

This last point identifies a profound difference between the unilateral trade actions proposed in this study and *gaiatsu* or 'foreign pressure' applied by the USA against Japan in the 1980s. Many of the previous bilateral US trade negotiations with Japan have focused on the export sector of the Japanese economy, including automobiles, consumer electronics, film, and semiconductors. There the interests of the USA and of innovative Japanese firms have been fundamentally opposed, although US interests are arguably well aligned with those of Japanese consumers. In contrast, many recent US trade negotiations with Japan have turned to the 80 percent of the Japanese economy in the uncompetitive domestic sector. Here the USA can and should take pains to stress that the deregulatory and social reconstruction goals pushed by innovative US firms are not only also in the interests of globally competitive Japanese firms, but are absolutely essential for the growth and prosperity of Japan as a whole.

Post-*gaiatsu* trade actions by the USA must seek *total ecosystem reform*, or an integrated package of reforms throughout Japanese business ecosystems. If we re-examine the Japanese domestic ecosystem for pharmaceuticals displayed in Figure 4.2, we find important linkages across the components. MHW price regulations are thoroughly destructive, yet so long as doctor demand remains so pathological, it is difficult for MHW to deregulate prices fully. The clinical trial system in Japan is grossly provincial and incompetent, yet reform of that system will require institutional reform and significantly greater funding for the biomedical science base in Japan. Greater funding for basic science will require savings through reduction of overconsumption of medicines. And so on around the ecosystem.

This study proposes that the USA seek ten specific reforms of the Japanese domestic ecosystem for pharmaceuticals, grouped into four major areas.

Pricing

1. End the doctor's margin The 'doctor's margin' is at the core of the corruption and inefficiency (both static and dynamic) of the Japanese pharmaceutical industry. Among the many deleterious effects of the doctor's margin are several that exclude foreign pharmaceutical

innovations.   The increased costs and idiosyncratic skills needed for
distribution of drugs in Japan exclude most foreign firms from the market.
Doctor preference for high-priced drugs materially contributes to the shorter
product life of new drugs in Japan. And these shorter life cycles artificially
favor   non-innovative   domestic   products   over   significant   foreign
innovations. The doctor's margin should be abolished, at the minimum by
direct MHW regulation of wholesale prices and at best by banning
wholesale discounts off NHI retail prices.

2. *End price vintaging-* The MHW-imposed steady reductions of prices
based on the age in Japan (or vintage) of new drugs is anti-innovative and
exclusionary. This regulatory tactic directly and clearly causes the ultra-
short product life of new drugs in Japan that excludes many foreign drugs.
Price vintaging also nullifies intellectual property rights of patent holders in
Japan, both directly by stripping innovators of their ability to price their
innovations adequately and indirectly by shortening product lives. For at
least the life of the Japanese patent, MHW must be proscribed from
imposing any reduction off the launch price of a new drug.

3. *Institute a 100-percent-of-US-price floor* The bilateral USA-Japan MOSS
talks of 1985–86 set a 50 percent to 200 percent band for the launch price in
Japan of new drugs relative to the US price. MHW-set prices in Japan are
simply too low on average, and drive the exclusion of foreign products from
Japan. The MOSS band is too wide, and in particular the 50 percent floor
tolerates and encourages lowball pricing by MHW. Low MHW regulated
prices also nullify intellectual property rights for patented medicines.
Ideally and in the long term, MHW price regulations should be discarded in
favor of market-based pricing. MHW must publicly commit itself to such
deregulation within a set time frame. In the short term, the backward nature
of Japanese medical demand for pharmaceutical products may require some
level of price controls.   Any such short-term controls must, however,
explicitly proxy market-driven prices.   As the largest, the most
sophisticated, and a price-unregulated market, the US pharmaceutical
industry serves as a completely appropriate proxy to determine market-
driven prices. This floor should be set at 100 percent of US prices and
should apply without discrimination to all recent drugs sold both in Japan
and in the USA, including those of Japanese innovators.

4. *Move drugs to OTC status* Unusually few drugs are sold in Japan over
the counter (OTC) directly to consumers without doctor prescription.
Creation of a vibrant OTC market in Japan will promote innovation in
several ways. First, OTC products encourage knowledge and independence
of Japanese consumers, and creation of a large OTC market will

significantly improve their sophistication. Second, moving products currently under NHI reimbursement to OTC status will save significant revenues for insurers, and these revenues can then be used for price increases for important new drugs. Third, ending the anti-innovative and exclusionary features of the Japanese pharmaceutical market will severely challenge many Japanese drug firms. Creation of a significant domestic OTC market will provide a graceful exit for some of these firms, as they redirect their business from trivial 'innovations' sold to doctors under the current corrupt system to OTC products sold directly to Japanese consumers.

5. Encourage generic drugs Generic drugs are legal copies of formerly patented molecules, and as such are supposedly chemically and biomedically identical to the original molecules. Generic drugs are priced at a fraction of the cost of original products they copy, in large part because generic manufacturers need not pay for extensive research and testing prior to launch. While generic products exist in Japan, they have only the most minimal sales. MHW has no policies to promote their usage, and the doctor's margin ensures that doctors and hospitals are strongly discouraged from prescribing them. Greater use of generics, like greater use of OTC products, will encourage patient knowledge of costs, reduce overall health care costs and provide a graceful exit for non-innovative Japanese pharmaceutical firms.

Registration

6. Institute timing deadlines The registration and clinical trial process in Japan has almost completely collapsed for innovative foreign drugs since 1992. Gross delays between the filing of a New Drug Application (NDA) in Japan and MHW approval have greatly increased since that year. These delays are transparently exclusionary and anti-innovative. In 1992 in the USA, as Congress considered the Prescription Drug User Fee Act (PDUFA), the FDA publicly committed itself to a rigorous schedule for approval of US NDAs. If the FDA in the USA can promote innovation and public health through adherence to strict schedules for approval of NDAs, then so can and so should the MHW in Japan. Note that this proposed reform is based on outcomes (actual formal approvals) not processes (a good effort, with some sort of explanation from MHW for delays).

7. Institute a 'rule of three-of-four' The greatest delay in the registration process comes not after an NDA is filed with MHW, but rather during the clinical trials that precede NDA filing. As the discussions in this study of the clinical trial system in Japan make clear, process-oriented rules will have virtually no effect on the Japanese clinical trial system. Specifically, process-oriented rules on Japanese acceptance of foreign clinical trial data are a waste of time. Instead, outcome-oriented rules are inescapable to force Japan to take the politically difficult steps necessary to truly reform its corrupt clinical trial system. Japan must commit itself to a verifiable and rigorous standard for approval of pharmaceutical innovations: 80 percent of all drugs launched in three of the four largest pharmaceutical markets (Britain, France, Germany, and the USA) must be approved by MHW within one year of their NDA filing in Japan.

Demand

8. Institute patient information systems The passive and ignorant demand by Japanese patients works against significant pharmaceutical innovation. Since US pharmaceutical innovation is skewed towards significant drugs while Japanese innovation has been skewed towards minor, ineffective, and imitative drugs, this backward demand is a nontariff barrier for US firms. Basic steps towards social construction of informed and active demand by Japanese patients would involve simple package inserts (or comparable accompanying literature) for all prescribed medicines and some form of direct advertising to patients by pharmaceutical firms.

9. Launch managed care Balancing medical costs and benefits is an inescapable component of any efficient health care system. In Japan, this balancing is performed extremely poorly, and is often little more than cost-suppression through anti-innovative and exclusionary price controls. Yet removal of price controls will require some new systems that encourage doctors to prescribe cost-effective medicines while discouraging prescription of cost-ineffective ones. It is increasingly clear that some form of managed care is essential towards this end. The creation of new social systems is a complex and long-term process, and in Japan must be adapted to local cultural values. The social construction of the Japanese automobile industry (sketched in Figure 2.3) took almost a decade, and represented a brilliant act of organizational entrepreneurship. In constructing this business ecosystem, A.G. Toyoda and his domestic competitors did not copy the US system as pioneered by Henry Ford, but rather adapted the US system for Japan and in the process significantly improved it. A comparable act of organizational entrepreneurship is desperately needed in the Japanese health care system

Science Base

10. Greatly expand science funding The US government spends $14 billion each year (roughly $55 per citizen) for biomedical research through the National Institutes of Health. Japan reportedly spends almost ¥375 billion per year (roughly $24 per citizen at an exchange rate of 120 yen per dollar). For Japan to match US per capita spending on biomedical R&D, it would have to double current levels of government spending. It must be stressed that the effects of greater basic R&D in Japan will be felt throughout its health care ecosystem. Increased basic R&D shifts the balance of influence and power within the medical profession away from private practitioners towards scientists. It also shifts the tone and nature of choice among competing technologies towards evidence-based medicine, on a par with prevailing practice in the USA and northern Europe. It is important to note that elimination of overconsumption and ineffective medicines in Japan would save more than five times the proposed increase in basic science expenditures. Thus any claim that Japan cannot afford greater basic research is utter nonsense; the reality is that Japan has starved basic science (and the doctors who conduct it) in favor of a corrupt and politically motivated support for the incomes of private practitioners (who provide the backbone of the JMA).

11. Reform science governance Expansion of the biomedical science base in Japan will require not only greater expenditure, but vastly greater coordination among the three ministries that oversee such funding: the Ministry of Education (MOE), the Ministry of International Trade and Industry (MITI), and MHW. Unlike supply articulation industrial policies of the 1950s and 1960s that were exclusively coordinated by MITI, or the demand articulation policies for cellular telephones that have been coordinated by MPT, industrial policies for pharmaceuticals face the challenge of fragmented ministerial authority. In the case of health care research, the vast bulk of current expenditures are the responsibility of MOE.

Several points should be made on this package of proposed reforms. First, these reforms are unmistakably post-*gaiatsu*, both because their goal is integrated reform of an entire ecosystem and because Japanese pharmaceutical firms will actually gain global competitiveness with adoption of the reforms. In pursuit of these reforms, the USA should stress their interrelatedness and the enormous benefits that ordinary Japanese citizens would receive from them. It is imperative that the USA break from its *gaiatsu* tradition and appeal directly to Japanese citizens to explain its positions and seek support. It is also imperative that US trade negotiators seek alliances with Japanese interests that will benefit from reform, such as leading Japanese pharmaceutical firms, MITI officials, and research physicians.

Second, half of the proposed reforms (the first, second, third, sixth, and seventh) are directly pursuable via unilateral US action under Section 301 of the 1974 Trade Act. Section 301 has been amended over time by the Trade Agreement Act (1979), the Trade and Tariff Act (1984), and the Omnibus Trade and Competitiveness Act (1988). Five practices are identified (the doctor's margin, price vintaging, low MHW-set price levels, delay in MHW review of NDAs, and discriminatory delay in execution of clinical trials – in part due to exclusion of foreign clinical trial data). As this study has demonstrated, these practices are 'unfair and inequitable' for US pharmaceutical firms and they inappropriately exclude most US innovations from the second largest pharmaceutical market in the world. These practices clearly fail to meet the various standards set by Congress to determine unfairness and inequity of foreign exclusion. The Japanese government has been made well aware of the exclusionary nature of these practices (most recently in the MOSS talks of 1985–86 and the Structural Impediments Initiative of 1989–90), and the Japanese government has not kept its agreements reached under these negotiations. The remaining five proposals are arguably not pursuable under Section 301, and if resisted by Japan might be dropped in bilateral negotiations with Japan. It is important, however, for the USA to push these remaining proposals 'in the court of public opinion', regardless of the actual course of formal negotiations with the Japanese government.

Third, the proposed unilateral actions are arguably consistent with US international obligations under the WTO. The US government, particularly the Congress, has clearly and repeatedly stated its belief that unilateral action under Section 301 remains completely appropriate under the WTO. The United States Trade Representative (USTR) Office has stated:

> Congress would not have approved the WTO if they felt we were relinquishing all use of Section 301 irrespective of whether the issues were adequately covered by the WTO Agreement. We didn't agree to the WTO on those terms, and nobody in the world thinks we did. (quoted in Stokes, 1995)

The key phrase in this statement is 'adequately covered by the WTO Agreement'. The WTO Agreement does not in fact cover structural impediments to trade, or exclusionary policies that are not explicit and formal acts of government. Thus, exclusionary aspects of the Japanese pharmaceutical ecosystem, such as the corruption of the clinical trial system or the barriers raised by the doctor's margin, are not actionable under the WTO. Initial supporters of the WTO have entertained hopes that the WTO would stretch GATT agreements to address exclusion due to acts by non-governmental actors. One such expression of hope was well put as follows:

> By participating in the WTO, states have agreed to curtail the opportunity to pursue unilateral gains in exchange for a system that functions through a multilateral framework. However, this compromise appears greater when private trade barriers are involved, for the GATT still primarily covers public barriers. Thus, although the WTO greatly reduces the scope of retaliation not authorized within GATT, the private barriers that Section 301 could have attached are not correspondingly reduced. This means, then that if the United States is to restrain its use of Section 301, the areas covered by the WTO must be expanded to compensate. The reduction in unilateral means must be countered by an increase in multilateral means. Therefore, the WTO must address anticompetitive policies in some manner. (Abels, 1996)

These hopes were dashed by rejection by the WTO in 1997 of the US case brought on behalf of Kodak. It is now clear that the WTO will not in fact address structural impediments.

TOWARDS A NEW GLOBAL POLITICS OF INNOVATION

Traditional economics regarded technology as fixed. Much of the popular press presents technology as the outcome of isolated entrepreneurial genius, as with Thomas Edison. This study has argued that innovation is socially constructed, and more than anything else is a result of collective political will. The pace of pharmaceutical innovation, the type of products discovered, the type of firms that innovate, even the existence of innovation itself are all politically based social constructions. Only a handful of nations have surmounted political hurdles to allow adequate pricing and sophisticated demand and regulation for new medicines.

We stand at the threshold of significant biomedical innovation, even for intractable problems such as AIDS, Alzheimer's disease, and cancer. Yet, ironically, the very pace of change that so excites us threatens the continued social construction of innovation for pharmaceuticals, by requiring a mounting share of national income to be devoted to health care. The rise of managed care in the USA offers profound organizational change that may well maintain an appropriate balance between the costs and benefits of medical innovation. It is far from clear whether Europe and Japan will correspondingly transform their own health care systems. In Japan, powerful special interests, embodied in the dual state, are arrayed against pharmaceutical innovation. The political will necessary for Japan to tear down the dual state, and rebuild a fully globalized and innovative economy, seems far beyond its existing political leadership. Further, global political institutions such as the WTO will prove almost useless in advancing innovation in Japan, much less in Europe.

Yet the USA can and must act to promote institutional change in Japan necessary to advance global innovation. As the second largest pharmaceutical market in the world, the size of Japan makes this action critical if global medical innovation is to continue.

References

Abels, T.M. (1996), 'The World Trade Organization's First Test: The United States-Japan Auto Dispute', *UCLA Law Review*, **44** (December), 467–526.

ACCJ (American Chamber of Commerce in Japan) (1997a), *Making Trade Talks Work: Lessons from Recent History*, Tokyo: ACCJ.

ACCJ (American Chamber of Commerce in Japan) (1997b), *1997 United States-Japan Trade White Paper Covering 38 Industry Sectors*, Tokyo: ACCJ.

Akira, K. (1993), 'Understanding Japanese Health Care Expenditures: The Medical Fee Schedule', in D.I. Okimoto and A. Yoshikawa (eds), *Japan's Health System: Efficiency and Effectiveness in Universal Care*, Washington, DC: Faulkner and Gray.

Anchordoguy, M. (1989), *Computers Inc.: Japan's Challenge to IBM*, Cambridge, MA: Harvard University Press.

Aoki, M. (1988) 'The Japanese Bureaucracy in Economic Administration: A Rational Regulator or Pluralist Agent', in J.B. Shoven (ed.), *Government Policy towards Industry in the United States and Japan*, Cambridge, UK: Cambridge University Press.

Aoki, M. and R.P. Dore (1994), *The Japanese Firm: Sources of Competitive Strength*, Oxford: Clarendon Press.

Arrow, K.J. (1962), 'Economic Welfare and the Allocation of Resources for Invention', in R.R. Nelson (ed.), *The Rate and Direction of Inventive Activity*, Princeton, NJ: Princeton.

Badaracco, J.L. (1985), *Loading the Dice: A Five-Country Study of Vinyl Chloride Regulation*, Boston: Harvard Business School Press.

Barber, B. (1995), 'All Economies are 'Embedded': The Career of a Concept, and Beyond', *Social Research*, **62**, 387–413.

Barney, J.B. (1986), 'Strategic Factor Markets: Expectations, Luck, and Business Strategy', *Management Science, 32*, 1231–41.

Barney, J.B. (1991), 'Firm Resources and Sustained Competitive Advantage', *Journal of Management, 17*, 99–120.

Bartel, A.P. and L.G. Thomas (1987), 'Predation through Regulation: The Wage and Profit Impacts of OSHA and EPA', *Journal of Law and Economics, 30* (October), 239–64.

Bartlett, C.A. and S. Ghoshal (1989), *Managing Across Borders: The Transnational Solution,* Boston: Harvard Business School Press.

Baum, J.A.C. and J.E. Dutton (eds), (1996), *Advances in Strategic Management: The Embeddedness of Strategy,* vol. 13, Greenwich, CT: JAI Press.

Berger, D. and I. Fukunishi (1996), 'Psychiatric Drug Development in Japan', *Science, 273* (July 19), 318–9.

Borrus, M., *et al.* (1985), 'Telecommunications Development in Comparative Perspective: The New Telecommunications in Europe, Japan, and the U.S.' Berkeley, CA: BRIE working paper.

Borrus, M. (1993), 'The Regional Architecture of Global Electronics: Trajectories, Linkages, and Access to Technology' in P. Gourevitch and P. Guerrieri (eds), *New Challenges to International Competition,* San Diego: University of California San Diego Press.

Calder, K.E. (1988), *Crisis and Compensation: Public Policy and Political Stability in Japan, 1949–1986,* Princeton: Princeton University Press.

Campbell, J.C. (1992), *How Policies Change: The Japanese Government and the Aging Society,* Princeton: Princeton University Press.

Carey, J. (1997), 'The Politics of Generics: Half the War Over Branded Drugs is Fought Outside the Lab', *Business Week,* (February 3), 128–32.

Carlton, D.W. and J.M. Perloff (1990), *Modern Industrial Organization,* Glenview, IL: Scott Foresman, 1990.

Chandler, A. (1990), *Scale and Scope: The Dynamics of Industrial Capitalism*, Cambridge, MA: Harvard University Press.

Christensen, R. (1998), 'The Effort of Electoral Reforms on Campaign Practices in Japan: Putting New Wine in Old Bottles', *Asian Survey*, **38** (October), 986–1004.

Clifford, M.L. (1994), *Troubled Tiger: Businessmen, Bureaucrats, and Generals in South Korea*, Armonk, NY: M.E. Sharpe.

Council of Economic Advisors (CEA) (1984), *Economic Report of the President*, Washington, DC: US Government Printing Office, especially chapter on 'Industrial Policy', 87–111.

Cox, G.W., F.M. Rosenbluth, and M.F. Thies (1999), 'Electoral Reform and the Fate of Factions: The Case of Japan's Liberal Democratic Party', *British Journal of Political Science*, **29**, 33–56.

Danzon, P.M. (1996), 'The Uses and Abuses of International Price Comparisons', in R.B. Helms, (ed.), *Competitive Strategies in the Pharmaceutical Industry*, Washington, DC: American Enterprise Institute.

D'Aveni, R.A. (1994), *Hypercompetition: Managing the Dynamics of Strategic Management*, New York: Free Press.

Davis, G.F. and W.W. Powell, (1992), 'Organization-Environment Relations', in M. Dunnette *Handbook of Industrial and Organizational Psychology*, vol. 3, 2nd edn, Palo Alto, CA: Consulting Psychologists Press.

DiMaggio, P.J. and W.W. Powell (1983), 'The Iron Cage Revisited: Institutional Isomorphism and Collective Rationality in Organizational Fields', *American Sociological Review*, **48**, 147–60.

DiMaggio, P.J. and W.W. Powell (eds) (1991), 'Introduction', in *The New Institutionalism and Organizational Analysis*, Chicago: University of Chicago Press.

Dobbin, F. (1994), *Forging Industrial Policy: The United States, Britain, and France in the Railway Age*, New York: Cambridge University Press.

Dosi, G., L.D. Tyson, and J. Zysman (1989), 'Trade, Technologies, and Development: A Framework for Discussing Japan', in Johnson, *et al.* (1989).
Economist (1993), 'Japan's Drugs Industry: Medicinal Madness', (March 27), 73.

Economist (1995), 'Second Time Around', (August 12), 51–52.

Economist (1996), 'Japan's Sickly Drug Firms', (October 19), 65–66.

Economist (1997a), 'Under the Knife: Japanese Medical Suppliers', (September 13), 65–66.

Economist (1997b), 'Japan: Bitter Pill', (November 8), 21–22 and 42–43.

Economist (2000), 'Battle of the Airwaves', (July 29), 57–8.

Farrell, J. and G. Saloner (1986), 'Installed Base Compatibility: Innovation, Product Preannouncements, and Predation', *American Economic Review*, **76**, 940–955.

Fitzpatrick, M. (1997), 'Cellular Success Paves Way to Deregulation', *Communications International*, **24**:3 (March), 27–28.

Flanagan, S.C. and A.-R. Lee (2000), 'Value Change and Democratic Reform in Japan and Korea', *Comparative Political Systems*, **33** (June), 626–59.

Foray, D. and C. Freeman, (eds) (1993), *Technology and the Wealth of Nations: The Dynamics of Constructed Advantage*, London: Pinter Publishers.

Freeman, C. (1987), *Technology, Policy, and Economic Performance: Lessons from Japan*, London: Pinter Publishers.

Friedland, J. (1994a), 'Now You're Talking', *Far Eastern Economic Review*, **157**:7 (February 17), 42–44.

Friedland, J. (1994b), 'Forceful Persuasion: Motorola Wins Access to Japanese Market', *Far Eastern Economic Review*, **157**:12 (March 24), 56.

Fukushima, M. (1989), 'The Overdose of Drugs in Japan', *Nature*, **342** (December 21), 850–51.

Gerlach, M.L. (1992), *Alliance Capitalism: The Social Organization of Japanese Business*, Berkeley: University of California Press.

Ghemawat, P. (1984), 'Capacity Expansion in the Titanium Dioxide Industry', *Journal of Industrial Economics*, **33** (December), 145–63.

Gibney, A. (dir.) (1988), 'Manufacturing Miracles: A Japanese Firm Reinvents Itself,' [videotape, 35 minutes] San Francisco: California Newsreel.

Giddens, A., *Modernity and Self-Identity: Self and Society in the Late Modern Age*, Palo Alto, CA: Stanford University Press, 1991.

Gilbert, R.J. (1981), 'Patents, Sleeping Patents, and Entry Deterrence', in S.C. Salop, (ed.) *Strategy, Predation, and Antitrust Analysis*, Washington, DC: Federal Trade Commission.

Grabowski, H.G. (1980), 'Regulation and the International Diffusion of Pharmaceuticals', in R.B. Helms, (ed.), *The International Supply of Medicines*, Washington, DC: American Enterprise Institute.

Grabowski, H.G. and J.M. Vernon (1990), 'A New Look at the Returns and Risks to Pharmaceutical R&D', *Management Science*, **36** (July), 804–21.

Goozner, M. (1995), 'AIDS Puts Japan Society on Trial: Suit Says Foreign Made Products Deliberately Kept Out', *Chicago Tribune*, (April 4), 1.

Granovetter, M. (1985), 'Economic Action and Social Structure: The Problem of Embeddedness', *American Journal of Sociology*, **91**, 481–510.

Hamilton, D. P. (1996), 'Japan AIDS Scandal Raises Fear the Safety Came Second to Trade', *Wall Street Journal*, (October 9), A1 & A6.

Hamilton, G. and N.W. Biggart (1988), 'Market, Culture, and Authority: A Comparative Analysis of Management and Organization in East Asia', *American Journal of Sociology*, **94**, S52–S94.

Hart, J. A. (1992), *Rival Capitalists: International Competitiveness in the United States, Japan, and Western Europe*, Ithaca: Cornell University Press.

Helm, L. (1993), 'A Vaccine that Comes up Short: Safe Products Were Available Abroad, But Japan Wanted to Develop its Own: Death and Illness Resulted', *Los Angeles Times*, (May 3), p. D1.

Helms, R.B. (ed.) (1975), *Drug Development and Marketing*, Washington, DC: American Enterprise Institute.

Helms, R.B. (ed.) (1981), *Drugs and Health: Economic Issues and Policy Objectives*, Washington, DC: American Enterprise Institute.

Holden, C. (1993), 'Taxol Gains Quick FDA Approval', **259** *Science*, (January 8), 181.

Howard, M. C. (1983), *Antitrust and Trade Regulation: Selected Issues and Case Studies*, Englewood Cliffs, NJ: Prentice-Hall.

Howells, J. and I. Neary (1995), *Intervention and Technological Innovation: Government and the Pharmaceutical Industry in the UK and Japan*, London: Macmillan Press.

Hughes, T.P. (1983), *Networks of Power: Electrification in Western Society, 1880–1930*, Baltimore: Johns Hopkins University Press.

Ibrahim, Y.M. (1997), 'Finland: An Unlikely Home Base for Universal Use of Technology' *New York Times* (Monday, January 20), A1 & C6.

Ikegami, N. (1992), 'The Economics of Health Care in Japan', *Science*, **258** (October 23), 614–8.

Ikegami, N., W. Mitchell, and J. Penner-Hahn (1996), 'Pharmaceutical Prices, Quantities, and Innovation: Comparing Japan with the U.S.', *Pharmacoeconomics*, 424–33.

Ikegami, N., S. Ikeda, and H. Kawai (1997), 'Why Costs Have Increased Despite Declining Prices for Pharmaceuticals in Japan', working paper.

ITU (International Telecommunication Union) (1995), *Communication Indicators for Major Economies, 1995*, Geneva: ITU.

Jackson, J.H. (1989), *The World Trading System*, Cambridge, MA: MIT Press.

Japan Pharmaceutical Manufacturers Association (JPMA) (1995), *Data Book 1995*, Tokyo: JPMA.

Jewkes, J., D. Sawers, and R. Stillerman (1958), *The Sources of Invention*, London: Macmillan.

Johnson, C. (1982), *MITI and the Japanese Miracle: The Growth of Industrial Policy, 1925–1975*, Stanford, CA: Stanford University Press.

Johnson, C. (1989), 'MITI, MPT, and the Telecom Wars: How Japan Makes Policy for High Technology', in Johnson, *et al.* (1989)

Johnson, C., L. D. Tyson, and John Zysman (eds) (1989), *Politics and Productivity: How Japan's Development Strategy Works*, New York: Harper Business.

Johnson, C. (1993), 'Comparative Capitalism: The Japanese Difference', *California Management Review*, **35** (Summer), 51–67

Johnson, C. (1995), *Japan: Who Governs?* New York: W.W. Norton Company.

Kester, W.C. (1991), *Japanese Takeovers: The Global Contest for Corporate Control*, Boston: Harvard Business School Press.

Kessler, D.A., A.E. Hass, K.L. Feiden, M. Lumpkin, and R. Temple (1996), 'Approval of New Drugs in the United States: Comparison with the United Kingdom, Germany, and Japan', *Journal of the American Medical Association*, **276** (December 11), 1826–31.

Kimura, B., A. Fukami, S. Yanagisawa, and K. Sato (1993), 'The Current State and Problems of Japan's Pharmaceutical Market', in D. I. Okimoto and A. Yoshikawa (eds), *Japan's Health System: Efficiency and Effectiveness in Universal Care*, Washingon, DC: Faulkner and Gray.

Klevorick, A.K., R.C. Levin, R.R. Nelson, and S.G. Winter (1993), 'On the Sources and Significance of Interindustry Differences in Technological Opportunity', Yale University working paper.

Kochan, T. A., H. C. Katz, and R. B. McKersie (1986), *The Transformation of American Industrial Relations*, New York: Basic Books.

Kodak Corporate Information (1997), 'An Overview and Summary of US Submissions to the WTO Dispute Settlement Panel', @ http://www.kodak.com/ aboutKodak/bu/cpa/JPMarketBarriers.

Kogut, B. (ed.) (1993), *Country Competitiveness: Technology and the Organizing of Work,* New York: Oxford University Press.

Krattenmaker, T.G. and S.C. Salop (1986), 'Anticompetitive Exclusion: Raising Rivals' Costs to Achieve Power Over Price', *Yale Law Journal,* **96**, 209–95.

Kruger, A.O. (1990), 'Free Trade is the Best Policy', in R.Z. Lawrence and C.L. Shultze (eds), *American Trade Strategy: Options for the 1990s,* Washington, DC: Brookings Institution.

Krugman, P.R. (1987), 'Is Free Trade Passé?' *Economic Perspectives,* **1** (Fall), 131–44.

Kuttner, Robert (1984), *The Economic Illusion,* Boston: Houghton Mifflin.

Lawrence, R.Z. (1984), *Can America Compete?* Washington, DC: Brookings Institution.

Lawrence, R.Z. (1991), 'Efficient or Exclusionist? The Import Behavior of Japanese Corporate Groups', *Brookings Papers on Economic Activity,* **1**, 311–30.

Levin, R.C., W.M. Cohen, and D.C. Mowery (1985), 'R&D Appropriability, Opportunity, and Market Structure', *American Economic Review,* **75** (May), 20–24.

Levin, R.C., A.K. Klevorick, R.R. Nelson, and S.G. Winter (1987), 'Appropriating the Returns from Industrial R&D', *Brookings Papers on Economic Activity,* **3**, 783–820.

Lincoln, E.J. (1990), *Japan's Unequal Trade,* Washington, DC: Brookings Institution.

Lipasti, I., M. M. Martii, and J. A. Quelch (1989), *Nokia-Mobira Oy: Mobile Telecommunications in Europe,* Boston: Harvard Business School Case 9-589-112.

Marshall, A. (1919), *Industry and Trade*, London: Macmillan.

Marshall, A. (1920), *Principles of Economics*, 8th edn, London: Macmillan.

Masaru, K. (1997), 'Voter Turnout and Strategic Ticket-Splitting under Japan's New Electoral Rules', *Asian Survey*, **37** (May), 429–40

Maruyama, H., J.H. Raphael, and C. Djerassi (1996), 'Why Japan Ought to Legalize the Pill', *Nature*, **379** (February 15), 579–80.

Mason, M. (1992), 'United States Direct Investment in Japan: Trends and Prospects', *California Management Review*, (Fall), 98–115.

Matsushita, M. (1991), 'The Role of Competition Law and Policy in Reducing Trade Barriers in Japan', *World Economy*, **14** (June), 181–97.

Mikitaka, M. and J.C. Campbell (1996), 'Evolution of Fee-Schedule Politics in Japan', in N. Ikegami and J.C. Campbell, (eds), *Containing Health Care Costs in Japan*, Ann Arbor, MI: University of Michigan Press.

Millstein, J.E. (1983), 'Decline in an Expanding Industry: Japanese Competition in Color Television' in J. Zysman and L.D. Tyson (eds), *American Industry in International Competition: Government Policies and Corporate Strategies*, Ithaca: Cornell University Press.

Montague, J., A. Nordhaus-Bike, and K. Sandrick (1996), 'How to Save Big Bucks' 70 *Hospitals and Health Networks* (January 1), 18–22.

Mulgan, A.G. (2000), 'Japan: A Setting Sun?' *Foreign Affairs*, **79** (July/August), 40–52.

Myers, S.C. and C. Howe (1997), 'A Life Cycle Model of Pharmaceutical R&D' working paper, MIT Program on the Pharmaceutical Industy.

Narisetti, R. (1997), 'P&G Uses Packaging Savvy on Rx Drug', *Wall Street Journal*, (January 30), B1 and B9.

National Economic Research Associates (NERA) (1993), *Financing Health Care with Particular Reference to Medicines: Volume 7, The Health Care System in Japan*, London: NERA.

Neff, R. (1997), 'Unlocking Japan-At Last? It's No Stampede, but Foreign Investment is on the Rise', *Business Week*, (April 14), 56–57.

Nelson, R.R. (ed.) (1993), *National Systems of Innovation*, New York: Oxford University Press.

Nelson, R.R. and S.G. Winter (1982), *An Evolutionary Theory of Economic Change*, Cambridge, MA: Belknap Press of Harvard University Press.

Odagiri, H. and A. Goto (1996), *Technology and Industrial Development in Japan: Building Capabilities by Learning, Innovation, and Public Policy*, Oxford, UK: Oxford University Press.

Parker, J. (1988), 'Who Has a Drug Lag', working paper, University of Otago, NZ.

Peltzman, S. (1974), *Regulation of Pharmaceutical Innovation: The 1962 Amendments*, Washington, DC: American Enterprise Institute.

Penrose, E.T. (1959), *The Theory of the Growth of the Firm*, Oxford, UK: Basil Blackwell.

Pfeffer, J. and J.R. Salancik (1978), *The External Control of Organizations: A Resource Dependence Perspective*, New York: Harper and Row.

Piore, M. and C. Sabel (1984), *The Second Industrial Divide*, New York: Basic Books.

Pisano, G.P. (1991), 'The Governance of Innovation: Vertical Integration and Collaborative Arrangements in the Biotechnology Industry', *Research Policy* **15**, 237–49.

Porter, M.E. (1990), *The Competitive Advantage of Nations*, New York: Free Press.

Powell, W.W. and L. Smith-Doerr, 'Networks and Economic Life', in N.J. Smelser and R. Swedberg (eds), *The Handbook of Economic Sociology*, Princeton, NJ: Princeton University Press, 1994.

Prestowitz, C.V. (1988), *Trading Places: How We Allowed Japan to Take the Lead*, New York: Basic Books.

Pollack, A. (1993), 'Now It's Japan's Turn to Play Catch-Up' *New York Times* (Sunday, November 21, Business Section), 1 and 6.

Pollack, A. (1994), 'Stunning Changes in Japan's Economy' *New York Times* (Sunday, October 23, Business Section), 1 and 6.

Pollack, A. (1996), 'As Consumer Electronics Evolve, Can Japan Rule?' *New York Times* (Monday, October 7), C1 and C4.

Quick, P.D. (1984), 'Business: Reagan's Industrial Policy', in J.L. Palmer and I.V. Sawhill, *The Reagan Record: An Assessment of America's Changing Domestic Priorities,* Cambridge, MA: Ballinger, for the Urban Institute.

Quinn, J.B. (1992), *Intelligent Enterprise: A Knowledge and Service Based Paradigm for Industry,* New York: Free Press.

Ramseyer, J.M. and F.M Rosenbluth (1993), *Japan's Political Marketplace,* Cambridge, MA: Harvard University Press.

Reich, M. R. (1988), 'Why the Japanese Don't Export More Pharmaceuticals: Health Policy as Industrial Policy', *California Management Review,* **32**, 124–49.

Reich, R.B. (1983), *The Next American Frontier,* New York: Penguin Books.

Reich, R.B. (1985), 'Bailout', *Yale Journal of Regulation,* 163–224.

Reich, R.B. (1990), 'Commentary', in R.Z. Lawrence and C.L. Schultze (eds), *An American Trade Strategy: Options for the 1990s* Washington, DC: Brooking Institution.

Ross, C. (1993), 'An Apology for AIDS: Compensation for Japanese Hemophiliacs with AIDS', *The Lancet* (June 19), 1585.

Ross, C. (1996), 'AIDS Shakes Up Japan's Status Quo', *The Lancet* (April 6), 961.

Rumelt, R.P. (1984), 'Towards a Strategic Theory of the Firm', in R.B. Lamb, (ed.), *Competitive Strategic Management,* Englewood Cliffs, NJ: Prentice-Hall.

Sachs, J. (1994). 'Lessons from the Frozen North' 333 *Economist* (October 8), 76.

Salop, S.C. and D.T. Sheffman (1983), 'Raising Rivals' Costs', *American Economic Review* 73, 267–71.

Salvaggio, J. (1995), 'Japan's Big Year' 4 *Digital Media* (April 10), 11–15.

Scherer, F.M. (1994), *Competition Policies for an Integrated World Economy* Washington, DC: Brookings Institution.

Scherer, F.M. and D. Ross (1990), *Industrial Market Structure and Economic Performance* 3rd edn, Houghton Mifflin.

Schmalensee, R. (1978), 'Entry Deterrence in the Ready-to-Eat Breakfast Cereal Industry', *Bell Journal of Economics* 9, 305–27.

Schultze, C.L. (1983), 'Industrial Policy: A Dissent', *Brookings Review* (Fall), 3–12.

Seligmann, A.L. (1997), 'Japan's New Electoral System: Has Anything Changed?' *Asian Survey* 37 (May), 409–28

Selznick, P. (1948), 'Foundations of the Theory of Organization', 13 *American Sociological Review* 13, 25–35.

Simison, R.L. and J.B. White (2000), 'Reputation for Poor Quality Still Plagues Detroit: Ratings Show US Car Makers Lag Behind Foreign Rivals Despite Years of Effort', *Wall Street Journal* (May 4), B1 & B4.

Smith, C. (1989), 'On the Same Wavelength: Tokyo agrees to US Demands on Mobile Phones', *Far Eastern Economic Review*, 145:29 (July 20), 56–57.

Solomon, S.D. (1993), 'Things the Tortoise Taught Us', *Technology Review* (May/June), 20–27.

Staelin, D. H., et al. (1989), 'The Decline of US Consumer Electronics Manufacturing: History, Hypotheses, and Remedies', *The Working Papers of the MIT Commission on Industrial Productivity*, Cambridge, MA: MIT Press.

Steslicke, W.E. (1973), *Doctors in Politics: The Political Life of the Japan Medical Association*, New York: Praeger.

Sunao, O. (1988), 'The Ossification of University Faculties', *Japan Quarterly* **35** (April), 157–62.

Teece, D.J. (1986), 'Profiting from Technological Innovation: Implications for Integration, Collaboration, Licensing, and Public Policy', *Research Policy,* **15** (December), 286–305.

Teece, D.J., G. Pisano, and A. Shuen (1997), 'Dynamic Capabilities and Strategic Management', *Strategic Management Journal* **18**, 509–33.

Thomas, L.G. (1990), 'Regulation and Firm Size: FDA Impacts on Innovation', *Rand Journal of Economics* **21** (Winter), 497–517.

Thomas, L.G. (1994), 'Implicit Industrial Policy: The Triumph of Britain and the Failure of France in Global Pharmaceuticals', *Industrial and Corporate Change,* **3**, 451–89.

Thomas, L.G. (1996), 'The Two Faces of Competition: Dynamic Resourcefulness and the Hypercompetitive Shift' *Organization Science* **7** (May–June), 221–42.

Thomas, L.G. (1998), 'Spare the Rod and Spoil the Industry: Vigorous Competition and Vigorous Regulation Promote Global Competitive Advantage', working paper.

Thomas, L.G. and G.W. Waring (1999), 'Competing Capitalisms: Capital Investment in American, German, and Japanese Firms', *Strategic Management Journal,* **20**, 729–48.

Thompson, J.D. *Organizations in Action,* New York: McGraw Hill, 1967.

Tyson, L.D. (1991), 'They Are Not Us: Why American Ownership Still Matters', *The American Prospect* (Winter).

Tyson, L.D. (1992), *Who's Bashing Whom: Trade Conflict in High-Technology Industries,* Washington, DC: Institute for International Economics.

Uriu, R.M. (1996), *Troubled Industries: Confronting Economic Change in Japan,* Ithaca, NY: Cornell University Press.

US Congress House Committee on Science and Technology, Subcommittee on Science, Research, and Technology (1979), *Oversight-The Food and Drug Administration's Process for Approving New Drugs* Washington, DC: US Government Printing Office.

US Congress, OTA (Office of Technology Assessment) (1993), *Pharmaceutical R&D: Costs, Risks, and Rewards*, OTA-H-522, Washington, DC: U.S. Government Printing Office.

US GAO (General Accounting Office) (1980), *FDA Drug Approval-A Lengthy Process that Delays the Availability of Important New Drugs*, HRD-80-64, Washington, DC: US GAO, May 28.

US Trade Representative (USTR) (1994), *Annual Report*, Washington, DC: USTR.

Vogel, D. (1992), 'Consumer Protection and Protectionism in Japan', *Journal of Japanese Studies*, **18** (Winter), 423–34.

von Hippel, E. (1988), *The Sources of Innovation*, New York: Oxford University Press.

Wade, R. (1990), *Governing the Market: Economic Theory and the Role of Government in East Asian Industrialization*, Princeton, NJ: Princeton University Press.

Wardell, W.M. (1973a), 'British Usage and American Awareness of Some New Therapeutic Drugs', *Clinical Pharmacology and Therapeutics*, **14**, 1022–34.

Wardell, W.M. (1973b), 'Introduction of New Therapeutic Drugs in the United States and Great Britain: An International Comparison', *Clinical Pharmacology and Therapeutics*, **14**, 773–90.

Wardell, W.M. (1974), 'Therapeutic Implications of the Drug Lag', *Clinical Pharmacology and Therapeutics*, **15**, pp. 73–96.

Wardell, W.M. and L. Lasagna (1975), *Regulation and Drug Development*, Washington, DC: American Enterprise Institute.

Wardell, W.M., (ed.) (1978), *Controlling the Use of Therapeutic Drugs: An International Comparison*, Washington, DC: American Enterprise Institute.

Weber, J. (1997), 'The Battle of Blockbuster Heart Drugs: About to be an Also-Ran, Bristol Gambles on a Costly Heart Study and Wins', *Business Week* (January 27), 93–100.

Weidenbaum, Murray (1988), *Rendezvous with Reality: The American Economy After Reagan*, New York: Basic Books.

Wernerfelt, B. (1984), 'A Resource-Based View of the Firm', *Strategic Management Journal*, **5**, 171–80.

Whitley, R. (1994), 'Dominant Forms of Economic Organization in Market Economies', *Organization Studies*, **15**, 153–82.

Williamson, O.E. (1968), 'Wage Rates as Barriers to Entry: The Pennington Case in Perspective', *Quarterly Journal of Economics*, **85**, 85–116.

World Bank (1993), *The East Asian Miracle: Economic Growth and Public Policy* Oxford: Oxford University Press.

Yamamura, K. (1982), 'Success that Soured: Administrative Guidance and Cartels in Japan' in K. Yamamura (ed.), *Policy and Trade Issues of the Japanese Economy: American and Japanese Perspectives*, Seattle: University of Washington Press.

Yoon, S. (2001), 'The Musty Smell of Success', *Far Eastern Economic Review* (January 25), 32–5.

Yoshikawa, A. (1989), 'The Other Drug War: US-Japan Trade in Pharmaceuticals', *California Management Review*, **31** (Winter), 76–90.

Yoshikawa, A. (1993), 'Doctors and Hospitals in Japan', in D. I. Okimoto and A. Yoshikawa, (eds), *Japan's Health System: Efficiency and Effectiveness in Universal Care*, Washington, DC: Faulkner and Gray.

Zukin, S. and P. DiMaggio (eds) (1990), *Structures of Capital: The Social Organization of the Economy*, Cambridge, UK: Cambridge University Press.

Zysman, J. and L. D. Tyson (eds) (1983), *American Industry in International Competition: Government Policies and Corporate Strategies*, Ithaca, NY: Cornell University Press.

List of acronyms

AIDS	Acquired Immune Deficiency Syndrome
ASEAN	Association of South East Asian Nations
AT&T	AT&T Corporation (USA)
BMS	Bristol-Myers Squibb Company (USA)
DDI	DDI Corporation (Japan)
DRAM	Dynamic Random Access Memory
DVD	Digital Versatile Disk
FDA	Food and Drug Administration (USA)
FTC	Fair Trade Commission (Japan)
FTC	Federal Trade Commission (USA)
GAO	General Accounting Office (USA)
GATT	General Agreement on Tariffs and Trade
GCP	Good Clinical Practice
GDP	Gross Domestic Product
GJMA	Greater Japan Medical Association
GSM	Global System for Mobile Communications (mobile telephony standard)
HIV	Human Immunodeficiency Virus
IBM	International Business Machines, Inc. (USA)
IMS	IMS Health, Inc. (USA)
IPF	Innovation Possibility Frontier
IRB	Institutional Review Board
ITU	International Telecommunications Union
JMA	Japan Medical Association
JPMA	Japan Pharmaceutical Manufacturers Association
LDP	Liberal Democratic Party (Japan)
MHW	Ministry of Health and Welfare (Japan)
MIDAS	MIDAS^{TM} is an IMS database system
MITI	Ministry of International Trade and Industry
MMR	Measles, Mumps and Rubella (triple vaccine)
MOE	Ministry of Education (Japan)
MOF	Ministry of Finance (Japan)
MOSS	Market-Oriented Sector-Selective
MPT	Ministry of Posts and Telecommunications (Japan)

NCI	National Cancer Institute (USA)
NDA	New Drug Application
NEC	Nippon Electric Company (Japan)
NHI	National Health Insurance (Japan)
NIH	National Institutes of Health (USA)
NMT	Nordic Mobile Telephone (mobile telephony standard)
NTT	Nippon Telephone and Telegraph (Japan)
OTA	Office of Technology Assessment (USA)
OTC	Over-the-counter (pharmacy drugs)
PCS	Personal Communications System (mobile telephony standard)
PDUFA	Prescription Drug User Fee Act (USA)
PHS	Personal Handyphone System (mobile telephony standard)
RCA	Radio Corporation of America (USA)
R&D	research and development
RFS	Reimbursement Fee Schedule (Japan)
SII	Structural Impediments Initiative
SNDA	Supplementary New Drug Application
USTR	United States Trade Representative
VCR	Video Cassette Recorder
WTO	World Trade Organization

Index

References are to persons, practices, and organizations in Japan except where stated. Page numbers in italics indicate figures. Page numbers in bold indicate tables.